How to
THRIVE
with Adult
ADHD

How to
THRIVE
with Adult
ADHD

7 Pillars for Focus, Productivity and Balance

DR JAMES KUSTOW

Vermilion
LONDON

4

Vermilion, an imprint of Ebury Publishing
Penguin Random House UK
One Embassy Gardens, 8 Viaduct Gdns,
Nine Elms, London SW11 7BW

Vermilion is part of the Penguin Random House group of companies
whose addresses can be found at global.penguinrandomhouse.com

Penguin
Random House
UK

First published by Vermilion in 2024

www.penguin.co.uk

A CIP catalogue record for this book is available from the British Library

ISBN 9781785044526

Typeset in 10/15.25 pt TT Norms Pro by Jouve (UK), Milton Keynes
Printed and bound in Great Britain by Clays Ltd, Elcograf S.p.A.

The authorised representative in the EEA is Penguin Random House Ireland,
Morrison Chambers, 32 Nassau Street, Dublin D02 YH68

Penguin Random House is committed to a
sustainable future for our business, our readers and
our planet. This book is made from Forest
Stewardship Council® certified paper.

The information in this book has been compiled by way of general guidance in relation
to the specific subjects addressed, but is not a substitute and not to be relied on for
medical, healthcare, pharmaceutical or other professional advice on specific
circumstances and in specific locations. Please consult your GP before changing,
stopping or starting any medical treatment. So far as the author is aware the information
given is correct and up to date as at July 2024. Practice, laws and regulations all change,
and the reader should obtain up-to-date professional advice on any such issues. The
author and publishers disclaim, as far as the law allows, any liability arising directly or
indirectly from the use, or misuse, of the information contained in this book.

CONTENTS

INTRODUCTION

Whether you have been diagnosed with ADHD or it is something you suspect you have, this is the right book for you.

It could be that you are festering on an endless waiting list to be assessed, coming to the gradual realisation that the process is not going to be all that straightforward. You may be feeling fed up and increasingly hopeless. This book has been written for you.

Or it may be that the early novelty and excitement following your ADHD diagnosis is starting to fade. Perhaps, after a few haphazard attempts at making well-intentioned changes to your life, old habits and patterns are creeping back in. You may be feeling deflated and frustrated. This book is most certainly for you.

Perhaps the honeymoon period that you experienced on your ADHD medication has ended, and you are coming to terms with the fact that there is a lot more work to be done, but you're not quite sure where to start. Please don't panic; you have picked the right book to serve as a guide.

Or possibly you have come to the decision, for whatever reason, that medication is just not for you. You may be considering next steps and an alternative strategy, but lacking in clear direction. Read on – this book was inspired by people like you.

You could be lacking conviction that you have the necessary resources to get a handle on things and the ability to make the changes you know are required. This book is definitely the one for you.

Or maybe this isn't about you, and you are reading this to help someone you love who is really struggling. Perhaps you want to understand a bit more about ADHD and get some pointers on how best to approach things and what to suggest. I have also written this book with you in mind, and you are certainly not alone.

Whatever brought you here, my aim is to provide a framework to supercharge your understanding, map your unique ADHD 'signature' (or profile) and carve out a path that, put simply, will make your life better, much better.

I want to emphasise that this is *not* a book heavily focused on medication, quite the opposite in fact. Though I address the important question of medication, briefly but comprehensively, in Part 3, my scope is much broader and introduces a multitude of other ways to not only manage your ADHD, but thrive with it. It is a guided process of change that aims to help you unleash your potential and become the best possible version of yourself. I feel confident that the approaches I share in this book can have a transformational effect on your well-being and self-concept, regardless of whether you have a formal diagnosis of ADHD, and whether or not you take (or plan to take) medication.

A BIT ABOUT ME

I have ADHD. There, I've done it! I've just officially 'outed' my ADHD and it feels good. I am confident that it will make the process we are about to undertake together a lot easier for me, and far more meaningful for you. I am James, and I'm a consultant psychiatrist based in the UK. Conveniently, as well as having ADHD, I also specialise in it professionally.

Looking back on my life, much of it lived without an awareness of my ADHD, I now see clearly that my journey to this point, both personally and professionally, has been dominated by an insatiable drive to first better understand, and then work out how to make good use of, my (secretly) different brain. It has been a riveting exploration of the mind–body system that has led me through medicine, into psychiatry and ultimately landing on a specialisation that involves helping others navigate the issue I, myself, have scuffled with since childhood.

I was diagnosed with Attention Deficit-Hyperactivity Disorder (ADHD) a short while after my thirty-fourth birthday. The diagnosis came just a few months after that 'lightbulb' moment; a moment that changed everything. I recall it vividly.

I was seated on a 747 jumbo jet, panting and sweating profusely as, seconds before, I had narrowly made my flight. I had literally squeezed myself through the closing airplane door capoeira-style, before collapsing into my seat, actively avoiding the disapproving eyes of my fellow passengers. I was in extremis following a tortuous run past what seemed like a never-ending expanse of airport gates, a plethora of sweat-blurred numbers.

Slumped awkwardly and twisted between layers of hand luggage and impulsive duty-free purchases I was already regretting, I cursed myself for having done it again. I wished that I'd taken a moment to register the enormous sign informing us of the '25-minute walk' to Gate 99.

Despite promising myself, the night before, that I would allow adequate time in the morning, I, yet again, got sidetracked, misjudged all timings, mislaid my passport and, five minutes into the taxi journey to the airport, asked the driver to turn back so I could 'quickly' check that I'd locked the front door.

This was not the first time this had happened. I had played out this strange ritual multiple times before. The stress of it all felt perversely exciting and energising, but oddly calming at the same time. As I fell into that seat, it was like I'd won a race and, at the same time, maximised my time in the airport (all very strange, I know, but welcome to the world of ADHD).

This stress-chasing, thrill-seeking, rollercoaster of a life lived (at least up until then) with unrecognised ADHD was all too familiar to me. *It's just the way that I am*, I had thought, *just a little bit quirky . . . and different.*

My lightbulb moment

As I settled, I pulled out some light reading from my overflowing rucksack – a handful of eye-catching articles that had been selected and torn out of the mountain of unread, guilt-inducing, psychiatric journals that had started invading our living space months before.

I eventually managed to latch my focus onto the article and slipped into 'the zone'. I was suddenly hit by an overwhelming resonance: 'Oh, my goodness,' I inwardly exclaimed, 'this article is describing me! That's it! That's what it is. I think I have ADHD.'

You need to understand that, by that point, I'd completed a five-year stint at medical school, worked as a hospital doctor for a similar time and was part-way through an intensive 'on the job' training to be a psychiatrist. Yet somehow, bizarrely, I remained ignorant of the reality of ADHD being a lifespan disorder. I had not appreciated that, in the majority of cases, this 'childhood condition' continued into adulthood in some shape or form.

How could I have possibly missed that one? Why hadn't someone taught me this before? And, more importantly, why hadn't anyone worked out that I had it? These are questions some of you may relate to.

These powerful early suspicions were followed by a period of obsessive self-study, dissecting and grappling with the topic. Pretty much everything I read and watched reinforced to me, beyond reasonable doubt, that I indeed did have ADHD.

But how could I have ADHD? I initially thought to myself. I'd attended a respected school and university (admittedly struggling secretly through much of it). I'd endured a pretty gruelling, exam-fuelled medical and psychiatric training (which, to be honest, nearly finished me off). I'd captained numerous sports teams (but for some reason had missed the arranged transport to away matches on more than a few occasions and also got injured far more than others) and I'd held an array of (often impulsively adopted) leadership roles at both school and university. I was clearly functioning okay, at least on the outside, so how could I possibly have ADHD? Perhaps you've second-guessed yourself in a similar way? I really wish I had had a book like this to guide me through those tricky times. It would have answered so many of my questions and concerns.

As I slowly unpacked this conundrum during the years that followed, what I came to understand was that so much of my life up until that point had been fuelled by an unconscious, deeply held need to demonstrate both to myself, and the wider world, that I had worth – a form of compensation for my perceived 'weaknesses' and struggles. Essentially, this was an elaborate, internal ruse designed to ease the shame of a life spent (unknowingly at the time) sparring with this puzzling condition.

My diagnosis

I went on to have a really in-depth assessment with my now-colleague, friend and mentor Professor Philip Asherson, a world-respected adult ADHD researcher and an outstanding clinician, and, incidentally, the author of that 'lightbulb moment' article I had read on the plane months before.

The assessment involved a detailed review of my life story to date and, at the end of it, a diagnosis of Adult ADHD – Combined Presentation (the more impairing subtype of the disorder, which we'll explore later in the book) was formalised.

Getting a diagnosis that helped make sense of many of my life's struggles was undoubtedly a pivotal moment in my life. I slowly began to understand myself better and gradually started to accept myself for who I was. I was now able to explain (not excuse) my difficulties within an ADHD framework, underpinned by pretty solid science, and this has had powerful shame-busting effects. The aspects I love about my ADHD brain are certainly counterbalanced by the very real struggles. Struggles, which I have to say, are much less difficult to handle when you understand and embrace them, rather than battle with and shame them. Over the last 15 years or so, working and (knowingly) living with adult ADHD, I have learned a lot – about ADHD and about myself. I no longer beat myself up or become too deflated when I occasionally misjudge something or mess up in some other way. That is just me and my ways, and I'm relieved to say that I now feel much more okay being me.

My credentials

As the Director of Education of the main professional organisation for adult ADHD in the UK, the UK Adult ADHD Network (UKAAN), I have had the privilege of helping shape the narrative and knowledge pool around adult ADHD in the UK over recent years. In addition to our training focus, our team has published important standards and guidance on the assessment process. My real passion lies in educating, speaking and now writing about this interesting topic, asking challenging and important questions along the way. I sense we are on the cusp of a wave of new understanding about what ADHD really is, hidden beneath the endless lists of symptoms and impairments.

As an open-minded and perpetually inquisitive psychiatrist, it has been my nature to experiment, explore and to take a few calculated risks along the way. I try to be open to new ideas that many are quick to dismiss. And I've sought to look under the hood and make sense of the approaches I encounter that appear to have particularly potent or positive effects on the brain and body. Endlessly mesmerised by the stunning workings of the physical body, I especially love finding tools and techniques that essentially 'hack' our normal physiology; shifting psychological blocks, processing trauma and neutralising charged emotions.

I have had to tread cautiously, straddling the world of mainstream western medical practice, and a diverse range of novel, sometimes odd-looking, ways of working with mind and body. I am committed to helping others on this journey, and this book and programme are the vehicles to achieve that goal. There are a lot of us out there, but the majority don't yet realise that it's ADHD that underpins their struggles. Many also don't appreciate, as I didn't, that it so often continues into adulthood.

This book is the weaving together of years of experience, both personally and professionally. Based on my experience, the seven pillars in Part 2, many of which introduce new and cutting-edge ideas, have the potential to have a transformational effect on the richness of your life.

Evidence-based, but open and non-judgemental

Where available and worthy of inclusion, I have referenced some of the evidence that supports my recommendations. The reality, however, is that I cover some areas that currently lack a robust evidence base. For the most part, this is because the necessary studies simply haven't yet been conducted. In these situations, I have based my guidance on 'expert opinion' and common sense, rooted in years of life and clinical experience.

In some areas, I have extrapolated findings from other related fields, including from the far more extensive pool of research on children and adolescents with ADHD. And, in places, where my experience tells me it is warranted, I have unashamedly broken new ground, introducing exciting new ideas and approaches that are not covered elsewhere in the adult ADHD literature.

For those of you who wish to keep things simple, I direct you to two groundbreaking papers: the first is called 'The World Federation of ADHD International Consensus Statement', published in 2021 by leading US ADHD researcher, Dr Stephen Faraone and team, and it is freely available online. This paper comprises over 200 evidence-based statements about the disorder taken from high-quality studies. It doesn't cover all of the areas I am interested in, but it does a pretty impressive job overall and it is an obvious starting point when seeking science-based answers to a range of ADHD-related questions.

The second, for those of you who want a slightly deeper dive, is the 2018 'Updated European Consensus Statement' on diagnosis and treatment of adult ADHD of which, I was a co-author. Taken together with the original edition from 2012, it provides a comprehensive clinical overview of what we currently know about adult ADHD, in a digestible yet scientific style.

HOW TO USE THIS BOOK

Over my career, I have met so many people who, like me, had that ADHD 'lightbulb moment' well into their adult life. It's often a profound experience with huge potential for personal development and growth.

Over recent years, there has been an explosion of interest in adult ADHD, waves of articles and conversations surfacing online, a steady stream of celebrities 'outing' their ADHD, with more and more people questioning whether ADHD could explain their difficulties. In many cases it does, given the large numbers that remain undiagnosed.

With so much information out there, it can be difficult to know where to start. This is where this book comes in. If you're anything like me, however, faced with a new project of this nature, you are likely experiencing a flutter of excitement, together with a serving of apprehension, possibly bordering on concern.

As a consequence of my ADHD, I have really struggled to engage with the written word. This was not ideal given my curious mind and hunger for knowledge. So, when it came to pass that I would be writing my own book, I worked hard to get the formula right. I assume that your mind, like mine, needs lots of structure and signposting to stay connected and to learn. I have therefore tried to start with the basics, to keep things concise and build gradually.

A great deal of thought has gone into the presentation of the material, to really optimise things for you. I am referring to the level of detail included, and of course the structure and style. I know we are not all the same, but this approach would have worked well for me. I hope it does for you too.

The book is divided into three parts:

1. **Part 1** introduces the topic and lays the foundations. This section provides a comprehensive, but digestible, overview of the nature of adult ADHD and how it is diagnosed.
2. **Part 2** comprises the seven pillars, the central hub of the book. I have structured the majority of the practical guidance into this staged, seven-pillar plan. The goal is to support you to improve your focus, productivity and overall life balance, and learn to skilfully manage your ADHD.
3. **Part 3** starts by overviewing the conventional medical management of adult ADHD, most notably the use of medication (stimulant and non-stimulant). I have tried to capture the shiny and the not-so-shiny aspects of taking medication for ADHD. I show that, although effective in many, it is not a panacea for all of life's struggles, nor is it the greatest of society's evils, as sometimes portrayed. I also introduce a range of creative workarounds to deal with stubborn and resistant symptoms.

Your journey undoubtedly starts with information – learning about ADHD, but also about yourself, and where and why things go wrong.

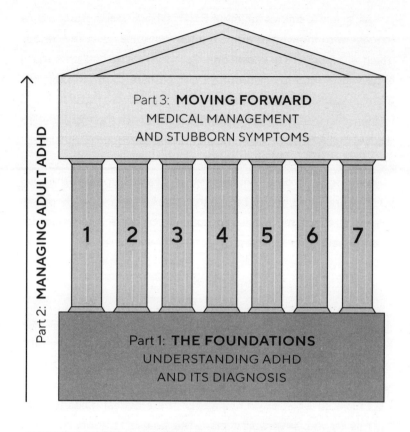

THE SEVEN PILLARS (Part 2):

1 NURTURE A GROWTH-ORIENTED MINDSET

2 ANCHOR YOUR SLEEP

3 TAKE CONTROL OF YOUR TIME

4 MANAGE YOUR ENVIRONMENT AND INPUTS

5 NOURISH AND MOVE YOUR BODY

6 REDUCE YOUR TOXIC LOAD

7 REGULATE YOUR EMOTIONS

The structure of this book

I recommend that you initially concentrate your efforts on these foundational chapters in Part 1, deepening your understanding of what ADHD really is and how it has shaped your life experience. This will set the scene and inform your strategy for engaging with it.

As we build up these foundations, my hope is that you begin to broaden how you think about ADHD, consolidate your understanding, and foster more self-awareness and sensitivity.

Then we will move from the 'What?' of Part 1 to the 'How?' of Part 2. As you progress through the seven pillars, at whatever speed feels right for you, you will experience your self-care steadily improving in real time, together with a slow rebuild of your self-respect and worth.

The order in which I have presented the pillars is intentional, with each building on the last. Ideally, try to implement and adjust to each new intervention before moving on to the next one. This gradual stepwise 'building-in' of positive change, in my experience, really is the key to success. The shifts you make using this approach are far more likely to hold, weaving themselves effortlessly into the fabric of your everyday life experience. Saying that, there really are no rules, so proceed as you wish, without any fear, shame or guilt whatsoever. This book is intended as a non-judgemental and usable resource for you to engage with in whatever way feels right for you.

I want to, from the very start, quash the illusion of there being a miraculous solution in my approach, or any other book or approach for that matter. This is not to minimise the very real excitement that commonly bubbles up when you find answers, or explanations, that make some sense of the years of strife and misdirection that you may have endured. Or to underplay the relief that can flood in when you find something that works for you and actually alters the way you think, feel and act. It's just vital that you see this process of self-development as lifelong, progressive and dynamic.

Grab a notebook and pen

You may be comfortable writing notes directly into the margins of this book (and I certainly won't discourage this), but it is something I have always personally felt a little uncomfortable doing. So why not buy yourself a small blank notebook to accompany you on your journey, and to document it along the way? If you want to elevate the status of this notebook, you can refer to it as your 'Thrive Journal'.

It's your choice, but I think it may help as, at various points, I will be proposing some brief mind-sharpening reflective exercises (nothing too arduous, don't worry). There are also likely to be a few practical nuggets – material that particularly resonates – that you feel compelled to jot down somewhere as you read, so you can refer back to it at a later stage.

Whereas before you may have been fumbling around clumsily in the dark of the forest, searching for answers and direction and possibly having the occasional lucky win, I hope this process brings an awakening; a warm, glistening and expanding light, that will illuminate a well-trodden path for you to follow (of course allowing for a bit of ADHD-esque sidetracking along the way).

THRIVING WITH ADULT ADHD

Embedded within the book, and concentrated in the seven pillars that follow, is a practical framework to facilitate positive change. As well as learning to negotiate the hurdles, I also want to help you identify and harness those powerful 'adaptive' traits that ADHD can bring. Over more recent years, ADHD has been referred to by some as a 'superpower'. Given the very real suffering, this is understandably a controversial statement. Personally, I believe that, with the right care and attention, paired with a lifelong commitment to self-development and a honing of strengths, ADHD can indeed be associated with brilliance. That is our ultimate goal, and one that I recognise may feel unattainable from where you presently stand. However, as you delve deeper into the book, taking one small, manageable step at a time, the pendulum should begin to settle and steady. The idea is that incremental shifts and welcome changes unfold and evolve in a naturally paced and unforced way, and that they are sustained.

With more calm and stability you will be freed up to divert a larger proportion of your energy into your relationships with others, and into creative exploration and expression – less juggling and less firefighting, and much more direction and flow.

From my perspective, thriving with ADHD involves remaining 'on track' for more of the time than you are 'off track', and striking a healthier balance across the various expressions of your life, including life/work, rest/play, engagement/independence, but also in terms of life management – specifically how you manage your *sleep*, your *diet*, your *finances* and your *time*.

Most importantly, you will feel a heightened sense of satisfaction with your life and path, now much more focused on enjoying and enhancing the journey, rather than a mindless bolt to the finish. Having carved out your unique niche and purpose, you may well transition into the stage of striving for mastery in whatever it is you're passionate about.

There will, of course, continue to be frustrating problems and ordeals that challenge you, and annoying and stubborn residual symptoms to contend with, but they won't faze you nearly as much as before. You will navigate and negotiate them far more skilfully and pick yourself up more quickly when you have the occasional slip-up, learning so much along the way.

As you gradually elevate and open yourself, there may also be a process of spiritual growth and 'awakening', slowly manifesting, often in unexpected ways.

This, in my experience, is what it means in real terms to thrive with adult ADHD. This is where we are heading! I am honoured to be with you on that journey, a journey that I myself have been on for a little while now. A journey that never actually ends.

> **Exercise: Initial reflections and your commitment**
> I encourage you to take a moment to explore and (if you feel inspired) capture in words what you feel as you read these introductory reflections.
>
> - Do you closely identify with any of the descriptions?
> - How are you feeling about your future?
> - How motivated are you to work on yourself and embark on this expedition?

PART 1

LAYING THE FOUNDATIONS

In this part, before diving into the seven pillars, we'll explore in some depth the question of what exactly ADHD is, summarising our current, still somewhat limited, understanding. I'll introduce the main symptoms and common impairments, and share what we know about longer-term outcomes, if things are left unchecked.

Using a model I have developed, that I am introducing here for the first time, I will try to capture what ADHD *really* looks like in adults.

We'll then move on to the diagnosis of adult ADHD, starting with the question of screening and what should make you consider ADHD as a possibility. I will guide you through what the process looks like from early suspicions to assessment and provide top tips along the way. We'll also look at whether getting assessed is something you really need to do.

Let's get started.

WHAT IS ADHD?

ADHD is usually associated with childhood, which makes the concept of adult ADHD surprising to some. It is the most common 'neurodevelopmental disorder' in childhood, affecting about 6 per cent of children globally. What many do not realise is that it also affects at least 2.5 per cent of adults.

ADHD, by definition, is a 'disorder'. In plain speak, it is a right old pain in the backside. Its manifestations are broad and can be quite different from person to person, which makes it tricky to describe to others and to get taken seriously. The fact of the matter is that ADHD *is* serious – very serious – and the world is only just realising that.

Those of us with ADHD often realise that we are 'different' in some way. Our behaviours, emotions, responses, sensitivities and patterns will often jar with convention and create disharmony in relation to others and, importantly, ourselves. If ADHD is not picked up and addressed, we tend to mask and muddle our way through, collecting considerable shame, confusion and sometimes trauma along the way. We commonly take things into our own hands and try to find ways to minimise the impact of the symptoms.

Importantly, when it comes to diagnosing ADHD (the subject of the next chapter), the 18 'symptoms' listed in the *Diagnostic and Statistical Manual of Mental Disorders* (*DSM-5*) that are explored, and scored, as part of the assessment process don't get anywhere close to capturing the real-life experience of actually having ADHD as an adult.

These 18 symptoms (which can be found in the Appendix on page 283) have been selected because they have been shown in studies to be best able to *differentiate and distinguish* ADHD from other disorders, than other symptoms tested, a fact that is often overlooked. The way ADHD really shows up in adults is far more subtle and multilayered compared with this rather sterile and superficial symptom list that so commonly gets bandied around as the official descriptor of ADHD.

To further muddy the water, this list of symptoms was in fact created with children – not adults – in mind, before there was widespread recognition and acceptance that ADHD is a lifespan condition. For this reason primarily, the current symptom list is far from ideal for adults.

One of the problems for adults is that it overemphasises the hyperactivity features (allocating 6 of the 18 symptoms to hyper-activity), when we know that this is not so much of an issue in adults, at least not overt physical hyperactivity (the hyperactive mind is another thing altogether, of course – more about that later). Additionally, the list lacks sufficient focus on problems related to both *executive function* and *emotion regulation*, both of which are central to ADHD.

All too often, we end up conceptualising ADHD based solely on this somewhat narrow (and child-centric) symptom list used as part of the diagnostic work-up. I have developed my own model, which I feel illustrates far better how ADHD looks in adults.

A NEW WAY OF UNDERSTANDING ADULT ADHD

According to our current way of describing it, ADHD is a dis-order characterised particularly by persistent and impairing features of **inattention** (including distractibility, disorganisation and forgetfulness), **hyperactivity** (of both body and mind) or **impulsivity** (of actions and words), or aspects of all three. Most of those affected also experience **emotional dysregulation**, or mood instability, in addition to the features listed above.

Personally, I find it most helpful to think of ADHD simply as a disorder of regulation (or a 'dysregulation disorder'). This aptly describes my personal experience, and that of the many patients I have worked with, where pretty much all difficulties experienced relate back to an issue with one's ability to regulate . . . something. *Too much. Too little. Can't start. Can't stop. Too fast. Too slow. Too long. Too short. Too hot. Too cold.* This allows an appreciation that some of the features of ADHD result from over-regulation, while others are associated with under-regulation – in many ways, this explains the marked variability in the way that ADHD looks to the naked eye.

Underpinning the capacity of any system to regulate is its ability to put the brakes on; to *inhibit* action. In ADHD there is a demonstrated problem with inhibition, sometimes called 'disinhibition'. This disrupts attentional processes and underlies the problems with executive function. It also drives ADHD's hyperactive impulsive and emotional symptoms. In fact, inhibition is linked to pretty much all aspects of ADHD.

Executive functions

There are a number of features of ADHD that result from problems with what are termed 'executive functions'. These include a range of cognitive (thinking) processes and skills that are thought to originate in the brain's prefrontal cortex (the bit at the front, behind the brow). They are involved in the planning, monitoring and successful completion of a task, and in the achievement of goals.

This disordered regulation, characterised by problems with inhibition, plays out in many different areas of one's life, both mentally and physically.

I have identified ten key areas that get dysregulated in adult ADHD, which I call the **'Ten Domains of Dysregulation'**. This model aims to capture the essence, woven together with the science, of ADHD. The domains are supported by current and, in some places, cutting-edge scientific understanding.

Associated with each of the ten domains are a set of symptoms, or *features*, that occur due to disordered regulation, or 'dysregulation', of that domain. The model also captures the various *outcomes*, both negative (adverse) and positive (adaptive), that are linked to ADHD. (I have not assigned these outcomes to specific domains as, in many cases, they straddle multiple.) You may recognise some of these features in yourself.

This model will give you a framework to work with that will provide you with a deeper and more sophisticated understanding of the disorder, support and broaden your process of self-analysis and help guide what you might do to improve things.

Amber warnings

There are a handful of general clues to the possible presence of ADHD, or what I call 'amber warnings'. I have captured them here in the form of a few initial screening questions:

- Have you always had the feeling that you were 'different' from others (with attempts to mask that difference) and is there a pattern of lifelong difficulties, in multiple areas, that haven't been explained or formulated adequately?
- Do you or your family members have ADHD or any other neurodevelopmental problems such as tics or Tourette's

syndrome, dyspraxia (or developmental co-ordination disorder, DCD, as it is now known), dyslexia or autism?
- Do you have any other common comorbidities that are associated with ADHD? (Mental or physical health – see page 59.)
- Do you resonate strongly with someone you know who has ADHD, or find yourself migrating towards people who have ADHD?
- Do you find it challenging to maintain things like relationships, jobs, emails, finances and healthy practices, despite noble intentions?
- Do you often feel like you are 'chasing your tail', 'juggling too many balls', 'firefighting', 'winging it' or 'in catch-up mode', but never seem to be able to get on top of things?
- Do you have a spread of ADHD-type features from the ten domains listed below?

Domain 1: Attention and executive functioning

ADHD, in part due to its confusing name, has traditionally been associated with having a lack, or 'deficit' of attention (referred to as inattention or distractibility). There are, in fact, a few different types of attention, for example, focused attention, selective attention, sustained attention, and so on.

It is the form of attention that carries into the future, that is related to goal acquisition and task completion, i.e., sustained attention and its counterpart, *persistence*, that is disproportionately affected in ADHD – this explains the difficulty people with ADHD very often have with sticking with things to completion.

The features of ADHD that are linked to these attentional aberrations, some of which are considered executive functions, include problems with *distractibility* (the ability to resist responding to distractions which requires good inhibition), *working memory* (which is the temporary 'holding in mind' form of memory that facilitates task completion) and *task re-engagement* (getting back on track after being knocked 'off-task' by an interruption).

Equally impairing in many, however, is the challenge of 'hyper-focus', which is in direct contrast to attention deficit. These are periods of super-intense focus, where there is an inability to pull away from a task and shift focus. With hyperfocus, there is clearly still an issue with regulation and inhibition, but this time playing out in the opposite direction.

Features of the attention/executive function domain

- Problems resisting distraction both by internal thoughts and sensations (mind-wandering) and by external stimuli (distractibility), and difficulty sustaining attention in tasks and activities – experienced as getting sidetracked, recurrently needing to go back and reread paragraphs of text, often needing to ask people to repeat questions and having lots of half-read books and half-finished projects.
- Evidence of hyperfocus: being able to focus for hours on end on a narrow interest (yet struggling to focus in many other situations that interest you less).
- Forgetfulness (usually affecting the 'hold it in mind' or working memory, for example, forgetting people's names, what you went to the shop to buy and appointments) and poor follow-through on well-intentioned promises or commitments made to others.
- Procrastination over almost every task (except those that excite or interest you, or where there is a serious consequence of not doing it).

- Disorganisation (and inefficiency) in tasks and activities, with difficulty with prioritisation and decision-making, forward planning, being on time, following instructions carefully and doing things in the correct order or sequence, and difficulty sticking to time, meeting deadlines and managing personal health, relationships and finances.
- Difficulty sticking to routines, and then getting back on track when routines are broken (for example, by a holiday or illness).
- Recurrent mistakes, and periods of crisis and overwhelm.

Domain 2: Activity

In young children, hyperactivity is often quite prominent, and it has become a hallmark symptom of ADHD. This is not the case when it comes to adults, though. With age, the hyperactivity reduces, partly because it is not socially acceptable to be balancing on bannisters and swinging from signs in your thirties. In many adults, the hyperactivity seems to get turned inwards and is experienced as inner restlessness, a state of heightened vigilance or agitation.

Hyperactivity in all its forms is explained by a problem with inhibition. Although the current criteria focus mainly on the *physical* (i.e., excessive or irrelevant movement or activity – termed 'motor disinhibition'), hyperactivity can also apply to both *speech* ('verbal disinhibition') and *thought processes* ('cognitive disinhibition').

Although ADHD is typically associated with excessive activity (physical, verbal and mental), at the other end of the activity spectrum, those with the condition can also struggle with apathy and boredom, and experience significant issues with drive and motivation. Again, due to inhibitory challenges, there is a relative disregard of the future and later consequences, both positive and negative, and a preference for the here and now, which has an impact on motivation.

Features of the activity domain

- Difficulty staying still (physical restlessness or overt hyperactivity).
- Non-stop mental activity (mental restlessness).
- Talking excessively.
- Difficulty stopping what you are doing and relaxing, and use of external aids or substances to quieten a busy body and mind.
- Physical and mental exhaustion (leading to burnout if left unchecked).
- Apathy and motivational issues, and boredom.
- Social withdrawal.
- Overexcitement.
- Sexual issues due to apathy or excitability.

Domain 3: Impulse

Problems with the regulation of impulse (of words, thoughts and actions) can be a highly destructive feature of adult ADHD. Again, issues with impulse control result from a problem with the braking system. Verbal, cognitive (thinking) or motor (physical) disinhibition drives the features we understand to be linked to impulsivity and hyperactivity.

Impulsivity (and impulse control issues) can be toxic to relationships, and markedly increase the risk of substance misuse, disordered eating, self-harm, aggression towards others and accidents.

Features of the impulse domain

- Problems delaying gratification and weighing up consequences of actions.
- Disordered eating (undereating, overeating and mindless eating).
- Self-harming (difficulty regulating strong emotions).
- Careless driving, road rage and other risk-taking activities (acting without thinking).
- Interpersonal (relationship) conflicts – due to speaking without thinking and a lack of reciprocity (the give-and-take) in communication.
- Alcohol and substance misuse (especially nicotine, cannabis, caffeine or cocaine), often initially employed as a form of 'self-medication', and impulsive decision-making about whether to start, and when to stop.
- Spending money impulsively and making unnecessary 'in the moment' purchases.
- Other addictive tendencies, for example, excessive screen use, gambling, pornography, and so on.

Domain 4: Emotion

Emotional dysregulation is present in the majority of adults with ADHD (some studies suggest over 90 per cent). Although not listed as a core feature in ADHD's diagnostic criteria, most would agree it should be. Again, it is linked to disinhibition, but this time in the emotional domain.

Features of the emotion domain
- Anxiety (numerous manifestations, often including generalised and social anxiety).
- Rapid mood shifts, sometimes referred to as mood instability – ranging from anxiety to excitement, to boredom, to sadness or shame . . . all in the space of a few hours.
- Being quick to anger and getting easily frustrated.
- Excitability and the expression of raw, unfiltered emotion.
- Difficulty relaxing and unwinding, due to background worry.
- Heightened sensitivity to rejection and criticism, and often carrying a heavy burden of shame.

Domain 5: Reward/pleasure-seeking

Those with adult ADHD commonly struggle with addictive tendencies of all varieties, due to the difficulty they experience in regulating their brain's reward system.

There typically exists an under-rewarded baseline state, which predisposes people to seek out reward, in the form of dopamine-boosting activities (dopamine is a brain chemical or 'neurotransmitter' that plays a role in pleasure and motivation, among other things). This can involve migrating towards pleasurable activities, but also towards conflict, as there is an unconscious gravitation to the dopamine-fuelled calm after the storm.

There is clear overlap with the impulse domain, and the tendency of being in the here and now, with a relative disregard for future consequences.

Features of the reward domain
- Novelty, risk-taking and sensation-seeking behaviour.
- Alcohol and substance misuse (especially nicotine, cannabis, caffeine or cocaine), process (or behavioural) addictions, including overeating and overspending.
- A tendency to generate conflict or crises unconsciously, in an attempt to self-regulate.
- Boredom, with short-lived interests and endeavours.
- Difficulty delaying gratification and inhibiting drives.
- Being 'in the moment' (difficulty prioritising and thinking of future impact).

Domain 6: Sensory processing

Many adults with ADHD (and ASD, autism spectrum disorder) have sensory processing issues, and they can experience both sensory under- and over-reactivity. This multidimensional problem can be impairing in a range of different ways: it can aggravate the other symptoms of ADHD, drive sensation and thrill-seeking behaviours, and result in overwhelm and isolation (as a result of shielding from sensory overload).

Features of the sensory domain
- Sensory over-reactivity.
- Sensory under-reactivity.
- Sensation-seeking behaviours and activities.
- A tendency to get overwhelmed, leading to dissociation and 'shutdown'.

Domain 7: Time appraisal

Those with ADHD very often have deficits in their ability to appraise, or estimate, how long things are going to take (with both under- and overestimation).

When looking retrospectively, people can struggle to know how long something they did took or how long ago it happened. This can have significant 'knock-on' effects and can result in difficulties in multiple areas.

Features of the time domain
- 'Time blindness' (issues with estimation or perception of time, including during examinations or tests, or when planning journeys).
- Time-management issues (leading to lateness, with a negative impact on productivity and relationships).
- Running out of time (unfinished exams and projects, breached deadlines).

Domain 8: Sleep–wake (circadian) rhythm

There are well-established variations in the circadian rhythm in those with ADHD. Sleep-onset and wake times are typically shifted later, a phenomenon which results in later bedtimes (and possibly wake times).

In many, particularly when the demands of life require an early start to the working day, this can result in the progressive accumulation of a 'sleep deficit' (with a resultant aggravation of other symptoms, and educational and occupational problems).

Some will go on to develop complete 'sleep reversal' (which involves being awake during the night and asleep during the day) which, for obvious reasons, can be highly impairing on many levels.

Features of the sleep domain

- Delayed sleep and wake times.
- Going to bed late, in part due to difficulty stopping an activity.
- Sleep deficit.
- Sleep reversal.
- Daytime tiredness (with knock-on effects on work function and learning).
- Features suggestive of an independent sleep disorder, like obstructive sleep apnoea or restless legs syndrome (see page 97).

Domain 9: Immune function (and inflammatory status)

The data is still only just emerging in this area, but those with ADHD are more likely to have evidence of immune system dysregulation. Studies show much higher rates of allergy and asthma (examples of immune over-reactivity) and autoimmunity (a misdirected immune response) in people with ADHD.

Additionally, and likely linked, there are significantly raised levels of inflammatory markers (or tests) in those with ADHD. These compelling associations, which point to a more somatic (physical) and multisystem disorder, may in time provide important clues as to the biological drivers of ADHD symptoms (extending beyond a disturbance in brain chemistry). Mast cell activation disease (a seemingly common syndrome of immune over-reactivity) may be a particular issue in those with ADHD, but this needs more study (we'll explore this in more detail in Pillar 6).

Features of the immune domain

- Heightened sensitivity (and, in some, multiple chemical sensitivity).

- Higher levels of inflammation, in multiple body systems.
- Increased pain levels and possibly more pain syndromes, for example, fibromyalgia.
- An association with fatigue states, for example, chronic fatigue syndrome (CFS)/ME (which are likely to have an immune basis, but this remains controversial).
- More infections, and recurrent infections, such as tonsillitis.
- More allergies, intolerances and sensitivities, and higher rates of autoimmunity.
- Features indicative of mast cell activation abnormalities (for example, higher rates of asthma, allergies including hay fever, Long Covid syndrome and hives).

Domain 10: Arousal and energy expenditure

Those with ADHD commonly have difficulty regulating their arousal levels and energy expenditure. This can quite often manifest in a 'boom and bust' pattern of functioning (for example, excessive energy, followed by collapse).

Features of the arousal/energy domain
- A 'boom and bust' pattern of energy expenditure, with difficulty pacing.
- Physical and mental exhaustion (leading to features of burnout in some).
- Problems with blood sugar regulation.
- Sleep disturbance.
- Hyperfocus and perfectionism.
- Excitability.
- Under-arousal and motivational issues.

- A dysregulated stress response, leading to a heightened state of vigilance.
- Features suggestive of dysautonomia (dysregulated autonomic nervous system – ANS – function), for example, orthostatic intolerance (symptoms on standing) including dizziness and fainting, and postural orthostatic tachycardia syndrome or POTS (a very fast heart rate when standing).

ADHD in women and girls

In childhood, ADHD appears to be more common in boys, with about a 3:1 male to female ratio. This gender discrepancy is likely to be explained, at least in part, by the fact that many girls with ADHD are missed – either undiagnosed or misdiagnosed. This may be because girls have been shown to have less overt ADHD symptoms – in particular, less hyperactivity and impulsivity – meaning that they are more likely to be overlooked. Masking (the use of compensatory behaviours to cover up difficulties) is also very common. With increased awareness of the disorder over recent years, there has been a relative surge of diagnoses in adult women.

Whether or not they are diagnosed, girls with ADHD are more vulnerable to bullying and, as they transition into adolescence and early adulthood, they are often more sexually active than their peers, with obvious risks. They may engage in other risk-taking activities, sometimes with the goal of fitting in. If impulsivity is present, this may be associated with self-harming behaviour. Low mood and emotional dysregulation are prominent features, and it is not uncommon for women to attract labels of 'anxiety' or 'depression', and for the ADHD to be missed. Women also seem to have more physical health issues than men with ADHD, especially fatigue and pain.

MID- TO LATE ADULTHOOD

Problems from early adulthood may continue, plus issues adjusting to certain phases and transitions, including marriage, job changes, pregnancy, having children and parenting, menopause, retirement, physical illness, loss of parents.

EARLY ADULTHOOD

Problems with engagement in higher education, work-related difficulties (lateness, absenteeism), relationship dysfunction (quickly bored, conflict), challenges with 'out of nest' independent living (including suboptimal self-care), mental and physical health problems, substance use, self-esteem issues and accidents (including car accidents and unwanted pregnancies).

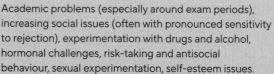

ADOLESCENT YEARS

Academic problems (especially around exam periods), increasing social issues (often with pronounced sensitivity to rejection), experimentation with drugs and alcohol, hormonal challenges, risk-taking and antisocial behaviour, sexual experimentation, self-esteem issues.

EARLY SCHOOL YEARS

Disruptive/hyperactive behaviour, attention-seeking (class clown), social issues and academic struggles start to emerge.

INFANCY AND TODDLER YEARS

Inability to settle, sensory differences, sleep and feeding issues.

ADHD across the lifespan

Symptoms may become more pronounced during periods of transition (for example, leaving school), and are commonly exacerbated by hormonal changes – during the menstrual cycle, pregnancy and the menopause. Oestrogen levels reduce markedly during weeks three and four of the menstrual cycle and around the menopause period, resulting in a correspondent reduction of dopamine. If you are seeing a specialist, get their advice on managing these vulnerable periods. They may recommend increasing your dose of ADHD medication at these times, or in some cases adding in an antidepressant or hormone replacement therapy.

Negative (adverse) outcomes

ADHD is serious, and something you most definitely want to know about. It is certainly not a minor or glamorous condition to have, as it is sometimes portrayed in the media, and there are several evidence-based negative outcomes associated with having it (especially if untreated), including:

- Underachievement (relative to potential) – academic, employment and financial.
- The huge toll taken on the body and mind through years of unhealthy compensatory behaviours, such as routinely using high stress to activate yourself.
- Financial problems and debt.
- Self-neglect and poor self-care.
- Injuries and accidents (including road traffic accidents).
- Relationship dysfunction and breakdown (including family members, friends, colleagues and intimate relationships) and higher rates of social isolation.
- Work-related issues (impaired work function, higher rates of unemployment and sickness including burnout).
- Parenting challenges, which can be further compounded if the child has ADHD themselves.

- Associated physical health issues, for example, sleep disorders, cardiovascular and autonomic dysfunction, obesity, epilepsy, hypermobility syndromes, sexually transmitted diseases, diabetes, asthma, allergy, autoimmunity, fatigue and pain syndromes, recurrent infections and inflammation.
- Anxiety and mood disorders, and higher rates of psychological trauma.
- Shame, demoralisation, social anxiety and self-esteem issues.
- Antisocial behaviour and criminal activity (often of an impulsive nature).
- Addiction – both substance and process (or behavioural) addictions.
- Increased health and social care use (including emergency department attendances).
- Reduced life expectancy and higher suicide rates.

Positive (adaptive) attributes

Despite the many negative outcomes listed above, adult ADHD does seem to confer some potential benefits in some individuals, such as:

- Productive hyperfocus.
- Divergent and innovative thinking (often translates to creativity).
- Problem-solving skills (often good in a crisis).
- Resilience and tenacity.
- Empathy, compassion and a forgiving nature.
- Fairness and a strong moral compass.
- Healthy risk-taking and spontaneity, and the learning and growth that comes with it.
- Fun-loving and playful (often great with children and pets).
- Engaging, funny and charismatic. Often the 'life and soul' (and the last to leave the party).
- Passionate and motivated (but generally in short bursts, and with a narrow focus).

Exercise: Adult ADHD and me

Using the 'Ten Domains of Dysregulation' model as a framework, I invite you to now capture your current symptoms and difficulties, linked to each of the domains, in your Thrive Journal or on the grid on pages 40–1. This important reflective exercise is designed to map out what I refer to as your 'ADHD signature' and establish an accurate and detailed baseline from which to build.

You can even record a personal narrative, or a conversation with someone you trust, where you explore your ADHD signature verbally. Whatever approach suits you best is fine, but I really encourage you to record it in some way for safekeeping.

Under each domain heading, start to build in the detail, listing your *specific symptoms or difficulties*. I have provided a few pointers below to help guide you regarding the type of content to include and on pages 38–9 you'll find a template for recording your answers:

1. Attention/executive function
- Any attentional issues? Is the problem harnessing attention or sustaining it?
- What impact do your attentional difficulties have?
- Are there any problems linked to hyperfocus?
- What factors influence your ability to concentrate?

2. Activity
- Hyperactivity or inner restlessness?
- Apathy, boredom or motivation problems?
- Any difficulty slowing down and taking rest?

3. Impulse
- Any impulsivity in terms of words, thoughts and actions?

- Any fallout from the impulsivity in terms of relationships, substance use, disordered eating, self-harm, anger management issues or accidents?

4. Emotion
- Are your emotions often dysregulated?
- Do you have a low tolerance of frustration or anger, or get easily overwhelmed?
- Are you highly sensitive to rejection and criticism?

5. Reward/pleasure-seeking
- Do you feel that your baseline state is under-rewarded (where normal pleasurable activities just don't hit the mark)?
- Are there any addictive problems (to alcohol or substances, or 'process addictions', such as pornography, gaming or gambling)?

6. Sensory processing
- Are there any sensory processing differences? Do they cause you problems or impact other symptoms?
- Do you often get overwhelmed due to sensory issues, or do you isolate yourself for protection?
- Are there any sensation-seeking behaviours (and, if present, are your addictive tendencies linked to sensation-seeking)?

7. Time appraisal
- Do you have 'time blindness', where you struggle to estimate how long things take?
- Are you very often running late or rushing?
- Do your time-management issues impact your relationships and productivity?

8. Sleep–wake (circadian) rhythm

- Are your sleep and wake times shifted later than usual, and what effect does this have?
- Do you often find yourself building up a 'sleep deficit', or ever slip into 'sleep reversal'?
- Do you have (or suspect) any other sleep-related issues, for example, restless legs syndrome, periodic limb movements, insomnia or obstructive sleep apnoea?

9. Immune function (and inflammation)

- Is there any evidence (or family history) of immune system dysregulation?
- Any immune over-reactivity (for example, intolerances, allergy, asthma, eczema or hay fever)?
- Any autoimmune-related issues?

10. Arousal and energy expenditure

- Do you have a 'boom and bust' pattern of functioning?
- Are there any 'energy drains' that may be stealing energy from your attention, such as pain, visual problems or lax joints?
- Is there any evidence of ANS dysregulation (or dysautonomia), for example, temperature regulation issues or cold extremities, symptoms on standing (relieved by lying flat), 'brain fog', hypervigilance, low energy, weakness or gut motility issues?

Once you have listed your specific features within each domain (if there are any), move on to the outcomes. First take a moment to evaluate the broader impact (the longer term, higher-level nega-tive or *adverse* outcomes) of your ADHD on your career, relationships and self-image, and capture these in the designated

ATTENTION

_____
_____
_____
_____
_____
_____
_____

ACTIVITY

_____
_____
_____
_____
_____
_____
_____

SENSORY

_____
_____
_____
_____
_____
_____

IMMUNE

_____
_____
_____
_____
_____
_____

SLEEP

_____
_____
_____
_____
_____
_____

NEGATIVE OUTCOMES

_____
_____
_____
_____

IMPULSE

_____
_____
_____
_____
_____
_____
_____
_____
_____

EMOTION

_____
_____
_____
_____
_____
_____
_____
_____
_____

TIME

_____
_____
_____
_____
_____
_____
_____

ENERGY

_____
_____
_____
_____
_____
_____
_____

REWARD

_____
_____
_____
_____
_____
_____
_____

POSITIVE ATTRIBUTES

_____
_____
_____
_____

Mapping out your ADHD signature

box. These may include relationship dysfunction, career or work-related problems, accidents, physical health problems and low self-esteem.

Finish by highlighting (in the box on page 41) a handful of positive attributes (*adaptive* outcomes) – those ADHD-linked traits where you excel and that make you special.

Studies have demonstrated that ADHD lies on a spectrum that everyone falls somewhere on, and that it is about degree. It's a bit like high blood pressure: everyone falls somewhere on the blood pressure range, however, at some point, towards the upper end of the scale, it becomes problematic, it becomes a disorder – hypertension – that requires treatment.

If, having reviewed the ten domains and completed the reflective exercise above, you feel ADHD is a distinct possibility, read on. In the next chapter, we'll be looking more closely at what is involved in screening and assessing for ADHD, and what is required to make a formal diagnosis. For now, though, let's take a look at the causes of ADHD so you can continue building your knowledge.

WHAT CAUSES ADHD?

When it comes to the question of cause, the truth of the matter is, no one really knows for sure. The majority of cases of ADHD are considered 'idiopathic', that is, they don't have a definable, identifiable cause. What we can say is that it is 'multifactorial', with a variety of different mechanisms contributing to one (or more) final common pathway.

Experts have established that the condition is associated with depleted (or dysregulated) levels of the brain chemicals (or neuro-transmitters) dopamine and noradrenaline. However, this is only looking from one narrow angle at a condition that is likely to have many faces. Certainly, the medications currently prescribed in ADHD work by boosting the circulating levels of these brain chemicals, addressing these presumed deficits. They may, however, also be working in other ways, perhaps including through their side effect of slightly increasing blood pressure and blood supply to the brain.

As with most mental health conditions, the current understanding is that ADHD is the result of **genetic factors** (variants in the genetic code, which is written into the DNA of our cells) causing a particular vulnerability. Importantly, there is no single gene that causes ADHD, rather multiple genes acting together and collectively increasing the chance of having the disorder. Various studies have shown that the heritability (or genetic weighting) of ADHD is around 70–80 per cent. That is high! In fact, of all mental health conditions, ADHD is right up near the peaks of the heritability scale. By way of comparison, the heritability of depression is around 30 per cent.

Environmental (or external) factors then interact with those genes and, in some cases, lead to ADHD symptoms. Several studies have sought to identify the environmental (external) triggers of ADHD, and those that have been linked with ADHD include:

- exposure to tobacco, alcohol, drugs and certain medications during pregnancy
- high blood pressure, stress, obesity and low vitamin D levels in the mother during pregnancy
- preterm (premature) birth, hypoxia (a lack of oxygen) during the delivery, low birth weight and brain injuries in the infant (these particular factors are thought to directly cause ADHD in some)
- childhood exposure to second-hand cigarette smoke
- exposure to certain environmental toxins
- iron deficiency
- low fatty acid blood levels
- artificial food colourings
- developmental trauma
- poverty

However, except in rare cases, it is virtually impossible to isolate any one specific environmental cause at an individual level, especially given the interaction with genetics. Despite much discussion and debate, there is no good evidence to support the notion that television, sugar, poor parenting or even social media can actually cause ADHD (although the latter certainly needs more study).

There are still so many unanswered questions around the causes of ADHD, but with an ever-increasing amount of data being fed into genetic studies and new insights emerging about the physical health problems that cluster together with ADHD, I feel we may be on the cusp of being able to answer a few more of them.

Is ADHD a disorder of the brain?

Whether driven by genetic or environmental influences (or a combination of both), it is important to consider whether ADHD is solely a disorder of the brain. Conventional wisdom, and a considerable body of research, would suggest that ADHD is indeed a disorder of brain structure and function.

Seemingly supportive of this view, recent genetic studies confirm that most of the genes that have been linked to ADHD do indeed have brain effects. The full story, however, may not be that simple, as genes commonly have a range of different functions. In the case of ADHD, some of the genes being identified also seem to have a variety of immune-related (and other) effects, an understanding which may in time provide further insight into what I suspect is a more system-wide disorder.

Our current, western medical model promotes the naive notion that illnesses must be either 'physical' (body-based) or 'mental' (brain- or mind-based), the implication being that there is some sort of impermeable boundary between what are perceived to be two distinct entities. From my perspective, this long-outdated Cartesian view has done a great disservice to western medicine and has been hugely divisive at many levels.

Everything I have gleaned during my professional career tells me that this could not be further from the truth. Consequently, for many years now, I have adopted a far more systemic perspective that integrates mind and body, physical and mental, as one. It seems obvious really and it is the foundation of the seven pillars in Part 2.

The contribution of traumatic stress

Traumatic stress, left in the wake of a highly distressing or catastrophic event, may overwhelm the normal processing ability of the brain and, in one of many manifestations, result in PTSD (post-traumatic stress disorder). PTSD occurs more commonly in those with ADHD, probably because of the heightened sensitivity-dysregulation dynamic.

Trauma presents in many guises, however, and mood dysregulation is a prominent feature, with a heightened background arousal level and hypervigilance. Experiences of a traumatic nature are distressing to recall, as the memories remain encoded in a bundle with raw emotion and lots of uncomfortable bodily arousal. I refer to this package of memory-linked emotion and physiology as a 'traumatic charge', a charge which gets activated by some form of memory trigger, commonly of a sensory nature.

Left unchecked, these unprocessed charges can dysregulate the system and, in some cases, may mimic the symptoms of ADHD. If the trauma occurs early in life, it may be better understood as the direct cause of the ADHD, rather than a masquerader. Either way, it is important to be mindful of the impact of trauma and how it may relate to ADHD.

Central to understanding trauma is recognising the avoidance patterns it leads to. As an attempt to minimise the distress associated with triggering, people work hard to avoid exposure, and they carefully navigate around any reminders of the event or events. This has the effect of narrowing and limiting one's life experience. Traumatic avoidance is sometimes confused with the procrastination and withdrawal that can occur in ADHD.

If you think you are struggling with unresolved trauma, please seek out appropriate support, which often includes trauma-focused psychotherapy, ideally (in my opinion) using an approach that engages the body.

CONDITIONS THAT TRAVEL TOGETHER WITH ADHD

Research has shown that there are certain conditions (both physical and mental) that occur more commonly in those with ADHD than they do normally. **'Comorbidity'** is the term used to describe the relationship between these conditions. The relationship could be due to shared genetics, or it may be that one of the conditions in some way drives, or facilitates, the other. For example, ADHD causes stress, and having chronically high stress makes developing an anxiety disorder much more likely. Therefore, there is a higher prevalence of anxiety disorders in those with ADHD.

Conversely and theoretically, the relationship could be working in the other direction – it could be that the other disorder is causing the ADHD presentation; however, aside from an example like a head injury, that is a bit more complicated to make sense of and throws up all sorts of challenges. Given that we don't fully understand ADHD, and the fact that adult diagnoses are increasing, with many cases seemingly emerging in adulthood for the first time, this idea might actually be worth entertaining.

Mental health and ADHD

We have known, for a long while now, that ADHD co-occurs with certain other mental health conditions (such as mood, anxiety and substance use disorders) at higher rates than would be expected.

Those with ADHD have been shown to be at greater risk of having:

1. **Psychiatric disorders**, such as anxiety disorder, depression and bipolar disorder.
2. **Neurodevelopmental disorders and learning difficulties**, such as autism, DCD (developmental co-ordination disorder or dyspraxia), Tourette's syndrome and dyslexia.
3. **Alcohol and substance use disorders**, particularly nicotine, cannabis and cocaine.
4. **Chronic low self-esteem**, presenting with prominent shame, a bruised sense of self and self-efficacy, and a tendency to be highly sensitive to rejection and criticism.
5. **Sensory processing issues**.

A note on addiction

ADHD and addiction, of various forms, commonly co-exist. If you have ADHD, you are far more likely to develop an issue with addiction. Looking in the other direction, individuals who experience addiction are also much more likely to have ADHD. There are multiple pathways from ADHD to addiction – they include the impulsivity and reward deficiency inherent to the condition, a response to negative life experience (linked to the ADHD), a consequence of self-medicating the symptoms of ADHD and the bruised self-esteem that is so common in the disorder. From the best available data, in the general population, between 2.3 and 41.2 per cent of adults with ADHD will also have some form of substance use disorder (compared to between 0 and 16.6 per cent in those who don't have ADHD). In a clinic population, the rates in those with ADHD go up to 82.9 per cent. Looking at the other side, a study found that one out of every four (25 per cent) adolescent and adult patients with a substance use disorder has ADHD.

In addition to **substance-related addictions**, there are a broad range of **behavioural, or 'process', addictions**. Among others, the list includes binge eating, watching pornography, having sex, working, shopping, social media, gambling, gaming, eating and self-harming.

Sadly, many who suffer addiction, including many with ADHD, are too ashamed to admit it to themselves or others. Aside from the physical health damage that may result from the behaviour in question, the denial, guilt and secrecy can plague lives for years and delay seeking out the required help.

If you recognise yourself in any of the above, please reach out to a professional for help – you are certainly not alone and addiction *can* be overcome. (See Resources, page 287 for support organisations.)

Physical health and ADHD

Studies conducted over recent years have highlighted intriguing comorbidities between ADHD and various physical health (or somatic) conditions. Research from Sweden and Japan has high-lighted stronger than expected associations with obesity, sleep disorders (including sleep disordered breathing), epilepsy, diabetes (Type 2) and high blood pressure.

While these could be argued as being logical and explainable in terms of the negative lifestyle impact of ADHD (for example, poor sleep and nutrition, higher stress levels, substance use, and so on), there are a handful of associated physical health issues that are rather more intriguing, as they can't easily be explained using this logic:

- allergies
- autoimmunity
- asthma
- pain
- hypermobility

My suspicion is that these somatic associations may well, in time, provide clues to the underlying drivers of the condition in some; however, this idea is highly controversial as it challenges the fundamental premise that ADHD is a neurodevelopmental disorder solely affecting the brain.

Should ADHD be seen as a 'disorder' or just a 'difference'?
ADHD is a form of neurodivergence, a term which focuses on the differences in brain structure and function that underlie the variations in how people process and experience the world around them. 'Neurodiversity' is usually used to describe neurodivergent individuals at a group level.

Neurodivergent people often find themselves disadvantaged in environments that have been optimised for the majority who aren't neurodivergent (often referred to as neurotypicals), but they may be advantaged in other settings, and with respect to certain skills or characteristics.

So, do we need to label this difference as a disorder? Does a focus on deficits lead to stigma, low self-esteem and impaired well-being? Should we not be reframing things to focus more on the strengths associated with neurodiversity?

These are all very important questions and, broadly speaking, I am in favour of much of what the neurodiversity movement stands for. I support its noble mission to try to create a more open and accepting society.

For me, it is quite simple, however: someone who has a few ADHD traits, but is not really struggling too much, is quite different from someone who is showing clear signs of dysfunction in multiple areas of their life. If it causes 'dis-order' over a sustained period, assuming the necessary environmental adaptations have proved unsuccessful, I would call it a 'disorder'. We are dealing with a condition for which there are recognised and effective treatments, and it is important to be able to identify, through robust assessment, those who are eligible for these treatments.

ADHD can be a highly symptomatic and destructive condition, particularly if not proactively managed. We must not minimise the huge burden that sufferers experience, and removing it from the realm of disorder, as some argue for, would likely do that. Making a diagnosis opens up additional options for intervention, including medication, which have the potential to be life-changing.

Wow, that was quite a journey. There's lots of information in this chapter, I know, but please don't panic. What I really want is for you to have developed a felt sense of what this entity we call ADHD really looks like, and how it typically plays out. Knowledge is power.

In the next chapter, we'll explore the formal adult ADHD assessment, as we now move from the 'What?' to the 'How?'

ASSESSMENT AND DIAGNOSIS

In the last chapter we explored the complexity of ADHD and I introduced how it can be best understood as a 'disorder of regulation'. In this chapter, I'll discuss a key, and often life-changing, moment in your ADHD journey: getting assessed and diagnosed.

Unfortunately, the diagnostic journey is not always a streamlined and efficient one. Lack of government resources and rising numbers of people globally seeking assessment have meant long waits, paired with increasingly loud voices challenging the validity of people's experience. More people are going private, but this is not without its own challenges and is financially out of reach for many people.

Therefore, in this chapter I have provided some top tips on how to effectively navigate the journey. I have also suggested a structured approach for you to follow to capture relevant information, both for your benefit and as key supporting information to share with your assessor if and when the time comes.

Now, I am aware that you'll all be at different points on this journey, so this chapter may be more relevant to some of you than others. As I unpick the minefield of adult ADHD assessment and diagnosis, my hope is to address the questions that you may have.

If you have *not yet been assessed*, this chapter has been designed to help guide you through the process. Having done the 'Adult ADHD and me' exercise on page 36, you may suspect that you have the condition. I encourage you to be rigorous with yourself now and start to critically review the supporting evidence. On the basis of this mini-experiment, you can then decide if you need to take things further.

If you have *already been formally diagnosed* and you are reading or listening to this book to help enhance your well-being, you may already be familiar with some of the detail that forms the rest of this chapter. You may still wish to read on, as what I cover may provide additional insights, validate your experience of your assessment and, through the guided self-reflection, further develop your understanding of your ADHD and your life experience to date. This will help you to properly evaluate where things presently stand. Of course, if this is all too much, just skim through the text that follows or skip forward and get started with the seven pillars in Part 2.

FIRST STEPS

If you suspect that ADHD may explain your difficulties, you might be wondering, *What now?* Before you pick up the phone to your GP (or family doctor) and ask for a referral to a specialist, let's just pause for a moment and consider whether progressing to a formal assessment is something you really need to do.

I think that pursuing a diagnosis of ADHD should be considered as a last resort, after you have first done your homework and some groundwork. In my experience, there needs to be an initial phase of exploring and unpacking the difficulties that you are experiencing. Before going in search of a label and possibly latching on to ADHD as a watertight explanation for your difficulties, an honest appraisal is required as to the underlying causes of the problem, and the potential for reversibility. For example, if, having read through the previous chapter, deep down, you suspect that your difficulties may be even partially linked to unresolved traumatic experience, your use of alcohol or cannabis, or your junk food diet (all of which, by the way, are more common in those with

ADHD), it is important that you first try to address these reversible factors. It is only then that you will be able to properly see how the land lies.

By first optimising your self-care and lifestyle management, guided by the seven pillars in Part 2, you can then better determine if you are able to avert the need for assessment, diagnosis and possibly long-term medication. Of course, this approach may not be enough, but it could be worth having as an initial goal.

All that said, if, after a period of scrutiny and on the balance of probabilities, you do indeed think that you need to be assessed, in the first instance, go and speak to your GP and share your concerns and provide your rationale. As long as you put forward a reasonable case, and after a few additional questions, they should be comfortable to make a referral to a specialist service.

SCREENING FOR ADULT ADHD

There are a handful of tools that screen for the presence of adult ADHD and its associated impairment. These brief questionnaires are designed to guide decision-making and focus, and perhaps map progress over time.

Screening tools are most certainly not diagnostic, but they are a reasonable 'ballpark' guide. The two most commonly used in clinical practice are the **Adult ADHD Self Report Scale (ASRS)** and the **Weiss Functional Impairment Rating Scale (WFIRS)**, both of which can be easily accessed online.

Both tools can be helpful to guide thinking – the former on the likelihood of ADHD being present, and the latter on the scope of impairment – but I really think that the ten domains approach in the last chapter, along with the 'ADHD and me' exercise, provides a more extensive landscape for self-evaluation. I also find that the ASRS tends to throw up quite a lot of false positives.

I feel I need to introduce a note of caution here when it comes to the increasingly common practice of **'self-diagnosis'**. By this, I mean an individual coming to a relatively firm conclusion, perhaps on the basis of an online questionnaire or after reading some posts, but without a formal assessment, that they 'definitely' have ADHD.

It takes time and skill to properly evaluate for ADHD and it is not a diagnosis to make on a whim, or after a brief clinical encounter. It is not such a straightforward diagnosis to make as, unlike the symptoms we might observe in a psychotic illness like schizophrenia, such as delusions and hallucinations, which clearly lie beyond the scope of 'normality', the defining symptoms of ADHD are features that most can relate to (in some way, at some point). Everyone has experienced what it feels like to be a bit inattentive, or restless, or has acted slightly too impulsively, for example. This is not uncommon at times of high stress, or when sleep-deprived, overworked or hungover.

It is the chronicity, frequency and intensity of the symptoms, and the degree to which they negatively impact someone's life experience – it is the presence of 'impairment', which we'll discuss on page 60 – that shifts things out of the 'normal' zone and into the realm of 'disorder'. If it doesn't meet this impairment threshold, no diagnosis is made and we refer to these features as ADHD 'traits'.

If you do strongly suspect that you have ADHD and you are awaiting an assessment, there is a lot you can do to improve your situation – this book is an excellent starting point.

WHO CAN MAKE A DIAGNOSIS?

To carry out a 'clinical' assessment for adult ADHD, as well as having the required expertise in ADHD itself, the practitioner must have sufficient experience to be able to consider a range of other possible psychiatric conditions, that may be present alongside the ADHD or that may be masquerading as ADHD.

Critically, the diagnostician must also be able to screen adequately for underlying physical health problems (that could potentially be causing the ADHD-like symptoms) and ideally understand the various factors that may influence the prescribing of ADHD medication, if indeed this is indicated and wanted.

For these reasons, clinicians who carry out adult ADHD assessments have traditionally been psychiatrists, who are, of course, medically trained (and sometimes psychologists, who are not). Increasingly, however, and in line with the UK's NICE guidelines on ADHD, in NHS settings (and equivalent state-run healthcare systems in other countries) assessing clinicians will come from a range of mental health disciplines.

If you get referred to a specialist service within the NHS, there may well be a multidisciplinary team approach to your assessment, with different parts being done by different practitioners. There should, in my opinion, at the very least, be a degree of medical oversight. The reality of inadequate resources, however, means that state-run healthcare services need to find a viable way to deal with the ever-increasing flow of adult ADHD referrals.

In the private sector, there are a range of models that exist, from the single independent psychiatrist to a more multidisciplinary clinic-based model. There have been criticisms surrounding the standards of some private providers, especially the more commercially minded businesses that sometimes seem to prioritise throughput at the expense of adequate quality, sufficient 'quantity' (in terms of face-to-face contact time and thoroughness) and continuity, though this is not my experience of the increasing pool of well-trained, independent private psychiatrists who do things properly. I may be biased as I am responsible, as UKAAN's Director of Education, for coordinating most of the training provided in the UK, but I suspect most 'in the know' would agree with my appraisal.

In my view, the optimal (but not always possible) scenario is when a single experienced clinician, ideally a psychiatrist, journeys with you through the whole assessment process, and then carries you forward into the treatment phase. After all, a lot of what makes the experience of being assessed, diagnosed and treated nourishing and growth-promoting is the relationship and trust that forms between practitioner and patient. This approach is commonplace in parts of the private sector, and in some specialist NHS services.

In response to the debate around quality of assessment and the exponential spike in adult ADHD referrals over recent years, UKAAN has published consensus guidelines – 'The Adult ADHD Assessment Quality Assurance Standard' (AQAS) – that should clarify for both provider and patient exactly what the expectations are when it comes to adult ADHD assessments (see page 293 for a link to the AQAS).

Non-medical assessments for adult ADHD

Non-medical assessments for adult ADHD are relatively new phenomena, typically carried out in higher educational settings by trained special educational needs (SEN) practitioners. The main objective is to expedite the assessment process, and more quickly establish the diagnosis in students presenting with learning difficulties, to try to minimise the impact on their studies. These assessments, although robust and typically of high quality, are generally more heavily weighted towards how the symptoms are impacting on learning.

The assessment may result in a 'non-medical' or 'provisional' diagnosis of adult ADHD, which is generally sufficient for the student to access the necessary accommodations (for example, extra time or rest breaks in examinations, funding for disability support, and so on). If the student also wants to explore the option of ADHD medication, a supplementary clinical or medical assessment with an adult ADHD specialist needs to be organised. This will formalise adult ADHD as a 'medical diagnosis' and assess for the appropriateness of prescribing.

WHAT HAPPENS IN AN ASSESSMENT?

Following a GP referral to an adult ADHD service (or specialist), and sometimes after an unacceptably long wait, you will generally be sent a pre-assessment pack containing some information and various tasks. It will typically include some questionnaires and baseline scales (or screening tests) for you, and some of those close to you, to fill out and return – these may well include the two I mentioned on page 52, but there are a range of others. Some clinics conduct a brief screening interview to establish appropriateness.

You will then, hopefully, be offered an assessment appointment which will either be carried out remotely or in-person. The assessment may well take place over two sessions and, as a rough guide, if things are done properly, there should be at least two hours of face-to-face contact in total. It may well be longer depending on the level of complexity and skill of the assessing clinician.

The assessment generally starts with **an evaluation of your reported difficulties**, exploring and screening for the characteristic symptoms and impairment of ADHD in both the childhood years and adult life. This is usually done using a semi-structured diagnostic interview to help guide the discussion. The assessor should use open questions and encourage you to elaborate and reflect on certain themes, often with some gentle probing. They will be trying to elicit real-life examples of your reported difficulties, rather than simply relying on a 'tick box' approach, which is just not good enough.

Top tip

If you haven't done so already, I would encourage you to do the **'Adult ADHD and me'** exercise on page 36. Once populated, you can photograph it and either email it in advance of your assessment or print it out and take it along with you. This will show your assessor your ADHD-related difficulties and how they impact your life.

As you can see, the assessment is more than simply a 'snapshot' impression gained during the meeting. It is multidimensional and lifespan-focused. The assessor should take a detailed **developmental history**, which starts with the especially vulnerable perinatal period (that is the period before, during and after your birth). It then traverses your childhood years, particularly looking for clues to the presence of other neurodevelopmental disorders (for example, autism, tics/Tourette's syndrome, dyslexia or DCD), and other specific learning disabilities, including intellectual disability.

Exercise: Plot your life story

It may be helpful for you to provide a (one-page) written 'life story' or timeline to the person assessing you, ideally prior to the meeting. On one or two sides of paper, possibly in your Thrive Journal, capture poignant events and notable ADHD-related difficulties from your life – events and experiences that have shaped and defined you. Try to include detail relating to:

- **Pregnancy, birth and infancy:** include any details you know about your mother's pregnancy and your birth and early years:

- Were there any birth complications or issues with you achieving developmental milestones?
- What was your early temperament like? (Getting this information may require some additional detective work, but it is important.)
- **Childhood and adolescence:** here you should note relevant reflections from your nursery and school days:
  - How did you relate to others (both children and adults)? How were you perceived by others? How did you cope with your studies?
  - Include relevant detail about your peer group relationships, academic progress (and specific areas of difficulty), exclusions or expulsions, behaviour in class, antisocial activities, traumatic experiences and personal relationships.
  - Provide an appraisal of when problems started or escalated and reflect on life events and transitions that particularly stand out.
- **Adulthood:** think about important periods of transition, for example, leaving the family home, going into further education, starting your first job, getting married or divorced, retiring, and so on:
  - Consider key relationships (family, social and work-related) and important moments during your education and career to date. Again, try to provide an appraisal of when problems started, or escalated.

As well as guiding the path ahead, your life story will allow reflection down the line, on how things were pre-treatment, so you are better able to evaluate progress.

In addition to a deep dive into your ADHD features (past and present) and a decent developmental history, there are a number of **other areas** that are covered in a good-quality adult ADHD assessment:

- **Your mental health history**
  - The assessor will be screening for other common mental health problems (historically and current), particularly ones that may mimic ADHD (for example, bipolar type 2), and those that commonly co-occur with ADHD (for example, depression).
- **Your physical health history**
  - The assessor will be screening for common comorbidities, for example, obesity, allergies, hypermobility, asthma, epilepsy, diabetes, migraines, eye abnormalities and autoimmune conditions, such as psoriasis and ulcerative colitis.
  - This should include a consideration of sleep and diet (including your current, baseline, weight).
  - There will be an evaluation of your cardiovascular health (including a measurement of your baseline blood pressure and pulse rate) if medication is being considered.
- **Your family history**
  - There should be questions about the mental and physical health of family members, as this could influence how the assessor formulates your case, or the approach to treatment.
- **Informant perspectives**
  - Informant perspectives can be given in person, over the phone or by email. This is a key part of the process as they can give a valuable perspective and provide additional information that can serve to validate what you have said. Ideally, at least one should be someone who knew you during your childhood years (usually a parent or older sibling). If possible,

this should be supported by an account from someone who has known you over more recent times, as this will provide an insight into your current day-to-day functioning.

– School reports, if you can locate them, can also be a really great source of somewhat objective information about your childhood years, and how you were at school. In my experience, they can really add weight to the diagnosis. If you can't find your school reports, look for other forms of historical documentation that could prove helpful, for example an educational psychology assessment report.

• **An evaluation of functional impairment**

– Providing an employment history summary (or equivalent), with some accompanying notes containing your honest reflections, can be helpful and revealing.

MEETING THE THRESHOLD FOR DIAGNOSIS

With respect to ADHD, as we saw in the last chapter, the *DSM-5* is the most widely used diagnostic system (certainly in the UK) at the time of writing. This version of the *DSM* is the first to include minor adjustments to allow the criteria to be used in adults as well as children, with the increasing recognition that ADHD is a disorder that affects people right across the lifespan.

There are six *DSM-5* criteria (criteria A to E). The first, criteria A, essentially involves a **symptom count** (the list of 18 ADHD symptoms we discussed in the last chapter and which are included in full in the Appendix on page 283). The remainder of the criteria (B to E) relate to **age of onset**, the presence and scope of **impairment** and **exclusions** (that is, that the symptoms are not better explained by another disorder).

In terms of criteria A, the list of symptoms is divided into two categories – **Inattentive** (I) and **Hyperactive-Impulsive** (H-I) – with nine symptoms in each.

For older adolescents and adults (aged 17 and older), at least five symptoms are required in either category (or both) to meet this criteria. For a symptom to be present it needs to be *persistent* (lasting at least six months), *pervasive* (affecting multiple areas of your life) and *problematic* (interfering with functioning or development).

The decision as to whether or not to diagnose often boils down to the question of *impairment* – has a critical threshold of dysfunction been met in this person (that most would agree requires some form of intervention), in order that we can reasonably define this as 'disorder'?

Impairment can come in a variety of guises, some more obvious than others. It can extend to all areas listed below, and more:

- work functions
- family and social relationships
- coping with day-to-day activities
- accidents (particularly driving accidents)
- significant distress from the symptoms, and very low self-esteem
- marked emotional instability and behavioural problems
- severe sleep problems
- coexisting (or 'comorbid') disorders (for example, addiction, anxiety, depression, autism)
- related cognitive deficits, including specific learning difficulties

Importantly, it is still possible to diagnose ADHD in those who may be doing well in some areas of their life, so long as there is sufficient impairment in others. Equally, many people will display some traits, or ADHD-like tendencies, which are sufficiently compensated for, and not overly impairing. This is a difficult but important line for diagnosticians to negotiate, and understandably one that can be controversial, but this is no different from any other mental health disorder.

Factors that determine the degree of impairment

1. The **type of ADHD** – for example, having ADHD-Combined presentation has been shown to be more severe, compared with the other presentations of ADHD (we'll explore the types of ADHD below).
2. The **time of day** and the associated **demands**.
3. Whether or not ADHD **medication** is used, or has been taken that day.
4. The individual's **hormonal status** at the time (including phase of menstrual cycle and menopause).
5. The quality and duration of **sleep**.
6. The presence of coexistent **mental or physical health issues** (including other neurodevelopmental conditions, and alcohol/substance use).
7. **Gastrointestinal health** and other **nutritional factors**.
8. The individual's **stage in life**, and the associated **demands**.
9. The individual's level of **intelligence** and **motivation**.
10. The degree of **'scaffolding'** (support structures) in place.

The truth is that it boils down to a judgement call of the assessing clinician as to whether the threshold has been reached to warrant a diagnosis of ADHD. The impairment needs to be at least of *moderate severity*. A useful 'ballpark' is that the impairment should be to a degree that most would consider requires some form of medical (or social/educational) intervention, and where there are likely to be long-term negative implications for the individual, if left unchecked. (Note that the seven pillars in Part 2 and the Creative Workarounds in Part 3 will give you strategies for modifying your environment and changing things from the outside, which may limit or even neutralise the extent to which you are impaired.)

If a diagnosis is made, there is a 'specifier' according to the subtype (or 'presentation') of ADHD. This is not fixed and may change from day to day. At the time of assessment, if the criteria in both categories are met, then a diagnosis of **ADHD-Combined presentation** is made. If criteria are only met in the inattention category, a diagnosis of **ADHD-Predominantly inattentive presentation** is made. (Note: This diagnosis replaces the previously used name, ADD, or 'Attention Deficit Disorder'.) If criteria are only met in the hyperactivity/impulsivity category, a diagnosis of **ADHD-Predominantly hyperactive/impulsive presentation** is made.

Aside from the 3 types of ADHD presentation listed above, there is a further diagnostic category, **'ADHD in partial remission'** – this is where the full criteria were previously met, but this is no longer the case, yet there is ongoing impairment in social, academic or occupational functioning. Additionally, there is a (little known) optional, further stratification of the severity, into **mild**, **moderate** or **severe**, depending on the symptom burden and level of impairment.

Untangling the overlap with other mental health conditions

ADHD has a wide range of its own symptoms and, as we discussed in the last chapter, there is often more going on besides the ADHD which may be muddying the water. Some people will be misdiagnosed with ADHD when in fact something else is going on.

There is a 60–80 per cent chance that, if you have ADHD, you will have at least one other mental health condition, or 'comorbidity', over the course of your life. In fact, studies show that those with ADHD have an average of three additional comorbid mental health conditions. The mental health issues that journey together with ADHD shape how it manifests and it is expressed. And whether these other conditions are recognised, and how they are addressed, will radically influence the outcome.

Identifying and carefully mapping out exactly what is going on early in the process is important, as it may influence the approach and, more specifically, what you tackle first. Separating what is ADHD and what is comorbidity-linked can, at times, be challenging, and sometimes only becomes clear as the journey unfolds.

Keep in mind that it may not be 'one thing or the other' – both conditions could very well be present, especially given the high rates of mental and physical health comorbidity in ADHD. It's all a little technical and confusing, I know! That is precisely the reason that you need a professional with expertise in adult ADHD to help guide the process.

Finally, it can sometimes be challenging to differentiate the mood-related features of ADHD (which can include low self-esteem, emotional dysregulation, excitability, low motivation and apathy) from an independent mood disorder such as depression or bipolar disorder, or emotionally unstable (or borderline) personality disorder (or other responses to earlier traumatic experience or attachment disturbance, such as complex post-traumatic stress disorder – CPTSD). Mood-related features are likely to respond to ADHD treatment, whereas independent mood disorders will generally not (although the use of ADHD medication has not actually been studied in personality disorder or CPTSD, where it may be useful).

WHAT HAPPENS AFTER A DIAGNOSIS

Following a diagnosis of ADHD, there will, in all likelihood, be some discussion around certain themes, loosely referred to as **psychoeducation**. This is basically a download of what you need to know about ADHD in adulthood – the challenges you are likely to face, and the pitfalls to try to circumnavigate. Stigma, education, employment and relationships may be topics of discussion, together with safe driving and, more broadly, the need to be mindful of the higher risk of accidents in ADHD. You may also be cautioned about the lure of mind-altering substances and possibly about other unhealthy patterns of 'self-medication'.

The clinician will probably provide an overview of the treatment approach and services/options available locally, but ideally the emphasis should be initially centred on you adjusting to and coming to terms with your diagnosis, with the opportunity for questions.

A key take-home coming from this post-diagnostic debrief should be the critical importance of *working to your strengths* – first clearly identifying and then setting your life up around your strengths, skills and passions.

What I am describing here is, of course, the gold standard approach, so don't be too disappointed if it doesn't work quite like this.

The more detailed discussion about treatment, and medication specifically, if this is on the cards, is often scheduled for a subsequent session (we'll talk more about medication and other treatment options in Part 3, but feel free to look ahead if your follow-up session is due shortly). Separating the assessment and treatment session is, in part, so as not to overload you after what has likely been a long and emotionally laden day, but there are other reasons to do this.

My advice to you is as follows: before jumping in with more radical interventions such as medication, work through the seven pillars in Part 2 and attempt to incorporate some of the suggested lifestyle modifications, workaround strategies and environmental adaptations (known as environmental modifications). We can either alter our internal physiology and drives, or we can look to make changes to the outside, which is generally easier and often surprisingly impactful.

After reading this chapter, you may have concluded that you don't reach the threshold for diagnosis. If you are somewhere on the fence, using the tools and tips to come in the pillars in Part 2, you may be able to compensate sufficiently in your areas of struggle.

If you are debating going down the route of formal assessment, why not shift the order around? Try out some of the approaches in the pillars *before* getting assessed, to see if they help. After all, if they improve things enough, perhaps you can avoid a lot of unnecessary aggravation.

For those of you who have been formally diagnosed, if you are anything like me, as you confront and reflect on 'wasted years' and 'missed opportunities', you could be questioning, *Why wasn't my ADHD picked up earlier?* or feeling sorry for yourself and asking, *Why me?* What you are feeling is completely normal and you are in the right place. These emotional responses are valid and entirely understandable. You are where you are on this journey, but by virtue of the fact that you are reading this, you are being proactive and doing something about it.

Some of you may have already been prescribed medication, and many will have concluded that it can be useful, sometimes 'can't live without it' useful. However, you may also have realised that it will only ever take you part of the way. Again, this is where those environmental modifications come into the frame.

Let's now dive into the main event – my seven pillars – created to support you to thrive with adult ADHD, no matter where you are on your journey.

PART 2

THE SEVEN PILLARS: MANAGING ADULT ADHD

Harnessing the potential power of your unique ADHD brain requires you to discover ways of using it to your advantage, shifting those outcomes that we met in the first chapter away from *adverse* and towards *adaptive*. There is so much that you can do, but it is going to take the right mental attitude, a structured approach and an investment of energy.

Such an undertaking requires a multifaceted approach; one that considers mind and body, psychology and biology; that recognises and nurtures your brilliance; that proactively engages with others for support; and that reflects the complexity of you and your individual journey. The foundations are all now in place for us to embark on the seven pillars.

Whether you are pre- or post-assessment, on or off medication, family member or friend, the material included in this section should add tangible value to your self-development journey (or your ability to support the journey of a loved one).

Remember, not every suggestion will apply to you at the stage you are at. Please extract only what you need – engage with it more as a menu of options than a prescriptive 'must do'. There is no one size that fits all when it comes to adult ADHD, so try some stuff out and see what works.

Finally, when attempting to make any changes in your life, it is important that they are integrated actively and consciously, with an upbeat, welcoming and positive attitude. Changes that are actively resisted (termed 'egodystonic' in clinical psychology) will require a supersize serving of willpower to implement. When you resort to a 'high-effort–low-joy' strategy, the interventions have a high chance of losing steam, and ultimately failing.

Instead, I encourage you to build a buzz of excitement, and plan your strategy carefully. Try to drip feed mini-shifts progressively and incrementally, rather than attempting to do everything all in one go.

Exercise: Tailoring and targeting change

In the 'Adult ADHD and me' exercise on page 36, you mapped out your unique 'ADHD signature' – the particular cluster of difficulties and impairments that you experience. Take a moment now to refresh yourself on your day-to-day symptom and impairment profile.

If you feel motivated to build on this, I invite you to write 200–400 words about how you are feeling about your life presently. This is a facade-free zone, so no covering up or minimising. It should be a true appraisal of how you are currently doing. Then, identify some targets for change in relation to your ADHD. Doing this exercise before diving into the seven pillars will help focus the mind, inform your life choices moving forward and provide a framework for looking back and evaluating your progress over time.

You can use the prompts below as a starting point:

- What is healthy and positive about your life at present?
- Where do you feel you are not living up to your expectations of yourself?
- Can you identify key problem areas and think about what may be holding you back?
- Which areas do you want to focus on initially? You possibly have a wish to slow down, pull back or shed some of your current responsibilities that are weighing you down. Perhaps a desire to better regulate your emotional world or change the way you communicate and relate to yourself and others. Targets for change could include sleep, nutrition, physical exercise or other aspects of self-care. Or addressing or overcoming a block or barrier that stands in your way, such as a limiting belief or a festering addiction. It is really up to you.

Before we fire up the engines and move to countdown, an important caveat: when things don't work out on your first attempt, try not to despair. Take some time to stop and reflect on what didn't go to plan (as well as what went well), and then redirect your efforts and try something new, adapting your approach based on what you learned.

And get something clear in your mind from the very start: this change business is not a linear trajectory; it is a lifelong expedition that will present unpredictable twists and turns – it's just the way it is. Adopting an 'agile' and resilient mindset will serve you well, which happens to be the focus of the first pillar.

I invite you, whenever you feel ready, to tune in, orientate your intention to thrive as opposed to survive and, most important of all, do your very best to enjoy the ride.

PILLAR 1

NURTURE A GROWTH-ORIENTED MINDSET

The more I have experienced and observed, in both my personal and professional wanderings, the more I realise how important mindset is when it comes to managing ADHD. In the context of ADHD, 'mindset' encompasses the following themes:

- How you understand and make sense of your ADHD and associated difficulties.
- How you negotiate ADHD-related adversity (when things go wrong).
- How much toxic emotion (such as anger, guilt and shame) you harbour and carry with you, following that adversity.

I find that adults who have struggled during their life with undiagnosed ADHD (and a fair number of those diagnosed in childhood too) often have a tainted view of themselves and their ability to effect change – a resigned acceptance that they are in some way flawed or inferior. I don't know a single person with the condition who doesn't struggle, more than the average, with some form of shame-related intrusion – from the frustrating and embarrassing executive function mess-ups and impulsive 'I can't believe I said that' screw-ups, to the slowness, and the absentmindedness and the 'oh no, not again-ness'. You just can't get away from it.

Shame is just one 'block' or psychological barrier that risks impeding your progress, barriers that may lead to a degree of resistance to you fully accepting yourself and embracing your ADHD. In my experience, the most **common sources of resistance** broadly align with the following themes:

- A concern that ADHD is not a 'real' thing, and that you're making it up.
- A worry that there are far more needy people out there, that it's not so bad and that you're making an unnecessary fuss.
- A fear of being judged and stigmatised by others.
- A confusion about the boundaries between you and your ADHD.
- A self-pitying 'Why me?' preoccupation.
- Unhelpful limiting thoughts such as *I'm a failure, I'm flawed, I'm unworthy* or *It's just hopeless and futile*.

These psychological barriers are the hallmarks of what has been termed a 'fixed' mindset. This can also manifest as a fear of making mistakes and being judged in a negative light, as well as an avoidance of opportunities that challenge you. Or sometimes as a tunnel vision sprint to the finish line to be the winner, to be 'the best'.

Some of the **most common fixed-thinking traps** I see in those with adult ADHD include:

- **All-or-nothing thinking:** This is also referred to as 'black or white' thinking. You may catch yourself saying things like, 'If I can't give 100 per cent, it is not worth doing it at all', 'I'm either a good person or I'm an idiot' or 'My ADHD stops me from . . .' The reality is that things are rarely so clear-cut. We live in a world of uncertainty – the challenge is to embrace it and become more comfortable residing in the grey zone.

- **Overgeneralisation:** This is the trap of coming to further-reaching conclusions than there is evidence to support them. Ask yourself: Would others come to the same conclusion? And do you really have enough data to support your convictions?
- **Selective filtering (and discounting):** This is when we select only the information that supports our argument or position and discount the rest. This can play out when we are quick to notice and highlight our failures, but then neglect to acknowledge our successes. Being honest with yourself, do you focus more on the bad stuff or do you give things a fair appraisal?
- **Jumping to conclusions:** Sharing some features with 'all-or-nothing thinking' and 'selective filtering', this is where you make judgements and come to conclusions that you deem to be true, but which may well not be. Whenever you make bold statements, always stop and question the supporting evidence. Ask yourself if you are being balanced and reasonable. Jumping to conclusions can come in two common forms:
  1. *Mind reading*: This is where we think we know what other people are thinking (and, surprise, surprise, it often turns out to be a projection of our own anxieties).
  2. *Fortune telling*: This is where we believe we know what is going to happen before it does, based on limited data.
- **Magnification and minimisation:** These speak for themselves and again have overlap with some of the traps already described. Catastrophising, a form of magnification, involves giving more weight to the worst possible outcome or defining a situation as 'unbearable' or 'impossible', when it is just a bit uncomfortable. Do you find yourself overstating the negatives and underplaying the upsides in a situation? Does this happen when you think or talk about yourself, and how might someone else perceive this?
- **Emotional reasoning (being unduly led by emotion):** Here, we fall into the trap of assuming that our current emotional state reflects the external reality when it may well not. For example, if we are feeling very anxious when giving a speech, we may

conclude that we come across to the audience as a fraud. Just because it feels a bit uncomfortable inside, it doesn't necessarily mean that others see it that way.

- **Being led by thoughts:** With this trap, you may conclude that you feel a certain way, based on the content of your thoughts. In fact, it is very often the feeling (emotion or body sensation) that comes first, and the thoughts then follow in order to try to make sense of the feeling. Do your best to get below the thoughts and work out what is actually going on.

These limiting beliefs can be energy-draining and toxic. Left to brew, over time they are likely to promote self-hatred, confusion, fear and a victim mentality.

ADHD does indeed present complexity and bring certain challenges, but with it also come unique opportunities for growth and development – a chance to tune your brain and refine your approach and, over time, to allow your real potential and purpose to powerfully shine through. I can't think of a 'condition' in the mental health domain that has as much of a flip side as ADHD. In my experience, managed well, with the right support and scaffolding in place, and under the right conditions, it undoubtedly has the potential to drive excellence.

Having guided many hundreds of adults towards better management of their ADHD, I have come to appreciate that central to the success of skilfully negotiating these ups and downs is the cultivation of a growth-oriented mindset.

SEVEN STEPS TO NURTURE A GROWTH-ORIENTED MINDSET

According to US psychologist Carol Dweck, who popularised the terms in her book *Mindset*, having a 'growth' as opposed to a 'fixed' mindset, enhances well-being, and confers countless other benefits, as demonstrated by a raft of studies. She teaches that skills and intelligence can be honed and sharpened through dedication, hard work and the right mental attitude. The concept of a growth mindset centres on the notion that we're not simply born with a fixed skill set and pre-defined capability, but instead that we are fundamentally malleable, and have enormous potential to grow, adapt and improve.

With ADHD, a growth mindset is crucial as it allows you to reframe your perceived inadequacies and deficits as opportunities for learning and growth. A missed deadline, a late tax bill penalty or a mishap resulting from an impulsive decision cease to be representative of personal failure and riddled with shame. Instead, it becomes more about 'why', and what insights you can take from the experience that can inform future action.

With that in mind, let's now explore the ways in which you can foster a growth-oriented mindset.

Step 1: Challenge unhelpful thoughts

How we think about things is, in part, a product of our life experience. It is easy to see how, having lived a lifetime of ADHD's ups and downs, your thinking may be somewhat tainted. When faced with a new challenge, you may think, *I messed up when I tried it last time, so it's probably doomed from the start* or *I know I'm going to show myself up, so I might as well quit now.* Our thinking can become skewed and distorted, causing us to frame things in a way that leaves us feeling depleted and trapped.

These negative, distorted thinking styles don't always represent the reality of the situation and are often based on limited information. It's important to recognise these early and act quickly to avoid a spiralling effect.

One way to challenge these unhelpful patterns of thinking is with positive affirmations.

Exercise: Affirmation integration with acupoint tapping
Positive affirmations are statements used to bring about a more adaptive and resilient attitude. At the most basic level, positive affirmations involve choosing an upbeat phrase and repeating it quietly to yourself.

Affirmations have been shown to boost self-esteem and to motivate and drive change, combating rigid, subconscious 'scripts'. Studies in this area suggest that they can alter your concept of self and reduce the perception of external threat and defensiveness.

I find that combining the use of affirmations with tapping on acupuncture points dramatically enhances effectiveness. Acupoint tapping is employed by a variety of emotion/ trauma processing approaches, the most popular of which is Emotional Freedom Techniques, or EFT.

I will be discussing EFT in more detail in Pillar 7. To keep things really simple at this point, for the following exercise I have selected two important points for you to tap on: the two **collarbone points** on the upper chest, just below the junction of the breastbone and the two collarbones, on both sides, and the **karate chop point** on the outer edge of either hand (the padded area below the little finger):

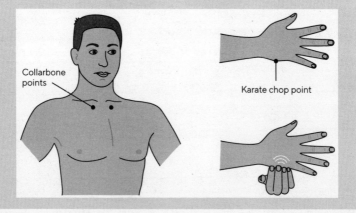

Collarbone points

Karate chop point

1. Decide which negative thought or block you want to tackle. You can select and, if necessary, adapt a statement from the list of problem-related affirmations in the box below and then write it down. Feel free to mix and match as you need. (Note: not all of the examples listed will be relevant to you, so, as you read through them for the first time, mark the ones that you relate to or that are most applicable.)

2. Commit a few minutes of your time and find a quiet space, free from distraction. Take a few slow, deep breaths and centre yourself.

3. Read the selected statement out loud, repeating it two or three times to yourself, tuning your mind into the words you are saying.

4. While you read, tap continuously on each of the two locations in turn. The frequency (or rate) should be approximately two to three taps a second. Switch from one location to the other about every ten seconds. When you tap, make reasonable contact, but not so firmly that you bruise or hurt yourself.

There is a growing body of research supporting the use of these tapping techniques in a whole range of conditions, including post-traumatic stress disorder (PTSD).

Menu of problem-related affirmations
- 'Even though I have lots of resistance to this ADHD thing, I choose to take time to look at it properly and access the support I need.'

- 'Even though it all feels a bit overwhelming at the moment, I choose to accept and embrace the challenge, and work out what I need to do about it.'
- 'Even though I am feeling sorry for myself, it is what it is and it's all going to work out okay.'
- 'Even though I sometimes feel like a waste of space and I don't really like who I am, I choose to let go of these unhelpful thoughts and start to believe in myself and my potential.'
- 'Even though ADHD affects every aspect of my life and it feels like a constant struggle, my intention is to try to centre my life around what I am really good at, and the things I love!'
- 'Even though I have this diagnosis that makes some sense of my behaviours and difficulties, I choose not to use it to my advantage or to excuse inappropriate actions, but instead give it the respect it deserves and strive to live well with it.'
- 'Even though ADHD is a pain in the backside, a perpetual annoyance, a constant irritation, I know there is a flipside. My unique brain works in interesting and creative ways and I choose to give it the space to show what it can really do.'
- 'Even though I am worried about what people will think and I hate having a label as it feels like an excuse, I choose to shed all this shame and start being kinder to myself so that I can become the best version of myself.'
- 'Even though I feel like a fraud, and that others are more deserving, I choose to embrace my ADHD wholeheartedly, and make the best of things.'
- 'Even though I feel confused and scared, my ADHD is probably here to stay so I will learn to live with it and try to make the best of my lot.'
- 'Even though I feel _____, I love and accept myself.'

Another effective way to counter negative thinking traps is to catch them early, scrutinise them and, if appropriate, think of a more accurate and balanced alternative – known as 'reframing'.

Reframing

Usually, it is possible to 'reframe' a situation, simply by viewing it in a different light, and adopting an alternative, more growth-oriented mindset.

If you recognise yourself in any of the thinking traps we explored above, try reframing:

- Broaden your lens and try to look beyond the original frame.
- Try to rationalise and normalise the situation. Remind yourself that you are where you are and, however much you might want to, you simply can't turn back the clock and undo what is already done. Tell yourself, *I am only human, and we all make mistakes* and *It's okay to feel this; it is part of the tapestry of life.*
- Find and celebrate the positives and try to see adversity as growth-promoting. Come up with another, more adaptive, way of looking at the issue. Think, *What is the potential upside? And what is the learning to take from this?*
- Ask yourself what a close friend would say to you about how you are thinking about this.
- In summary: catch it, check it and change it.

If the negative thoughts relate to how others might judge you or your contribution, I find that reminding yourself that we are all fallible and, ultimately, in the same boat, can really help. The reality is the other person is likely to be less bothered about you and your actions, and more concerned about how they themselves might be perceived – each party in their own self-conscious, paranoid bubble, worrying unnecessarily, and wasting lots of energy in the process.

Step 2: Use positive and energising language

Much like thought, speech is a powerful medium which deserves to be treated with respect. The words that we use and the tone in which we utter them significantly influence the way we feel about ourselves and our situation. Remember, words are an external representation of our beliefs. They can be used as a guide by us and others to the dynamics of our internal world.

It may take a bit of practice to first recognise when your words may be doing you or others harm, and then to rein in the impulse to speak negatively; however, it is worth the effort. Replacing loaded language and low-level hostility with more compassion and calm honesty can have a transformative effect on both your interactions and your sense of self.

Below is a selection of examples where our words (and self-talk) may be negatively impacting our behaviours, self-esteem, relationships and overall experience of life, together with some alternative approaches and practical suggestions:

Should've, could've

Try to avoid phrases like 'I should have . . .' or 'I could have . . .'; they just breed the toxic emotions of shame, guilt and regret. Try to think more in terms of 'I will . . .', 'I may . . .' and 'I choose to . . .'

Have to, need to

Try to banish loaded and pressuring words and phrases like 'have to', 'ought to', 'need to' and 'I must' from your vocabulary. Replace them with 'When I . . .', 'If I . . .' or 'I've decided to . . .'

Banish tough self-talk

Our self-talk can sometimes assume the tone of a critical parent or harsh teacher, also referred to having a 'critical super-ego'. This is in part linked to a life of ADHD-related setbacks, and probably also influenced by our tendency to be sensitive to criticism (a phenomenon that has been coined Rejection Sensitive Dysphoria or RSD – see page 209). Avoid self-deprecating self-chat such as *You fool, I'm always messing up, Typical!, I'm such a waste of space, or I'm an idiot*. As soon as you notice a harshness or hostility in your self-talk, stop and question what it is about and, if necessary, challenge and reframe.

'That's AWEsome!'

Make it a habit to notice and comment on the beauty and majesty of nature, people and the world. Generating and expressing feelings of awe has been shown to be great for our mental health and well-being. Be sure to find opportunities to translate this important finding into your day-to-day life.

Maintain a 'shame-free' policy

Avoid flippantly saying to yourself or others things like, 'Oh, what a shame!', 'Shame on you' or 'You should be ashamed of yourself!' It is not healthy to promote or assign to yourself or others the emotion of shame. This is a shame-free zone.

Don't say things you can't retract

Even in the heat of an argument, do your utmost not to say hurtful things to others like, 'I have always hated you' or 'I knew this relationship was doomed from the start!' Some words simply can't be undone.

Stop wasting your words

Finally, I am a believer in not wasting words generally, but especially not on things that you can't change. Attempt to keep your airwaves as clean and upbeat as possible.

By employing some of these strategies, you will hopefully nurture a more mindful, reflective and forgiving manner in which you speak about things.

Step 3: Foster self-belief and confidence in achieving goals

Our sense of self is so often negatively skewed in adult ADHD. Years of being told that you are 'too this' or 'too that' can take its toll and leave you feeling 'lacking' in some way. A growth-oriented mindset promotes an inner belief in your ability to overcome problems and navigate challenging situations.

Although we need to stay grounded and be mindful not to foster an overinflated sense of self, a 'can-do' or 'I will work it out' approach can be a game-changer. Self-belief and a sense of agency can often manifest as a passion for learning new things; a quest to improve knowledge, self-efficacy and even mastery in whatever area happens to interest you.

Learn to be proud of your achievements and successes, however small:

- Tidied up your room after months of procrastination: *'Big pat on the back!'*
- Updated your CV and applied for that job: *'A major win!'*
- Stopped yourself from impulsively blaming someone else for something that you know deep down was your fault: *'You're learning – great work.'*

These mini victories that you gain along the way, particularly if marked in some way, should serve as morale-boosting 'anchors' of progress. Acknowledge and celebrate them, as you would in a good friend or family member, demonstrating generosity and kind-heartedness towards yourself. This positive self-reinforcement really is the essence of a growth-oriented mindset.

When it comes to building self-confidence, it is also important to take the time to really work out where you shine in life.

Vision, intention and bundles of passion

In order to nurture a growth mindset, it is vital that you set explicit intentions as to what you want to happen with your life, rather than being swept along without a clear sense of direction or purpose. The exercise below will help guide your thinking around what you want to do with your life and inform your approach. Whatever goals you land on, the passion needs to be there, and a good rule of thumb is that it must inspire you sufficiently to get you up and out of bed on a chilly morning.

Exercise: The THRIVE method for achieving goals
I want you to think about your wider vision for your personal and work life, and envisage the steps or milestones along the way. Capture a few ideas in your Thrive Journal, possibly dividing them into short-, medium- and long-term life goals.

When it comes to actually achieving whatever it is that you are setting your sights on, I have created a system to help support you – a simple, digestible model that I have coined the 'THRIVE' method for achieving goals. I live by these rules, both personally and professionally, and they serve me well.

If I had to boil things down to a single overarching message, it would be to be explicitly clear in your vision and intention, to nurture an unwavering, upbeat stance that believes 'anything is possible' and to invest the required work.

I will introduce each theme of the THRIVE model in turn and provide some pointers and practical guidance below:

T = *Tenacity* *(the need for perseverance and a long-term perspective)*
Persistence and tenacity can be thought of as the (armoured) vehicles of sustained effort. They appear to be central factors in manifesting your dreams. When setting your vision, commit to achieving the desired outcome come what may, and then work hard to get yourself there.

H = *Have a clear vision*, *with defined goals and plans (and faith in your ability to achieve them)*
All achievements ultimately begin with an idea, which first needs to be explored and then captured in writing of some form. When doing this exercise, try to be explicit in terms of your destination and then link this to a step-by-step plan to get you there with Specific, Manageable, Achievable, Relevant and Time-bound (SMART) targets. Planning is necessary – things do not happen on their own.

R = *Resilience* *(in the face of inevitable setbacks)*
Setbacks should be seen as an integral part of the change process and they should certainly not lead you to impulsively abandon ship. Remember, much personal growth and new learning comes through adversity. When things don't go to plan, try to react mindfully, dust yourself off, work out what you have learned and how you might do things differently, and move forward emboldened.

I = *Interest* *(in your chosen endeavour)*
Having a passionate interest in the subject matter of your goals and aspirations is critical, especially in ADHD. Not dissimilar to medication, interest has the effect of literally neutralising (temporarily) many of ADHD's symptoms. If you lack passion, there is a high chance your commitment will wane over time.

It is important to select your goals and aspirations with your ADHD in mind and, as far as possible, play to your individual strengths and skills. This will help keep you engaged and motivated along the way, particularly when things get tough.

I would also suggest that, where possible, you try to organise your life in a way that shields you from doing those things you really dislike, or at least allows you to do them much less frequently. I am referring to the activities that consistently weigh heavily on you, the tasks and chores that you always seem to procrastinate on. Work to minimise your exposure to these time-consuming, energy-draining and life-plaguing struggles, and, if possible, even try to banish them from your life altogether. Cease endlessly struggling to master those things that have consistently defeated you.

You will of course need to find creative and innovative strategies, putting in place the required compensation to allow this to happen. For example, to avoid having to do any ironing, if ironing is particularly repellent to you, might involve you trading services with a friend. (We'll explore how to implement creative workarounds in Part 3, which you may find useful.)

V = *Vision-directed activity* *(and use of visualisation)*
Once your vision is clear and your goals have been refined, you then need to work out how you are going to achieve them, and then actually do it by building good daily habits. Good planning, using a project management-style approach (with phases, aligned objectives and visual reminders), helps to keep you on track and provides useful signposting.

Additionally, regularly engage your creative imagination and visualise, in your mind's eye, the path to your goal and the outcome itself, in all its splendour. Every step you take, and every move you make, should be aligned to your end-game vision.

E = Emotion-boosted (upbeat emotion supercharges intention)

Thoughts and, more specifically, intentions seem to be 'powered' by emotion and belief. I encourage you to play with this concept and try to bring extra passion and emotion into the mix as you work towards your goals, however small.

Equally important is not to allow excessively negative emotions to get in the way and pollute the process. Avoid wallowing, and wasting your energy on things that are no more. If you have temporarily lost your way, stop and reframe the situation. Tune into the bigger picture, refocus and just get on with it!

I encourage you to start thinking about how you are going to set up the mechanics of your life so the 'light' inside of you, however small and insignificant you deem it presently, has the best chance to shine brightly. Simply put, you've got to find your thing! And then set up your life so you can do more of that thing.

Nurturing this 'on-a-mission' mindset, as I refer to it, is the key to turning ADHD to your advantage and really thriving with it. Having a path to follow allows you to channel your often boundless (and sometimes misdirected) energy and passion into something real and tangible.

Step 4: Take (calculated) risks and embrace mistakes

Those with ADHD are most certainly not new to risk-taking. For many, living on the edge is our modus operandi, the output poorly regulated impulses, paired with powerful thrill- or sensation-seeking drives. At times, this can lead to problems, sometimes serious ones.

This risk-seeking nature can be countered, to a degree, in some, by the fear of getting things wrong and then being criticised, mocked or shown up. With such a powerful pull in the other direction, retreat may feel protective. This is commonplace in ADHD and many refer to this as RSD, a concept we'll discuss in more detail in Pillar 7.

Taking calculated risks, however, is necessary for growth. When you try something new and it doesn't work (or even if it works) you learn something, something that you may not have known before. For understandable reasons, this needs tempering in ADHD. When making a decision, especially when there is a reasonable chance that things won't go your way, it is important to try not to become overly attached to a particular outcome (despite your ideal wishes) and, as an extension, to permit yourself to occasion-ally mess up and fail graciously, without a strong emotional reaction or excessive self-deprecation. It's okay to feel frustrated, but it is also important to get back on track and keep going. (We will discuss mindful acceptance and letting go in Pillar 7.)

It isn't about avoiding difficult times; it's about picking yourself up and bouncing back stronger. It can take time and persistence to achieve your goals, and the setbacks need to be expected, planned for (as far as possible) and skilfully negotiated, without critical judgement. So, the next time you hit a problem or apparent barrier, take a moment to consider your response.

You are going to make mistakes, sometimes big ones. You will occasionally upset others, both with your full awareness and sometimes without appreciating it at the time. These mistakes are very likely to be a result of problems controlling impulses or regu-lating yourself in some other way, directly linked to your ADHD. And at times the symptoms and impairments of ADHD are going to overwhelm you, and you may be left feeling defeated and deflated.

You are going to have to learn not to scorn yourself so much. When things go wrong, face up to the situation head on, with hon-esty and an openness to reflect and learn. These setbacks are also the fundamental building blocks of personal growth and, in my experience, infused with the right mindset and approach, they may well supercharge that growth process.

So, the next time someone criticises or attacks you, despite that powerful internal drive to become defensive and assume the victim role, I want you to hone an ability to listen, openly reflect and calmly speak your truth. Where necessary, it is important that you own your mistakes with integrity, and then let them go. Try committing, with conviction, to discharging all the unhelpful emotions associated with the situation. Creepers like guilt and shame will no doubt toy with you and tempt you to remain embroiled, but you mustn't forget that you have a choice whether to entertain them.

If the other person chooses not to engage or isn't open to hearing what you have to say, then it becomes their issue. Do your utmost to explain: speak your mind as clearly as you can, and then, if they are unable to hear you, move on graciously but assertively. Gone are the days when you will allow others to bring you down excessively and dent your spirit if you have been misunderstood and have tried to rectify the situation. At the end of the day, when you mess up, what is most important is the underlying intention behind your actions.

Step 5: Remain mindful and firmly rooted in the present

Individuals who exhibit a growth-oriented mindset, similar to those with ADHD interestingly, tend to be quite rooted in the 'here and now', and less preoccupied and weighed down by things that have been and gone. Not overly dwelling on the past frees up energy and resources to be able to project forward and more effectively strategise. The difference, however, is that those with ADHD may be too rooted in the present, such that they lose a broader sense of perspective. And we know that the very nature of the executive function disturbance in ADHD is future-directed, impacting one's ability to complete tasks and achieve goals. This is an important differentiation: being 'in the moment', doesn't necessarily equate to being mindful and fully 'present'.

Individuals with poorly managed ADHD can also often get lost in the detail, become easily distracted and sidelined, spend disproportionate time rushing or being overactive and frantic, and they can, on a regular basis, become overwhelmed and effectively shut down by emotion. Unresolved trauma, which is so common in ADHD, is characterised by unwelcome intrusions of the past into the present. All of this 'noise' can serve as a serious distraction from the growth work, as it is often in the silence and stillness, and through presence of mind and body, that insights emerge and connections form. It is in this place that the real magic happens.

Attempt to connect with the beauty, love and joy in all your encounters, even the most raw and painful chapters of your life. You are where you are and, for the most part, it will be your mindset that defines your trajectory. Allow plenty of space for silence and quiet reflection, and try to get in touch with your deeper, more observing self. You may initially need to actively define and block time for this regenerative stillness, or you risk getting lost in the busyness of life.

Step 6: Redefine ordeals as challenges

With a growth-oriented mindset, challenges are positively embraced, and the learning they often bring is welcomed. The goal is to train yourself to shift your thinking into a more creative, accepting, optimistic and adaptive state, focused on finding solutions to the problem, not wasting time moaning about it. Ordeals are not uncommon in adult ADHD, and in the absence of an appropriate mindset, they can serve to further degrade confidence and lead to overwhelm. The exercise overleaf will help you to identify times in your life when adversity has brought growth.

Exercise: Reframe an ordeal

Think of an ordeal that you have had over the last ten years or so that has taught you something important; where, after the event, you may have thought, *If that hadn't happened, I wouldn't have* . . . In your Thrive Journal, jot down any memories that spring to mind.

When you are next faced with a setback or ordeal, through the fog of the stress, try to see the possible learning embedded within it. Reframe it as just another step in your journey of growth, and possibly an opportunity to elevate yourself in some way.

Step 7: Turn your focus outwards and help others

Those with ADHD tend to become a bit too 'self-focused' and can sometimes lose perspective of the bigger picture and the needs of others. Rather than becoming single-mindedly focused on achieving a goal and 'winning', try slowing down and taking stock. Look around and take a moment to think about how you might reach out and support those in need.

You typically get back a lot more than you put in, and what goes around (commonly) comes around. Supporting others is a human drive, and luckily one that can be extremely nourishing for the giver – it also contributes to a sense of community, where everyone's needs are considered and valued, something that those of us with ADHD know is not always the case.

You may need to learn to loosen your grip on your (possibly overly principled) view of life. Everyone has their story and harbours a slightly different perspective on things – try to be compassionate and generous towards others and treat them as you would wish to be treated yourself. One aspect of this is training yourself not to gossip and speak unnecessary negatives about others, something that only serves to deplete you. Commit to spending more of your time spreading positivity – it is so much more uplifting!

Exercise: Select your top three mindset targets

1. Reflecting on this pillar, choose two or three themes or ideas that resonated with you and that you would like to implement or practise. You could type or write them in large print on a piece of paper and tack it to the wall near your bed.
2. Rate yourself on the (growth-to-fixed) 1–10 scale for the following categories:
   a. self-belief/confidence
   b. response to setbacks, mistakes or ordeals
   c. healthy experimentation and risk-taking
   d. ability to stay mindful and rooted in the present
   e. helping others
3. Circle the categories in which you scored above 5 – you may wish to include these as areas for personal development.

Cultivating a growth-oriented mindset is fundamental to managing your ADHD, but it's not something that happens overnight. Before I came to the realisation that I had ADHD, whatever I may have projected outwardly, inside I didn't feel that good about myself, or particularly hopeful that I had the resources to overcome what felt like insurmountable challenges. I would give myself a hard time, and curse internally. This was a skin that I needed to shed, to allow me to move forward, unburdened.

Nurturing a growth mindset took persistence, time and patience, but it allowed me to mature in my perspective, and I naturally started to become kinder and more forgiving of myself. All the previously harboured shame and secrecy has been replaced by an honesty and humility that others seem to really value. And they often respond with a vulnerability to match, that creates new connections and a sense of trust. These days, I am more open about my 'slightly quirky brain'. I am more comfortable telling people the areas in which I struggle, but also those where, under the right conditions, I can excel. Take me or leave me.

I encourage you to also embrace and celebrate your difference – both inwardly and, where appropriate, outwardly. The goal is to discard those redundant echoes of shame that you have no doubt attracted along the way. And as far as you can, try not to feel the need to prove *anything* to *anyone*. You are whole and worthy without any of your achievements or accolades, and equally you remain intact and unwaveringly lovable despite your accidental 'screw-ups'. The only person you can be truly accountable to is yourself, so carefully differentiate and distinguish what is within your boundaries, and sphere of responsibility and control, and what is not.

With the right mindset, you will be less likely to be held back by your ADHD. Rather, you will strengthen in the face of adversity and reach your goals through perseverance, despite the hardship. This should, over time, result in a far more meaningful and fulfilling life experience.

Having realigned your mindset so it is more likely to promote positive change and psychological growth, everything is now in place to transition to Pillar 2, which is concerned with optimising your sleep.

PILLAR 2

ANCHOR YOUR SLEEP

We all instinctively know that sleep is important. Studies have shown that it is critical for memory and other cognitive functions, as well as mood regulation. It clearly also plays a central role in physical and, in particular, brain health. Given that we spend about a third of our life doing it, it is probably worth paying careful attention to it and giving it the respect it deserves. This is particularly important for those with adult ADHD, for reasons we'll explore in this pillar. First, let's look at how much sleep we really need and the impact of sleep disturbance, especially on those with ADHD.

WHAT IS A 'SUFFICIENT' AMOUNT OF SLEEP?

It is generally accepted that you have had enough sleep when you wake naturally, without an alarm clock. If this is something that is difficult for you to evaluate, I would suggest that you aim for around seven to eight hours a night, which most would agree is pretty average for adulthood. Don't forget, however, that the amount of time we sleep at night typically reduces as we get older and varies between cultures. A clue that you may not be getting enough sleep is if you find yourself sleeping longer on the weekends than you do during the week.

People bandy around an array of terms when describing their sleep insufficiencies or peculiarities. When someone is not getting enough sleep, it is important to first differentiate between *sleep deprivation* and true *insomnia*.

Sleep deprivation

In sleep deprivation, people are depriving themselves, consciously or perhaps unwittingly, of adequate opportunity to get sufficient sleep. This leads to tiredness and sleepiness (they are in fact different) in the day, and a raft of negative physical health consequences. Importantly, in contrast to insomnia, in the case of sleep deprivation, spending more time in bed generally improves things.

Sleep deprivation reduces the speed at which our brain processes information, negatively impacts attention (especially the ability to rapidly switch attention) and impairs our ability to coordinate body movements.

Insomnia

When it comes to insomnia, there remains insufficient sleep even when there is adequate opportunity. So, spending more time in bed just doesn't help as that's not the underlying problem. Insomnia leads to tiredness during the day, but not always sleepiness, and, compared with sleep deprivation, it is associated with far fewer negative physical health consequences.

People with ADHD struggle with both types, but very commonly the executive dysfunction and sleep–wake rhythm disruption linked to ADHD drives a perpetual and pathological pattern of sleep deprivation. Sleep disturbance is particularly prominent in those with the combined or hyperactive/impulsive presentations of ADHD (see page 63). Over time, the chronic and ever-accumulating sleep debt can become toxic to physical health (impacting blood pressure among many other things), and it will certainly worsen ADHD symptoms.

In adults with ADHD, a shocking 80 per cent of us report going to bed later than usual. As the neurotypical world runs on neurotypical time, 60 per cent of those with ADHD end up experiencing daytime sleepiness and a range of other unhelpful symptoms. Adults with ADHD are commonly described in the sleep literature as 'evening types' (think 'night owls' who are more active in the evening and go to sleep later). It has also been shown that, on average, we take longer to fall asleep than our peers. This is referred to as 'prolonged sleep latency', and it is really common in adults with ADHD. Essentially, the sleep–wake cycle (or circadian rhythm as it is referred to) is *physiologically* shifted a little bit later. In effect, sleepiness just doesn't hit until way past our ideal bedtime.

Many of my patients tell me that they particularly appreciate the 'quietness' and reduced distractions of the twilight hours. For some, though, this late-night 'me time' is spent engaging in addictive, dopamine-boosting activities. These include drinking alcohol, bingeing on fast food and sometimes the use of other mind-altering substances. Cocooned away in the dark of the night, hidden from the shame-inducing eyes of others, there may also be an over-indulgence in pornography and other internet-based surfing, gaming or social media pursuits: *One more . . . and then I will definitely go to bed*. With pleasure centres firing hot, it can all just feel too enticing, understandable really given the system-wide regulatory challenges at play. Additionally, switching from one activity to another can cause real discomfort in those with ADHD. There is often simply not enough self-control to be able to shut down whatever has caught our hyperfocus, and to say, *Enough! It's time to stop now and get some sleep.*

The insomniacs among us (that's just over 40 per cent of those who are diagnosed with adult ADHD) will typically also struggle to sufficiently loosen the mental harnesses to be able to relax body and mind to allow sleep to come (and sometimes experienced as a low-level, hypervigilant threat state), which is often referred to as 'initial insomnia' by psychiatrists. People with ADHD describe difficulty 'switching off' an endlessly busy mind – this 'ceaseless mental activity', as it is sometimes called, can serve as an active repellent to sleep, making it an important target of treatment.

The reality is that many who harbour such a cacophony of pre-sleep intrusions will often, quite understandably, and initially quite unconsciously, slip into daily alcohol or substance use (often cannabis) in an attempt to quieten the 'noise'. In some, this will come at a cost, as addictive patterns may take root and physical health may suffer.

For others, it is the unwelcome awakenings during the night that trouble them, known as 'middle insomnia', though this is a bit less common in ADHD. Nightmares have also been shown to be more frequent in ADHD.

Becoming more aware of your own sleep and what is causing a problem for you is the first step to working out what to do about it. The exercise below will help you to identify those factors that contribute to your sleep problem so you can decide which steps to prioritise from this pillar.

Exercise: Chart your sleep problems

In your Thrive Journal, draw a pie chart (a circle made up of segments) and divide up the segments according to what you suspect to be the contributing factors to your sleep problem, noting the percentages. For example, 50 per cent going to bed too late, 30 per cent drinking wine, 20 per cent room too hot.

Once you have identified the main factors contributing to your disordered sleep, you can focus your management approach, as different problems require different interventions.

Of course, there may be more complex factors at play, which will require specialist input. These can include restless legs syndrome and other night-time movement oddities (which are present in 30–40 per cent of adults with ADHD), as well as obstructive sleep apnoea (a serious problem present in a staggering 30 per cent of adults with ADHD), where you basically stop breathing for a brief period during sleep. There is also a much higher chance of having bruxism (jaw clenching and teeth grinding) in ADHD.

The take-home message here is that if you suspect any of these more serious issues, go and speak to your GP about it. They may arrange some tests (possibly including 'sleep studies') or refer you to a sleep specialist.

Otherwise, I will assume that you are dealing with the more common challenges of a disordered or delayed sleep cycle, with difficulty falling asleep. If this is you, the first step is to apply the principles of what some refer to as 'sleep hygiene', though I prefer the term 'sleep optimisation'.

TEN TIPS FOR OPTIMISING SLEEP

A little while ago, I collaborated with my friend and colleague, national sleep specialist psychiatrist, Dr Hugh Selsick, to devise ten practical, evidence-based tips for optimising sleep. We have since adapted and updated this to have added relevance for those with adult ADHD. Most of what we recommend is rooted in solid science. Where there is limited guiding evidence, our recommendations are based on clinical experience and good, old-fashioned common sense. This practical resource has changed the way many of my patients think about sleep and I hope it will do the same for you.

1. Be guided by your body (and your level of sleepiness)

If you find yourself feeling tired or sleepy most of the day, on most days, then you are obviously not getting enough (good-quality) sleep at night. If, however, you feel alert most of the day, most days, with only occasional periods of tiredness or sleepiness, then you can assume you are getting sufficient sleep for you, regardless of how many hours you are actually sleeping.

2. Rise at the same time every day, seven days a week

This critically important bit of guidance will help establish and fix your circadian rhythm. Sticking to it should result in you feeling sleepy at the same time every night. Regretfully, this means a fond farewell to those weekend lie-ins which, when extreme, can cause a jetlag-like picture and take days to recover from.

3. Get outdoors (into natural light) as soon as possible after waking

When sunlight hits the back of your eyes it helps anchor your internal body clock and makes your sleep more predictable. It will also help you to feel more awake and alert during the day. A few minutes of natural light exposure is generally sufficient if the sky is clear and the sun is out. You should avoid staring directly at the sun and leave your sunglasses inside. Even if there is cloud cover, the natural light is still far more impactful than indoor artificial lighting; however, you will need to spend a little longer outside. Ideally, use the opportunity to take an energising morning walk which will confer additional benefits.

4. Reconsider daytime napping

If you experience difficulty sleeping at night, then you should avoid napping during the day. Napping does not catch up on sleep missed from the previous night. Rather, it steals sleep from the next one. Save the sleepiness for the night, when you'll get the most benefit from it.

If you don't experience difficulty sleeping at night, and you feel sleepy during the day, a nap can be helpful. Saying this, if you find that you need to nap frequently, it may indicate that there is a problem with your night-time sleep. Either you are not spending enough time in bed or there is something affecting the quality of your sleep. In the first instance, try increasing the time you spend in bed by 30–60 minutes, 6 nights a week for at least a month. If this does not make you less sleepy during the day, go and talk to your doctor.

5. Go to bed when (and only when) you are sleepy

If you go to bed before you are sleepy you will likely lie awake for a period of time. Conversely, if you feel sleepy but resist going to bed for a time, then you may not get sufficient sleep, and you are likely to feel sleepy during the day.

6. Use your bedroom for sleep (and intimacy) only

If you spend lots of time in your bedroom doing wakeful activities like working, studying, reading, watching TV, and so on, then your brain will come to associate the bedroom with wakefulness, and the act of going to bed may activate you. If you can't avoid spending time in your bedroom, create the important boundary between day and night in some other creative way (see page 106).

7. Address insomnia (both problems falling asleep and night-time waking)

If you go to bed and have difficulty falling asleep (initial insomnia) or wake in the night and struggle to get back to sleep (middle insomnia), get out of bed, go to another room and do something pleasant and relaxing. Ideally avoid stimulatory activities (for example, scrolling on your phone or doing work-related activities) and try to keep the lighting low. The key is to avoid going back to bed until you feel sleepy, which will ensure that almost all your time in bed is spent sleeping. After doing this for several weeks, the bed (and bedroom) will be so strongly associated with sleep, that merely the act of going to bed will make you feel sleepy.

8. Avoid taking your worries to bed

Try to build in a wind-down period before going to bed (see page 107 for more on this). At the beginning of that wind-down period, do something to draw a line under the day, perhaps have a warm shower, and psychologically orientate yourself towards sleep.

9. Introduce regular exercise

If done consistently, exercise can lead to significant improvements in sleep. It's probably better not to exercise in the two hours before bed as it can be too energising for some, whereas having a gentle stretch before bed can help relax the body without stimulating it too much. (See Pillar 5 for more on the benefits of exercise and stretching for adult ADHD.)

10. Dim the lights (but don't get too worked up about blue light)

It may be helpful to dim the lights at home (and on your devices) in the hour or two before bed, as light during the evening hours can be mildly alerting. It is fine to watch TV, but try not to sit too close to the screen – the further away you sit, the less light hits your eyes. The harmful effect of blue light emitted from screens has been overemphasised; the research findings do not actually support its role in disrupting sleep as strongly as many assume.

Exercise: Select your top three sleep optimisation targets
From the tips above, select the three that you think you are most likely to achieve and then diligently concentrate your efforts on them for a week. During the trial, note what you tried, monitor your sleep onset time, your night-time awakenings, your wake time and your sleep duration. You can add in any other variables you might have access to via smart technology (although this itself could be disturbing your sleep – see page 191 for more on this). Capture all this

data in your Thrive Journal or on your phone. This should enable you to better evaluate the impact of the changes you have made.

Once these changes have been integrated and consolidated, choose a further three to work on.

Now you have taken some important early steps to optimise your sleep, we're going to take a look at your morning and evening routines. Getting these important sleep-bridging phases running smoothly is the key to starting and ending your day on a positive and stable footing. I then find that the time in between feels more manageable to fill, and slowly but surely things start to fall into place.

ESTABLISHING A MORNING ROUTINE

A healthy and energising start to the day boosts well-being and can set you up for a much more positive and productive day, which makes the investment of time and energy worth it.

I am going to be honest with you right from the outset, particularly for those of you with external duties or responsibility: you are going to need to get your head round the idea of setting your alarm earlier than you currently do – perhaps even an hour earlier – to give yourself the time you need. Your immediate reaction to this breaking news may well be one of horror – 'I don't do early!' – but wait, hear me out.

Like most things in life, how well this works will come down to how much you decide to invest and how you frame it. Keeping in mind what we discussed in Pillar 1 about the importance of mindset, I encourage you to embrace your earlier morning start. Gracefully accept the challenge and make a commitment to running the experiments I propose overleaf. Make a decision that you are not going to moan or groan about it, but instead just dive in mindfully and see what happens.

Your main aim is to try to align your internal body clock with the natural rhythm of the light–dark, day–night cycle, which will generally involve you rising reasonably early in the morning, for example, between 6 and 8am. Even if it is a bit later, what is most important is that you maintain consistency in terms of your chosen wake time and that, as discussed above, you expose your eyes to natural light within 30 minutes of waking.

Your morning menu of options

Below are some ideas for your morning routine. This is not a strict guide as I understand that everyone's duties and responsibilities differ widely.

I have divided the menu into three steps, following a logical order, starting from the moment of waking, and ending at the point at which you launch into the main body of your day. The actual time of this launch point will obviously vary, but for many it will be between 9 and 9.30am.

You are not expected (and almost certainly won't have time) to do all of them. Just select the options that appeal and then test them out, possibly initially one by one. You may need to trial different combinations until you find what works best for you. Different days of the week, or periods of your life, may benefit from different selections. Importantly, whatever 'packages' you land on, ensure you give yourself enough time, so that you don't need to rush.

Step 1 (while in bed/on rising)

- **Consider replacing your alarm clock with a dawn simulator.** Traditional alarm clocks, with a shrill sound that abruptly jolts you into action, trigger the release of a flood of stress hormones, which is not great for the system. A dawn simulator is a specially designed alarm clock that integrates a 'natural' light, which progressively brightens, allowing your hormonal systems to adapt gradually, easing you more gently into wakefulness.

- **Avoid reaching for the snooze button – it's bad news!** Repeatedly pressing the snooze button on your alarm clock has the potential to devastate your morning routine. It's easy to lose track of the number of snoozes you have banked and, before you know it, you've lost important time and that flow state you were hoping for has been all but obliterated. Train yourself to get out of bed on the first awakening, possibly after a quick stretch (see below).

- **Do a gentle stretch in bed before rising.** Soon after waking, while still lying flat, take a minute or two to do a few gentle stretches. Try extending your arms and legs, then bringing your knees to your chest, followed by a gentle back twist. This will prime your body for more active movement, hopefully protect you against pulling anything and make getting out of bed that little bit easier. If, despite the stretching, you still feel resistant to getting up, simply count down from five to one, and then, without giving it a second thought, make your move.

- **Have slippers (and a dressing gown or hooded top) within easy reach.** Adding a layer of warmth when you get out of bed can be comforting, especially on chilly mornings.

- **Immediately drink a full glass of water to boost hydration.** You can keep this by your bed from the night before, which will mean that it won't be too cold for your still sensitive gut. If you are someone who often gets dizzy or lightheaded on standing (features that may be suggestive of ANS dysregulation), you may wish to add a tiny pinch of salt (less than a sixth of a teaspoon) to your morning water, blood pressure allowing, of course. There are also lots of salt/electrolyte preparations you can buy, but get advice from the pharmacist and check they don't contain too many nasties.

Step 2 (once out of bed)

- **Move into a brighter space and allow consciousness to re-enter (10 minutes).** Maybe enjoy a hot drink, and perhaps a brief morning encounter with whoever is around (including pets). Alternatively, take a few minutes to make a quick call to a loved one to say hi.
- **Try grounding through your breath, and ideally the soles of your feet (5–15 minutes).** Allow yourself a quiet moment to level for the day. Take a few slow, deep breaths, which should have the effect of connecting you with your body. If you have the option of doing the breath practice while standing or walking barefoot on some grass, ideally wet grass, then even better (though I appreciate that may not be possible for many). In fact, together with walking on wet sand, this is the ultimate in terms of 'grounding' (or 'earthing' as it is also known). Feel the energetic tingles radiating across the soles of your feet and notice how you feel afterwards. Have a read about grounding online. If you are not planning to do a more formal meditation practice as part of your morning routine, you can carve out a few mindful moments at this point.
- **Get out for a morning walk (15–45 minutes).** Time and weather permitting, quickly throw on some clothes and get out for a walk. Studies suggest that getting natural light exposure within 30 minutes of waking helps anchor your circadian rhythm. Omit this option if you are planning to walk or cycle somewhere, for example work, the school run, or your favourite cafe. You can even achieve your light exposure by simply opening your front door and stepping outside for a few moments.
- **Do a cardiovascular workout.** If you have the time, integrate a session of more vigorous cardiovascular exercise into your morning. Ideas include using an exercise bike while listening to a podcast, cycling or jogging to work (time efficient), following an online fitness, yoga or Pilates class, having a run round the local park or even trampolining or rebounding, ideally outside.

- **Prepare a nutritious and sustained energy-promoting breakfast.** Healthy breakfast ideas include porridge, eggs, avocado, sourdough toast, yoghurt, fresh fruit, grilled asparagus and chicory, or a bowl of microgreens with a citrus/apple cider vinegar and olive oil dressing. Alternatively, (if you own a juicer) you could make a fresh vegetable juice (with a little fruit added for taste, if necessary). If you happen to be doing intermittent fasting (see page 167), you may decide to skip breakfast altogether, but be careful if you are doing vigorous exercise, as you are likely to need the energy and sustenance.
- **Listen to an inspirational podcast/audiobook or read something interesting.** Have a listen or read while having breakfast or coffee, or while exercising/walking/making your way to work or college. Don't forget to charge your headphones the night before!
- **Mindfully meal prep for the day.** This could simply involve taking something you have pre-prepared or batch cooked out of the freezer for your lunch or dinner. Immediately put whatever you have prepared together with your other things by the front door, so you don't forget it.

On those occasions when, for whatever reason, you have a bit of extra time in the morning (perhaps on weekend mornings), you may wish to integrate a creative, nurturing, relaxing or growth-promoting activity, such as:

- drawing or painting
- journaling (perhaps detailing and reflecting on the previous day, your dreams from the night or simply how and what you are feeling)
- reading a book, magazine, paper or journal
- singing or dancing
- completing a crossword, or some other brain-boosting puzzle
- brainstorming a new idea or project
- reaching out to someone in need

Step 3 (before you start your day)

- **Bring your morning routine to a close with a 10-minute day planning session.** This is where you review and update your diary and work out your priority action list for the day. Some prefer to shift this planning session to the evening before. This 10-minute admin session will be time well spent, and it should improve the efficiency and overall flow of your day. I will expand on the approach to this planning session in the next pillar (page 116), which is focused on time and task management.

ESTABLISH AN EVENING ROUTINE

Many of us with ADHD get distracted with stimulating activities that can often absorb us late into the night, so, as I touched on earlier, it can be helpful to introduce a wind-down period, or pre-bed evening routine, to prepare the system for sleep.

Building in a semi-structured approach to these sundown hours has several important functions. At a simple level, it serves to draw a symbolic line under your day and progressively notch down your level of arousal. Getting this right will help promote better sleep. That said, it's important not to be too rigid and to avoid putting too much pressure on yourself. Due to the reality of life, maintaining a set evening routine simply won't be possible every night, so perhaps aim for five nights out of seven, or at least enough to confer a sense of balance and routine. On occasion, despite good intentions, you may find your evening slipping away with some unplanned or spontaneous activity. When this happens, sometimes it is fine to just go with it and, importantly, you shouldn't give yourself a hard time. Remember, 'good enough is good enough'.

As with the morning routine, there are many different ways to fill the period of time that bridges late afternoon to bedtime. Again, my goal is not to dictate what you do, but rather to provide a range of options so that you can determine what works best for you and your personal set-up.

A menu for your evening routine

Step 1 (early evening)

- **Take a gentle walk**, ideally in a green open space, and (if lucky enough) watch the sun set. You could always engineer your journey home from wherever you have been so you integrate a 30-minute walk, possibly by getting off the train or bus a stop or two earlier. A brisk stroll may help you shed the stress of your day before arriving home.
- **Telephone a friend or family member** for a catch-up (perhaps during your walk).
- **Plan for the next day.** If you prefer to do next-day planning the evening before, dedicate 10–15 minutes to review and update your diary and work out your priority actions for the following day. (See Pillar 3 for a guide to a day planning session.)
- **Prepare a healthy evening meal**, perhaps with calming music or an interesting podcast playing in the background.
- **Allow yourself to get absorbed in a 'flow' state** by engaging in a creative or calming activity like sketching, painting, clay modelling, singing, dancing, playing an instrument or gardening.
- **Do a gentle yoga or stretching session.** You can improvise, follow an online video, join an established class or create an informal group with a couple of close friends.

Step 2 (mid-evening)

- **Tidy your bedroom** of clutter and change into comfortable clothes (putting away any stray clothes), but then don't linger in the room, which – as we discussed – should primarily be associated with sleep and intimacy.
- **Turn on the air filter in your bedroom if you have one**, to ensure clean air for your sleep environment.
- **Enjoy your evening meal**, and then try to avoid any subsequent snacking, to ensure a reasonable period for your gut to rest and regenerate, extending from the end of dinner to

breakfast the next morning (or possibly even lunch – see Pillar 5 for more on this).

- **Dim the lights, and your screens.** Consider protective blue-light glasses if doing close screen work.
- **Use an electric aromatherapy oil vapouriser** with calming essential oils like lavender and bergamot. Alternatively, you can add a couple of drops of the oil to the (inside) edge of your pillow.
- **Consider switching off your Wi-Fi at around 9 or 10pm.** Ideally use a timer switch for this, so you don't need to think about it. It will allow you to set a restart time in the morning. Although the use of mobile data remains an option, this additional hoop may hopefully discourage too much late-evening screen use.

Step 3 (late evening)

- **Enjoy a warming and soporific drink.** Chamomile tea, or something milky or malty, could be a good option.
- **Take a hot bath or shower** or even just do a hot foot soak (ideally with a small cup of Epsom salts).
- **Have a quiet read**, listen to some calming music or do some form of meditation.
- **Psychologically 'park' any worries you may be harbouring** by 'transplanting' them out of your head and onto paper. Keep your Thrive Journal close by.
- **Have a gentle stretch** or give yourself a relaxing foot (or head) massage, with or without massage oil.

Exercise: Build your morning and evening routines
- Select five items from both morning and evening menus that you are most drawn to.
- Order them in terms of ease.
- Then introduce one a week, starting with the easiest first.
- Start tomorrow, experiment and build up gradually.

Medication and supplementation for sleep issues

I see the use of strong sleeping medication, like the 'Z-drugs' (for example, zolpidem) very much as a last resort. Like benzodiazepines (for example Valium, also known as diazepam), they can result in dependency as well as next-day hangovers, which can worsen cognitive function. I would only ever prescribe these potentially addictive sleep medications in a crisis and, even then, only for a few days, just to help address a very disordered rhythm. I suggest you try to avoid them, as far as possible.

Sedating antihistamines, which include drugs like diphenhydramine (Benadryl), chlorphenamine, doxylamine, promethazine, hydroxyzine and ketotifen, can be really useful at times, on many levels. They may not be addictive, but they can still lead to a hangover effect, and long-term use has been shown to possibly affect cognitive function. Some of them (certainly the last two listed) will need to be prescribed. These medications can be surprisingly powerful so do treat them with respect.

Immediate release (IR) melatonin has traditionally been used ('off label' and by prescription only in the UK) and recommended in ADHD at doses of 1–3mg (based on the studies) to be taken about an hour before bed. The IR form only remains active for three to four hours, but there is a long-acting form, Circadin, that comes in 2mg doses and also needs to be prescribed. Melatonin may improve the sleep onset time in some, and it could have additional health benefits, but a recent study suggests that its use doesn't actually improve ADHD symptoms.

Supplements that have been used (with varying degrees of evidence supporting their use) include:

- valerian (possibly increases the neurotransmitter GABA which has a calming effect on the system; can cause sleeplessness in some; limited data)
- passion flower extract (early and limited data)
- glycine (improved sleep quality and onset found in a study)
- 5-HTP, a precursor of serotonin (some early data)
- L-theanine (limited data, may help more for those who wake in the night)
- CBD (some limited data)
- zinc (gently calming)
- magnesium (more of a mild stress reducer and muscle relaxant, working through an increase in GABA)
- vitamin B6 and GABA (see pages 178–9)
- ashwagandha (some benefit, especially at a higher dose of 600mg, demonstrated in a 2021 multi-study analysis)

Some of these supplements are dealt with in a bit more detail on page 196. If you do decide to try a supplement for sleep, it is a good idea to first discuss it with your GP. If what you try doesn't help noticeably, or is tolerated poorly, move on.

Now that your sleep cycle and the routines either side of it are anchored in properly, the next task is to fill and structure the remaining eight hours or so that fall in between. For many, but not all, that will be the typical working hours of 9am to 5pm. It feels more manageable to have to deal with this more limited 'prime-time' stretch each day, as opposed to having to plan out a whole 24-hour period. Next, we will address time and task management – the subject of Pillar 3.

PILLAR 3

TAKE CONTROL OF YOUR TIME

Time and ADHD don't sit that well together. In fact, as I have explained, at its heart, ADHD is a disorder of self-regulation, specifically impacting the brain's ability to organise itself over time and work step-by-step towards a future outcome, anticipating, making decisions and adapting along the way. The regulatory problems impact both memory (that is the 'working memory') and motivation, and they also drive a level of mind wandering and distractibility can interfere with the ability to sustain focus.

Without a framework to anchor you (and, believe me, most adults with ADHD don't have one), it is likely that you will be feeling a bit 'all over the place' inside: constant firefighting; juggling of too many balls; lurching from one deadline to another and exhausting yourself in the process; feeling that you are perpetually clawing your way from the edge. The chronic bodily state of low-grade threat and apprehension that this chaotic lifestyle promotes, if left unchecked, will progressively chip away at your health, degrading the hardware of your stress response systems. Many will turn to substances, or other mind-numbing addictive behaviours, to provide some respite from the never-ending 'down escalator' which they find themselves scrambling up. You may try to delude yourself that 'if only' you can make it to the top, and tick off everything that you need to do, 'then all will be fine'. If only it was as simple as that!

Existing in this 'crisis mode', over a stretch of many years, will likely take its toll on your life, not only on your self-care and health, but also on your relationships. And given finite time and resources, and inescapable real-life responsibilities like paying bills and keeping your job, you will no doubt prioritise income-generating work above all else. You may get stuck in a rut, where other facets of your life experience (your family and home commitments, and your friends and social life, just to mention a few) start to take a real hit.

But all is not lost. I, too, have struggled with my relationship with time, in various ways at different points in my life. As a child, I remember noticing that everything took me a bit longer than most of the other kids and, as a teenager and young adult, I, quite deservedly, attracted a reputation for being late, something I resented. When it came to journeys, in order to avoid squandering time, I would attempt to time things to the minute and would often make a game of it. I was regularly caught out, however, as I generally failed to factor in potential delays. And then there was the going out ritual – I used to, almost always, end up rushing to get ready when going out somewhere. Despite sound intentions, I would leave things to the last few minutes, with just enough time to spare, piggybacking on the adrenaline of stress to activate and motivate myself into action. These days, things are much more regulated due to the systems I have put in place. My aim in this pillar is for you to be able to do the same.

To mitigate, or minimise the effects of, these executive function deficits, the more compensation and external scaffolding you can introduce the better. In this pillar, I will share a selection of my favourite tools, systems and strategies to establish routine and promote more efficient time and task management. Having seen the positive effect this approach, or a variation of it, has had in many people that I've worked with over the years, I believe streamlined time and task management to be a linchpin of success and well-being. Once you get this working smoothly, even at a basic level, there is a reasonable chance that your day-to-day life will come into better balance. A well-oiled but simple system for managing time and tasks frees up bandwidth, allowing you to switch out of 'catch-up/fire-fight' mode, and into 'creative/relax' mode.

Before we get stuck in, I invite you to do the reflective exercise below to identify the areas you struggle most with when it comes to managing time and completing tasks. This will help you to focus on the elements in this pillar that are most relevant to you.

Exercise: Identify your time- and task-management burden
1. In 100 words, outline the main reasons that you think you struggle with time and task management.
2. What sorts of things do you find yourself procrastinating (putting off), and why do you think you do it?

STRUCTURE AND ROUTINE

I would first like to establish a few basic concepts, starting with the overarching importance of both structure and routine generally, and even more so when it comes to ADHD. By *structure*, I mean having specific and defined plans, with blocks booked into discrete time slots, which form a grid spanning 24 hours. Having structure means that, at any one time, you know exactly where you are meant to be and what you are meant to be doing. Having a day that has a predictable shape, with frequent and purposely located anchor points, and which rolls over to the night and then the following day with a tide-like rhythm, provides an important 'big-picture' framework to align to. Having structure fosters a sense of stability, which can have a grounding and regulating effect, and counter that pervasive inner feeling of chaos. External order is required to compensate for a sense of internal disorder.

By *routine*, I mean having fixed, scheduled activities and habits that repeat on a rolling basis, partly through association. Routine means that every morning/evening/day/week/month/year you do the same thing, at the same time. These routines get etched into your subconscious, requiring less work to maintain. Examples include:

- 'It's Monday – yoga night.'
- 'It's Sushi Saturday.'
- '1st of the month is billing day.'
- 'Take pills straight after brushing teeth.'

Those with ADHD sometimes resist excessive routine in search of novelty, but my experience is that overall it is worth striving for because of the stability it can bring. Changing things up within certain parameters, for example by altering your journey to work, can really help keep things fresh.

Both structure and routine are central to effective ADHD management. However, like everything in life, there needs to be a pragmatic counterbalance playing out here. The reality of life is that things don't always go as you hope they will. Meetings get cancelled, colleagues get sick, we miss a train, trip over and twist an ankle or wake up with a stinking cold that completely floors us. We may, at the last minute, have to shelve our previous plans to free ourselves up to support some else who needs us. This is just the nature and unpredictability of life.

For this reason, any system you establish must have a degree of flexibility built in, and you are going to have to develop an agility in responding to these unexpected diversions. It is important to accept and adapt to the reality on the ground, to quickly project ahead and, if necessary, alter your plans. There's no point wasting time feeling deflated and moaning about how 'everything is messed up'.

A reconfigured day, in the event of a diversion, can still be a successful and productive one. You should assume that disruptions to the smooth flow of your day will happen. When they do, your challenge is to tap into that growth mindset you nurtured in Pillar 1 and respond skilfully, without getting too ruffled or worked up. Your stress system really doesn't need any further dysregulation thrown in the mix, so try to take things in your stride and remain calm and focused. To be fair, as already discussed, individuals with ADHD can often be super effective in a crisis – when we need to, we are generally able to think resourcefully and on our feet. Try to harness this mindful hyperfocus when the inevitable disruptions arise, and then learn to calm the system down effectively once the crisis has abated.

Paper or electronic (or a hybrid approach)

Before we get going, you need to decide whether you are someone who will do better with a paper-based system for time and task management or if you are more suited to electronic devices. You may well already be using a combination of both, without having given it much thought, and that is fine too – whatever works for you, works! Let's just briefly consider the pros and cons of each.

With paper, the main advantage people cite is its accessibility – you can simply pick up your handwritten list or flip open your pocket diary and you're immediately where you need to be. Some also find the action of writing itself aids memory retention and, let's face it, for most, ticking or crossing things off is very satisfying. The real downside is that paper diaries (or loose pieces of paper or Post-it notes, as is more often the case) can easily get lost or stuck in the strangest of places. Although your phone can also go astray, of course, in most cases, the stored data will still be accessible.

The main advantage of electronic is the automated reminder function. Also, with the advent of cloud storage, information can not only be accessed on different devices, but also easily shared with others. The process of simply turning on or 'waking up' the device and logging in, however, can serve as a barrier for some. For most, though, online calendars are intuitive and easy to use.

PRACTICALITIES

The day planning session

Before we get into the depths of how to tackle time and task management, I want to highlight one key ingredient for success that we touched on in the last pillar – the day planning session. This is a brief, fixed, daily session dedicated to planning the stretch of time that lies immediately ahead, and should generally cover both home and work life life (although this will clearly vary according to what you do). This critical planning time is so often neglected by those with adult ADHD, probably because it feels tedious and time-consuming.

I encourage you to simply commit to 10 minutes. If, however, you get into it (and there is a reasonable chance that you will), you may choose to dedicate a little more time to it, though there is no need for it to be more than 20 minutes. The session can, of course, be done jointly with a partner or personal assistant (if you are exceptionally lucky!), either in person or remotely. Having a shared calendar that you are both able to view and edit makes this type of collaboration far more streamlined.

Most schedule this planning session at the start of their working day, which is a convenient bridge to what I call the 'prime time' of your day. Some, however, prefer to plan for the following day the night before. In this case, it shifts position to become part of your evening routine. Whatever approach you take, the important thing is to be consistent. Build this session into your normal daily rhythm and make it a habit, just like brushing your teeth (hopefully you brush your teeth). The small extra investment of time spent looking ahead to the next 12–24 hours will markedly impact how 'in control' you feel.

During this pivotal 10-minute review, you will refer to and update your two essential tools; your 'dump-all task list' and 'drop-a-block diary', which we'll explore now. Don't worry, I have done my best to keep things straightforward and clear.

When it comes to introducing a simple but reliable way of managing time and tasks – especially when there isn't one in place presently – it needs to be easy to implement and intuitive, and phased in one step at a time. That is what these tools are all about.

Essential tool 1: The 'dump-all task list'

This is the full list of all tasks that will need actioning at some point (usually within about three months). Essentially, this is the list onto which you 'dump' every task that arises, as it arises. This list does not include events which are already scheduled into your diary, but it may include tasks that don't have an obvious deadline, such as getting life insurance. It's up to you, but you may prefer to put things that need doing in the distant future into your diary.

Maintaining an up-to-date task list means there is less information for you to hold in your mind. It's freeing to get it out of your head, and reassuring to know that it is noted down somewhere that is readily and regularly accessed.

The dump-all task list is updated during your day planning session and at any point during the day as, and when, tasks arise. Specific actions may include adding new tasks, selecting priority tasks for the day ahead, ticking off completed tasks and adjusting priorities. Some find it helpful to introduce a colour-coding or flag system to help prioritise tasks. Whatever the approach you decide to adopt, keep it really simple, so you keep up the habit.

PILLAR 3

Defining actions

To counter overwhelm and reduce resistance, break larger tasks down into more manageable subtasks, or 'actions', a process known as 'chunking'. For example, 'sort out the kitchen' feels overwhelming and open to interpretation. However, when you break it down into the specific actions required – 'unload the dishwasher', 'take out the dustbins' and 'wipe all surfaces' – it feels more manageable. This is an important skill to nurture in ADHD.

As I will discuss, procrastination (the delaying or postponing of action) very often results from a feeling of not knowing exactly how or where to start, so defining your actions helps to limit this too.

When breaking down tasks, it can help to estimate approximately how long individual actions are likely to take, and to limit the duration. Ideally, I think any individual action should comfortably fit into a 30-, or maximum 60-minute time slot. This approach feels more manageable and helps keep boredom at bay, allowing for a natural breather in between actions. Many actions, often referred to as 'quick wins', will take much less time than this, possibly just a few minutes.

If you are looking for more structure, you can schedule the selected actions into specific locations in your day (or week), fitted around your existing diary commitments. You may find it is easier to create one or two dedicated 'actioning sessions' at fixed locations in your day (or week) into which the actions are slotted (see page 119).

The daily action list

From this 'dump-all task list', you will be extracting a handful of specific actions (usually about 3 or 4 at most) that you intend to complete over the subsequent 12–24 hours. This is the 'daily action list'.

The key here is not to overstretch yourself in terms of the number of actions you allocate for the day. And to try to get the balance right in terms of what actions you combine, avoiding taking on things that are too similar or too weighty.

For those of you who are early on in your journey and for whom the idea of having a list of daily actions is simply too overwhelming, I would suggest that you start very gently. Replace the daily action list with a 'weekly action list'. Weekly action lists (and weekly planning sessions) work in precisely the same way except that your expectations are lessened. Once the system is working well, you can then gradually build on it. It's far better to have realistic goals that are achieved (or exceeded), than to feel perpetually despondent regarding your progress.

The other thing that many find helpful is to write the finalised daily (or weekly) action list in big writing on a whiteboard (or blackboard), positioned somewhere prominent in your workspace or at home. Visual reminders, that you can't miss, can be so effective in ADHD. They will also help keep you on track when you are feeling a bit lost or unsure what to do next. You can wipe or tick things off as you go and, if you are on the move, you can even take a photo of it and save it as your screensaver if this helps.

Actioning sessions (optional)

This is the block of time in which you action the tasks that you have allocated yourself for the day (or week). Like the day planning session, actioning sessions ideally should be scheduled on a rolling basis, either daily or, when starting out, weekly. They should have consistent start and end times (for example, 8.30 to 9am and/or 5 to 5.30pm). The goal is to build them into your routine. You may have one actioning session for work and a separate one for your home life, but this obviously depends on your set-up.

Strategically locate these sessions just before more pleasurable or rewarding activities, like downtime, social time or mealtimes, rather than at the end of an intense period of work.

Into these defined windows of time (I would propose 30 or 60 minutes), allocate your selected tasks (or actions) for the day, extracted from your dump-all task list. Remember, an actioning session may have one or more tasks allocated. Allocate and combine tasks according to their likely duration, your interest/boredom level, what is involved and what other things you have going on that day.

Essential tool 2: The 'drop-a-block diary'

Working in unison with your 'dump-all task list' (and 'action lists') is the 'drop-a-block diary'.

Imagine your diary as an infinite 'grid' of empty 30-minute 'slots' of time, starting from the present moment and projecting forward months into the future. The grid spans day and night (24 hours) and includes weekdays and weekends (7 days a week).

This grid can be populated by a variety of different activities. Activities are considered in 30-minute 'blocks', which can, of course, be aggregated into longer time periods. As in the case of the 'actioning sessions', a 30-minute block may contain more than one action or activity.

To fill your diary, you simply need to drop activity 'blocks' into these 30-minute 'slots' within the 'grid', ideally filling ALL slots with one activity or another. Don't worry, 'activities' also include things like sleep, downtime and social time. I am certainly not suggesting that you need to be physically active and productive at all times; quite the opposite, in fact. You should, however, know what you are supposed to be doing at any point in time, with a quick glance at your diary.

Blocking out your diary and creating a schedule or plan for the day can be thought of much like laying a handful of further anchors that together provide a sense of stability and groundedness, and an hour-by-hour guide to follow. This has the effect of reducing overwhelm and, in turn, discouraging procrastination.

Block categories

You can create whatever categories that work for you and your life. In the box below, I have listed the ones that I think are most helpful, for most people, in three separate clusters. Feel free to use them as they are or adapt as you see fit.

PILLAR 3

Organisational blocks (fixed):
- *Day planning session* (x 1 daily, at the end of your morning routine or during your evening routine the night before)
- *Actioning session(s)* (x 1–2 daily/weekly)
- *Email review session* (x1 daily/weekly – see Pillar 4)

Basic 'housekeeping' blocks:
- *Sleep* (it is important to define your sleep window, as far as possible maintaining consistent sleep and wake times)
- *Morning routine* (see pages 101–6 – includes self-care, such as bathing and grooming)
- *Evening routine* (see pages 106–8 – again, includes self-care)
- *Meals* (be sure to protect time for meals, which are a form of downtime and act as important anchor points in the day)
- *Meal preparation* (often forgotten about when scheduling)

Additional blocks:

- **Work** (your approach to work-related blocks will vary depending on the type of work you do)
  (Note: Specifics such as the timing of meetings may be captured in a separate, possibly linked, work diary)
- **Exercise** (can include indoor and outdoor exercise, and walking or cycling between activities)
- **Social time** (either at home or out and about)
- **Downtime** (includes reading, watching TV, meditating, hobbies, and so on)
- **Travel and transition time** (ensure to build in enough transition or travel time, and factor in potential delays)

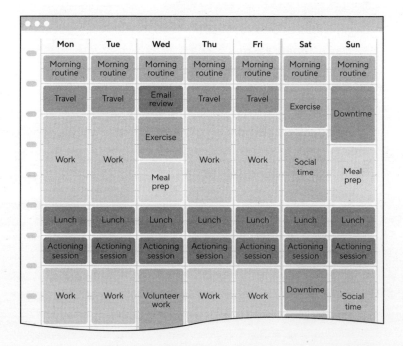

An example of different categories of *blocks* in slots

Exercise: Implementing the tools
(Time required = up to 3 hours, not necessarily in one sitting)

1. Select your tools and familiarise yourself with them (45 minutes).
2. Populate your dump-all task list (1 hour) following an email and paper review.
3. Open your drop-a-block diary. First establish and input your fixed blocks (including day planning sessions, actioning sessions, meals, work and sleep), with repeats and notification reminders where required (15 minutes).
4. Decide on your other block categories, and then populate your drop-a-block diary with (non-fixed) blocks for the next 4 weeks, with notifications where required (1 hour).
5. Tomorrow is your official launch (try to be disciplined with your day planning sessions and actioning sessions).

PILLAR 3

File management (digital and paper)
If you haven't already, consider signing up to a cloud-based digital file management system. Build yourself an intuitive, simple and user-friendly digital filing system where you can organise, save and easily access your digital documents both at home and on the move. In the settings, you can program the cloud system to automatically upload photos and videos taken on your smartphone.

When it comes to paper-based data, unless you are going completely paperless (which will mean you need to scan or photograph, and then upload and digitally file, important paper documents), you are going to need some sort of system to organise it. I encourage you to set up a simple paper-based filing system in a two- (or four-) drawer filing cabinet. Individual folders could include:

- health and well-being
- home administration
- work administration
- insurance documents
- other important documents
- tax-related

For small but important scraps of paper, receipts and business cards, it is useful to have an easy way of reliably capturing the information using your phone. You can do this either by taking a photo of it and then filing it on your cloud system or you can just save a typed note (but be sure to check accuracy). Whichever approach you choose, the key thing is to have a simple filing system set up in which to file it. Then you will be able to find it more easily down the line when you forget where you put it.

I would also encourage you to have a physical 'to-do' file where you store all the relevant papers for an upcoming task together, in a slip-in, hole-punched wallet. And when you encounter paper in the form of articles, flyers, brochures, magazines or handouts that you (really) want to read, I would suggest extracting the relevant pages and putting them in a visible 'to read' file or tray. Strategically locate this near your desk, bed, reading chair or toilet. (Note: Whenever the file or tray is approaching half full, dedicate half an hour, perhaps timed using a countdown timer, to sift through it. Read what really captures your interest and discard the rest. Be brutal – 'If in doubt, throw it out!')

FILLING TIME, PACING ENERGY AND ACHIEVING BALANCE

How you structure your day will depend on your demands and obligations. When scheduling activities, the goal is to promote a healthy balance and introduce enough variation to keep things fresh. You also need to pace yourself. Your energy reserves are finite, so you will need to judge carefully how to allocate them when orchestrating your day. Having lots of diversity is even more important if you have ADHD, due to the low tolerance of boredom or frustration.

Balance-promoting strategies
- Intersperse more sedate activities with more physical ones.
- Ensure you get adequate fresh air and natural light exposure.
- Schedule in rest breaks and protect mealtimes.
- Balance time spent alone and time spent with others.
- Be careful not to overcommit yourself and get overloaded and overwhelmed.
- Alternate work and non-work activities.
- Make sure you get enough sleep and try to maintain good blood sugar control (see page 165).

Avoid the common trap of telling yourself that you 'don't have time' for less pressured scheduled activities such as exercise, meals, social time, self-care and sleep. They are crucially important for well-being and emotional regulation, and improving these undoubtedly increases overall efficiency and productivity. If you find it difficult to give yourself 'permission', try redefining these balancing activities as a form of 'reward' that can be used to drive motivation in other more taxing tasks.

Like most things related to ADHD, how energy is regulated is laden with inefficiencies. Firstly, there is the problem of taking on too much. Unchecked, this can rapidly spiral into exhaustion, overwhelm and ultimately burnout. This overload issue results from a concoction of impulsivity, excitability, hyperfocus, perfectionism and some decision-making and working memory deficits thrown in for good measure. It's also the product of a distorted perception of how long things will take, known colloquially as 'time blindness'.

As well as misjudging and overfilling time, ADHD's impact on motivation, again a regulatory issue, can sometimes result in lots of empty, unstructured 'pacing' and 'fridge grazing' time. With all this unfilled space, we risk slipping into unhealthy or addictive patterns of behaviour that provide a degree of comfort or a brief respite. Remember, these behavioural defaults serve a clear function – to obfuscate and soften the inner discomfort of emptiness, boredom, apathy or underachievement that so commonly fills this void and oppresses the lives of those with adult ADHD.

In my experience, many adults with ADHD fall at the first hurdle as a result of sloppy scheduling (or no scheduling). Whether it is neglecting to allocate (sufficient) time for meals or transitions between activities, adults with ADHD so often make the mistake of setting unrealistic goals for the day, which can leave us feeling deflated and ineffective.

Many just pick themselves up and keep battling on, seemingly resilient as they bounce off setbacks, but, in the process, building up an ever-expanding energetic 'debt'. Over time, this will gradually wear the system down and, with dwindling reserves, subtle signs of strain may start surfacing, taking a creeping toll physically, emotionally and relationally. To limit this gradual energetic spiralling, have a look at my top tips for regulating energy expenditure in the box opposite.

Tips for regulating energy expenditure

- Overestimate how long things will take – I tend to add on 30–50 per cent to my initial predictions to be safe. When planning a journey, always build in some contingency in case things don't go entirely to plan.
- Conversely, edge slightly towards *under-* rather than overestimating what you think you can achieve in terms of your set tasks and activities for the day. It is far better to meet or exceed than fall short. To stay on track, set reminders and alarms/countdown timers to alert you when to wrap up and move on, and then, when prompted, act. Avoid trying to squeeze in too much and ending up perpetually rushing around. Where possible, run your schedule by someone else for a reality check.
- Avoid skipping meals (unless of course you are practicing intermittent fasting – see page 167) and ensure that you maintain optimal blood sugar control. This involves eating foods that provide sustained (rather than rapid) energy release and building in sufficient time for meal preparation. (We'll discuss nutrition in detail in Pillar 5.)
- Plan your day carefully so that there is adequate recovery and rest time built in.
- Make sure that you are sufficiently active during the day and avoid spending hours on end sitting in the same position, staring at the same screen, without a break. Get up and move around at least every 45 minutes, and regularly shift your focus away from the screen and look at something in the distance, preferably something green. Try to go outside and take a few deep breaths whenever you take a break.
- Integrate regular and varied forms of exercise to energise and recharge the system and be sure to get sufficient fresh air and natural light exposure each day.

- Allow yourself some flexibility when there are signs of slippage. If you sense that the plans you have scheduled for the remainder of the day are unrealistic and you don't think you will be able to catch up, stop and make a change – for example, cancel, delay or carry over – and do it as early as possible.
- Consider whether a scheduled in-person arrangement or meeting can take place remotely – by phone or via videoconferencing. Phone calls can be a bit less draining than video meetings. Saying that, try not to compromise too much on human-to-human contact which can be nourishing and energising.
- If you spend all your working time on site and you don't think it is necessary, explore with your employer the possibility of establishing a hybrid working model, perhaps going in every other day and working from home in between. As well as helping to conserve energy, it will free up time and introduce some variation which can help diffuse feelings of boredom and monotony.

RECOGNISING AND ADDRESSING PROCRASTINATION

Procrastination is *the action of delaying or postponing something that must be done*. It is such a common problem in ADHD that many see it as the hallmark of the condition in adulthood. It can impact one's ability to complete tasks which has a knock-on effect on productivity at home and in the workplace. It can cause us to lose faith in our ability and can lead us, and others, to conclude that we are 'lazy', when this is very often not an accurate representation of what is going on.

Along with most adults with ADHD, I used to procrastinate a fair amount! It can still be a problem at times, but I understand how to work with it better now. Tasks that I put off would weigh heavily on my mind and become much bigger intrusions than they were in reality. Although this has improved to a degree by implementing and maintaining the time- and task-management tools we explored earlier, I still sometimes find myself procrastinating. This is generally over mundane, administrative tasks (for example, car or tax stuff, non-urgent or monotonous jobs around the house, opening post, booking the dentist or optician, and so on). Procrastination can lead to a lot of mental anguish, and I always worry that it may, one day, have more damaging consequences than the occasional late payment fee or 'slap on the wrist'. As is the experience with many others, when I actually get round to starting the task, it is never as bad as I imagine. In fact, I typically get into it quite quickly, and sometimes even enjoy it; another paradox of ADHD.

The first moment you realise you are procrastinating is often when you notice that you have drifted into an 'escape behaviour'. These, sometimes unconscious, detours serve the function of putting off the activity that you are meant to be doing by filling the empty space. Common escape behaviours include checking emails or social media, watching videos on YouTube, taking a nap, smoking . . . or labelling and organising your sock drawer.

Procrastination is inherently not a good thing, since it often has negative consequences. Subjectively it is not a pleasant or welcome experience, yet, somewhat irrationally, we often continue to avoid what needs to be done. This suggests that what lies beneath the procrastination is registered as being even more uncomfortable than the inner conflict that surfaces when we catch ourselves doing it.

When thinking about how to tackle this common problem, we need to keep in the forefront of our mind the question: What lies beneath? There are many different manifestations of procrastination. What they have in common is a distorted, negative or unhelpful thought or feeling that is being actively repelled. It could be:

- an empty feeling of boredom or not being in the mood
- an assumption that it's not going to be much fun, and a desire to do something easier or more enjoyable
- an anxiety that it's going to take too long
- a concern that other things are more of a priority
- a lost feeling of having 'no idea where to start!'

As you can see, procrastination often involves a *magnification* of the perceived negatives, and a *minimisation* of the positive aspects of doing the activity. We also tend to *overestimate* how long it's going to take and *underestimate* how much we will enjoy it.

Ten tips for taming procrastination

1. The moment you realise you are procrastinating, acknowledge it: light-heartedly say out loud to yourself, 'James, you're procrastinating now.'
2. Then ask yourself, 'What do I have scheduled for this time?' Briefly pause for reflection, wrap up what you are doing, and redirect your attention assertively.
3. Reflect on what uncomfortable thought or feeling may be driving the procrastination. Then work towards a mindful acceptance of it and, with confidence, make a commitment to get started regardless. Some find it helpful to make a note of the worry, with a view to revisiting and exploring it later in the day (or not).
4. If the issue is that you are not sure where to start, make sure that the task has been sufficiently broken down (or 'chunked') into discrete behavioural steps, each with a clear launch point (see page 118 for guidance on this).

5. When redirecting your attention back to a task or activity, it can help to make some sort of bold and decisive move – perhaps stand up, clap your hands together and say out loud, 'Okay, enough procrastinating now, it's time to get started – 5, 4, 3, 2, 1.'

6. It can help to reframe the activity or action as a *challenge*, reminding yourself that it is time-limited and manageable. Reassure yourself that, in all likelihood, it won't be nearly as bad as you imagine once you get started.

7. Some find it helpful to visualise, in their mind's eye, the steps involved in completing a task, which has the effect of boosting pathways concerned with carrying out step-by-step actions or procedures. You can also try imagining the feeling of relief and satisfaction that will come once you have completed it.

8. Commit to a mere 10 minutes' work on the task. After the 10 minutes is up, reassess how you are doing and, if you still feel resistant, give yourself unreserved permission to stop. If you are happy and settled, then press on. Remember, *motivation generally follows action* not the other way round as most assume – you need to start and then you get engaged.

9. Build in a (healthy) reward (for example, a walk round the local park or a mini-stretching session) that you can only enjoy once you have completed the action or activity. Another approach is to set yourself a deadline or a time challenge.

10. Try pairing the action with a more pleasurable activity, such as doing the ironing while listening to the radio, tackling your monthly invoicing with a freshly brewed cup of coffee or listening to a podcast as you reorganise the shelves.

Exercise: Select your top five strategies for tackling procrastination
1. Select the five approaches that resonate with you most from the ten listed above.

PILLAR 3

2. Implement one a week for the next five weeks (every time you notice yourself procrastinating) and establish which ones work best for you.

So, there you have it – a whistle-stop tour through the practicalities of time and task management. Just do your best, building in the changes incrementally and not being too hard on yourself. I recognise this is a challenging area for many, so something is better than nothing.

In the next pillar, I remain with the important theme of organisation, but shift the focus to how we manage our physical *space*, and the endless flow of inbound *stuff* which populates that space.

PILLAR 4

MANAGE YOUR ENVIRONMENT AND INPUTS

Most of us intuitively recognise that the environment around us has an impact on our mental well-being. We know we feel full and cluttered in our minds when our living space is a mess, for example. In those with ADHD, a disordered environment, often brimming with stuff, is not an uncommon finding. And then there's the knock-on effect of clutter – not being able to find anything!

Until I understood my ADHD better and developed workable systems, I would regularly mislay personal items and waste lots of time searching and fretting. It wouldn't be uncommon to find me darting around the house, cursing obscenities under my breath, while searching for my keys or phone and leaving a trail of destruction in my wake. These days, pretty much every one of my possessions has a set place, preferably visible to the naked eye, and quite often labelled, which I've found can help quite a bit (though at times I can get a bit trigger-happy with the label maker).

Disorder in our immediate environment can leave us feeling stressed and just a little bit unsettled, weighed down and burdened by the ever-growing pile of dirty dishes squatting in the sink; increasingly incensed when we can't find a 'bloody lid' that fits 'that bloody, stupid Tupperware'; and deeply ashamed by an increasingly unruly wardrobe, while being secretly concerned about an equally secret hoarding tendency.

You may well have noticed that you feel less comfortable, or outright uncomfortable, in certain environments and that, conversely, you thrive in others – and that, when you do manage to clear the clutter and bring in more order, the sense of inner regulation and calm is almost palpable. The presence of a more tranquil external landscape clearly promotes a more harmonious internal world, and my mission in this pillar is to help you achieve that harmony.

To start with, I am going to guide you through the process of decluttering. Then, I will share some tips for managing key areas of your home, introducing simple and practical ADHD-friendly strategies that I know make a real difference. We'll then turn our attention to what I call your 'inputs', the unrelenting barrage of information that enters your conscious awareness minute-by-minute, hour-by-hour. Some of this information is unimportant (and simply needs to be filtered out), some may have utility down the line (and therefore requires cataloguing or capturing in some way) and a proportion is important (and requires you to take some form of action). We will explore ways to streamline things and protect you from getting overloaded.

Without a system you can quickly become snowed under, impacting your ability to maintain a sense of balance in the day-to-day management of your life. If you 'shutdown' or 'check out', the problems will typically start to pile up and become even more of a mission to rectify. I have no doubt that many of you will resonate with these descriptions and I hope the tips and strategies in this pillar will enable you to bring in more order. The first step in the quest for orderliness is to reduce the existing load.

DECLUTTERING

'Decluttering' is the process of removing things you do not need from a space, to make it feel more pleasant and less cluttered.

Aim to declutter each of your rooms about once a year. In this idealised world you would allocate one to two days per room. In reality, it is when the lack of order starts to feel oppressive or overwhelming, when you run out of storage space or when you struggle to find things that you need, that you consider a 'sort'.

Decluttering is only the first step. For this to really work, there needs to be a little activity on an ongoing basis to *maintain* things. This maintenance phase is far easier, however, when everything has its place.

How to declutter a space

When it comes to decluttering, you first need to commit (and block out) the time to do it, and then approach the process calmly and systematically. You may find it helpful to ask a friend or family member for help, to keep you on track and aid with decision-making. Where possible, try to reframe the project as a fun 'challenge'. In addition to recruiting someone for support, other strategies that can help include setting a time limit, building in a reward or putting some music in the background.

Below are my five top tips for decluttering:

1. **Everything in your home should have a defined place.** You can use labels to mark this space, ideally using a label-making device (my kids and I think labelling is the best thing since sliced bread, but my wife thinks we are all a bit bonkers). How far you take this is of course up to you, but most people with ADHD really benefit from visual reminders and prompts.
2. **When carrying out a declutter:**
   - Start with the *floors*. Put everything back where it belongs.
   - Then clear, and clean, all the *surfaces*.

PILLAR 4

- Only then, once the space is clear, do you tackle the *drawers* and *cupboards*.

3. **Allocate every loose item you come across to one of four separate piles.** Ask yourself, do you want to:
   - *Keep:* If so, you will need to return it to its home, or possibly find it a home.
   - *Discard:* Lose it, however difficult that might feel. Be bold, even ruthless!
   - *Donate:* To charity or friends/family – the donation pile should be transferred into bags and immediately put by the front door or directly into the car boot.
   - *Ponder:* There will inevitably be things you're not sure what to do with. If you are really conflicted, keep it (possibly in a 'ponder box') and review after three months. If the item has not been used, consider letting it go.

4. **Create a home for your 'daily carry items' (or DCIs).** Choose an easily accessible container, tray or drawer in which to store the items you carry with you outside the home on a daily basis, such as your mobile phone (have a charger and power source nearby), your keys, wallet, ID and glasses or sunglasses, but keep it at a reasonable distance from the front door. Get into the habit of immediately unloading your DCIs on entering your home (or workplace). Avoid leaving items in your pockets (you probably won't empty them later, whatever you tell yourself).

5. **Find innovative and practical storage solutions** (see pages 138–40 for more area-specific storage solutions).
   - Stacking storage boxes (possibly see-through) can be very helpful in allowing you to organise and easily access your possessions, but it's worth following these recommendations:
     - Keep related items together in a box, for example, present wrapping, sport equipment, Christmas decorations, and so on.

- Don't overfill the boxes and aim for a stack of no more than two to three boxes.
- Avoid storing the boxes away in remote places. The idea is that they are visible and easily accessible.
- Every time you fill a box, tape an index card (clearly listing the contents of the box) to the side of the box facing outwards, to ensure visibility.

- Store items that you need for the next day, such as gym kit, directly by the front door or packed into the boot of your car.

Five tips for dealing with annoying or stray loose items

1. Ask yourself if you have, at any point, needed to use it during the last year (this is the 'one-year rule'). If not, consider sending it on its way. You will probably not miss it and, frankly, life is just too short.
2. Remind yourself that, if needed, you will probably be able to source a replacement quite easily.
3. Avoid falling into the sticky, 'I may need it one day' trap. Remember, 'If in doubt, throw it out.'
4. Create a 'memories box' for those items that have little practical utility, but high sentimental value, for example, your favourite school football shirt or the ticket to your first stadium concert.
5. Create a 'miscellaneous box' for those items that you really aren't sure what to do with, including random spare parts and other important looking, but homeless 'bits and bobs'. Episodically, usually when the box is overflowing, sort through, keep what still feels important and discard the rest.

Ten tips for clothes management

1. Manage and periodically reduce your wardrobe. Consider a 'clothes declutter' every six months or so (see box on page 139).

2. Separate special activity clothes (for example, sportswear, gardening clothes and formal wear) from everyday clothes. These may be put on particular shelves (maybe the harder to access ones) or stored in index card-labelled boxes.

3. For hygiene reasons, store your outdoor shoes outside of your bedroom, ideally near the front door. Find a shoe storage solution that works for you, such as a drawer, rack or a (multiple compartment) hanging system, to avoid them permanently littering the hallway floor. Keep your indoor shoes (such as slippers or flip-flops) here to facilitate a seamless switch over.

4. Allocate one or more season-specific box(es) for stashing away your summer (or winter) clothes when they are not needed, freeing up accessible wardrobe space for the current season. Keep them somewhere nearby, so you can easily locate and resurrect them at the change of season.

5. Store your clothes rolled up (individually) in drawers to allow good visibility, compact storage and easy access.

6. After removing them at the end of the day, try to put your clean (enough) clothes back in the cupboard and the dirty items into the laundry basket, immediately. If it all feels too much and you decide to hang them over a chair, be sure to clear the pile every couple of days.

7. To avoid the monotony of pairing clean socks, consider replacing your existing socks (over time, if necessary) with only the two colours (or styles) that you wear most often. This makes pairing a whole lot easier, which will save valuable time in the long run.

8. Separate any clothes you are only keeping for sentimental value and keep them elsewhere (in your 'memories box' if this idea appeals).

9. Have a laundry basket for clothes that need washing (possibly with two compartments for splitting lights and darks upfront)

and a separate ironing basket for clothes that have been washed and dried (but still need to be ironed).

10. Schedule fixed days and times for clothes washing and ironing. Try not to leave wet clothes in the machine. They smell so bad, and you will only end up having to rewash them. Set a notification as a matter of routine.

The 'clothes declutter'

First, lay out all your clothes on the bed (you may wish to cover it with a sheet first to collect the dust). Then, one by one, handle each item of clothing and properly consider it. As with the room declutter, ask yourself if you want to *keep*, *discard*, *donate* or *ponder*. If you are conflicted and find yourself edging towards 'ponder' too often, try applying the 'one-year rule' or the 'hanger sign' technique:

- This novel approach involves lining up your clothes hangers with the hooks all pointing in the same direction to start with.
- Every time you wear an item, put it back into the wardrobe with the hook facing in the opposite direction.
- After six months, all unworn clothes (those with the hooks facing in the original direction) should be scrutinised.

PILLAR 4

Ten tips for kitchen management

1. Store kitchen items strategically, according to their use, for example, keep pots and pans close to the cooker, spices and oils near the hob, and so on.

2. Conduct an episodic cleanse of Tupperware (and other kitchen annoyances), disposing of unnecessary or odd items that have somehow found their way onto your shelves. Only keep Tupperware with matching lids (that fit properly) and, ideally,

    replace plastic with glass, to reduce your exposure to the chemicals that leach from plastic (see Pillar 6 for more on this).

3. Reserve the high shelves and cupboards for rarely used items, such as baking supplies, which may be more conveniently stored in easy-to-transfer boxes than kept loose.

4. Keep a single layer of items on a shelf to avoid clutter and allow easy access. Shelf dividers can be a practical way of doubling space.

5. Standardise your crockery: get rid of odds and ends and scrutinise the array of different-sized bowls and plates that so often cause cupboard and dishwasher chaos. As well as promoting more harmony in terms of 'shelf life', it will also make loading the dishwasher and drying rack so much easier.

6. Get into the efficient habit of batch cooking and freezing the extra food. You can also freeze and store leftovers following a meal (but wait for it to cool down a bit first). Every time you freeze something, note on the item the date it goes in and what it is.

7. Conduct a fridge cleanse every couple of months. Remove all contents, throw out perished items, clean (avoiding the use of harsh chemicals) and allow to dry. Then restock, reorganising everything properly to facilitate easy access. Do the same with your oven and the freezer (including an occasional full defrost when it gets overloaded or jammed with ice).

8. Have easily accessible dustbins, recycling bins or bags and food waste bins. Designate (with notifications) two set days a week for emptying the rubbish, recycling and food waste.

9. After every meal, immediately clear the dishes, dispose of the waste and wash up (or load the dishwasher). If there are multiple household members, create a rota or work together to get it done quickly. Maybe put on some music and try to make it fun. Finish with a quick (non-toxic) surface clean. (If you are feeling extra-motivated you can lay the table for the next meal to save time.)

10. Give meal planning a go and consider arranging a weekly food (or vegetable/fruit box) delivery (we'll discuss this further in Pillar 5).

MANAGING 'INPUTS'

At a very basic level, we humans function much like a computer. Incoming data, in different 'modalities', is registered by our multiple senses. The information is then transferred, organised and processed by our nervous system, and this generates some sort of response. If either our senses are impaired or the areas of our brain responsible for the information processing or task execution are wired slightly differently, there will be a knock-on effect in terms of outputs, affecting the overall stability of the system.

In ADHD, there are alterations to the brain that affect these important functions and dysregulate the system. They particularly impact the brain's ability to hold information 'in mind' with sufficient stability to allow the necessary steps that will culminate in the completion of an intended goal. Many things can go wrong along the way – too many simultaneous inputs and inefficient 'software' to organise the data can both quickly overwhelm the system. This typically results in either a state of shutdown and rigidity, or one of disorder and chaos. According to Dan Siegel, a Professor of Psychiatry in the US and respected author and thinker, these response patterns are shared with other systems where the individual parts are, for whatever reason, not properly integrated – leading to a state of rigidity or one of chaos.

A clue that there may be a problem in terms of the 'flow' of your inputs may include you feeling like you are in a state of perpetual 'catch-up' (but never actually catching up), paired with a rising sense of apprehension and doom in the face of an ever-growing cache of unanswered emails and unopened letters, or an out-of-control task list. Alarm bells should really start ringing when the

PILLAR 4

print on the higher peaks of the 'post mountain' begins morphing from an unassuming black to an alarming blood red.

Under pressure, you can become singularly focused and, in doing so, you may neglect other less pressing needs and responsibilities, just in order to stay afloat. A 'fight or flight' survival instinct kicks in, putting you in a continuous low-level threat state, and the system functions under strain. Left unchecked, you burn out.

Given the vulnerabilities ADHD confers, it's useful to get ahead of the curve and introduce compensatory strategies and effective aids to help your brain manage the flow. Otherwise, you may find yourself swimming against the tide.

Where to start

It makes logical sense that the centrepiece of effective flow regulation is a well-oiled system for time and task management. Getting this running upfront, at least at a basic level, will serve you well. If you haven't already, read through the previous pillar, where I have covered time and task management in detail. Putting in place the tools I've outlined there will give you a good head start.

Handling requests made of you

Where you have the option (and you deem it reasonable and appropriate), get into the habit of asking for a little space to consider requests made of your time. Before making up your mind, weigh up all relevant factors including the likely time commitment (doubled for safe measure) and whether or not the proposed deadline or delivery date is realistic. Perhaps discuss it with someone too.

If you know you are already overcommitted or you don't feel sufficiently motivated by an opportunity (which is not in your job description if it is a work request), don't be afraid to say 'No'. It is sometimes necessary to be assertive, and far better to respond with a decisive 'No' now, than to half-heartedly commit only to pull out sometime down the line.

Do your utmost to avoid the impulsive 'Yes', *even* if you feel honoured to have been asked. An overly accommodating attitude when considering invitations to take on extra responsibility is often underpinned by a sense of personal inadequacy and will likely lead to people taking advantage. Do not trick yourself into believing that, by volunteering for additional duties, you will somehow be making up for your perceived past 'failures'. There are people who will exploit this vulnerability. Don't be afraid to *respectfully* stand your ground and maintain the boundaries you deem to be important.

With any request that is made of you when you are on the move, and especially if you don't have the time or means to note it down properly, it is reasonable to ask for the request in an email or text.

If your boss is pushing you to take on more than your capacity allows, first take some time to gather your thoughts, then meet with them to talk it through. Without any emotional loading, or attitude, take them through your work diary and current commitments. Ask *them* for guidance as to what you should prioritise, given the 'unrealistic workload' for the 'available time'.

When you do agree to take something on, immediately make a note of it and then summarise your understanding, clarifying the important details, for example, 'So, my understanding is that you want me to . . .'

Agree it, note it, file it

Arrangements/appointments
Get into the habit of immediately inputting all arrangements and appointments directly into your (paper or digital) diary.

It's not complicated – just go ahead and drop a block into an available slot and give it a name. And be sure to capture any relevant contact and location information, for ease of reference. It's easy to digitally share the diary entry with someone else if you need to.

Tasks

Add all tasks, *as they arise*, to your dump-all task list. You may wish to mark or star the task as a priority if it is particularly urgent. If there are any paper documents associated with the task, you can keep them in your ring binder 'to-do' file.

Other gems and nuggets

You will, of course, be the recipient of other incoming information which doesn't fall into the category of arrangements, appointments or tasks, but which is nevertheless important or useful to retain. These will need to be added to one of a number of preconfigured lists. You can create any list that takes your fancy, of course, but here are a few ideas to ponder:

- food shopping list
- things to buy
- film/TV programme/book recommendations
- restaurant/holiday destination/places to visit recommendations
- gift ideas (me)
- gift ideas (others)
- passwords and other important reference information, such as bank account details (ideally, these need to be password protected)

Managing meetings, talks and important phone calls

Many find that taking notes during meetings or talks really helps them stay connected and sharpens focus. If it is an in-person presentation or talk, sit near the front of the room and, if you feel your attention is dwindling, try to engage with (relevant) questions, as this can help keep you tuned in.

On occasion, you may, with permission, be able to record a meeting (video/audio) so you can review the detail later; however, this is time-heavy and not an ideal strategy. It may be worth asking if you can get a copy of the presentation slides or notes for a meeting or lecture in advance, but be sure to save them immediately on receipt. This will allow you to briefly scan the material prior to the session, to familiarise yourself with the content. This may be a step too far, but it's worth a consideration.

If you have an important **telephone call** to make, whether work-related or otherwise, here is some guidance as to your approach:

- Have a pen and paper to hand. Before you start, put the title and date at the top of the page.
- Have any related documentation close to hand. Review and highlight relevant parts before the call to prepare and focus the mind if necessary.
- After a bit of introductory conversation, agree on the function of the call and, if appropriate, state how long you expect it to last.
- Start by summarising your current understanding of the issue under discussion.
- Make your points in a logical and structured way. Try not to get overexcited or to lecture the other person. Give them time to share *their* thoughts.
- At the end of the call, summarise the key points and clarify your shared understanding.
- If necessary, define specific 'actions' and a timeline for their completion. Add new tasks that arise to your dump-all task list immediately.

- Agree your next meeting date and time, and add this to your diary immediately.
- In a work setting, I think it is good practice to follow-up with a very brief email which just lists both parties' actions, for example, 'Thanks for the meeting. We agreed I would do . . . and that you would do . . . And that we would reconvene on . . .'

Reading (and audio)

So many of us with ADHD struggle with reading. Some require complete silence, while others find it easier to stay focused when there is a little low-level noise or some calming music playing in the background. Some lap up fiction and can't fathom how anyone could read non-fiction, and for others it is the exact opposite. Some tend towards extended periods of intense hyperfocus, and others prefer short bursts with regular breaks.

When it comes to reading, you really need to work out the medium, the environment and the approach that works best for you. Are you someone who likes the feel of a good old-fashioned book or do you respond best to a screen? If the latter, do you prefer a traditional white screen or the less intense black or grey options? Do you need to be sitting upright or do you read best when lying flat? And what about lighting? You get the idea – go ahead and experiment and find out what works for you. There are no rules here.

Over recent years, with the emergence of audiobooks, many, including myself, who had all but given up trying to overcome enduring and resistant reading blocks, have successfully migrated across to the spoken word. Audiobooks are an alternative way of accessing the wonderful world of literature, but, as deserving as they are of praise, they are not suited to all genres. Some technical, non-fiction books that have a lot of reference information, including boxes, diagrams and lists don't tend to work so well when spoken as opposed to read. The publisher often creates supplementary PDFs in this situation, which can be helpful, but it may be easier to go with a hard (or digital) copy in these cases.

When listening to audiobooks or podcasts, be sure to listen to a sample before purchasing to check you can tolerate the narrator's accent. It is also important to get your listening settings right. If the reading speed feels too slow, you can usually speed it up a bit. Faster speech can sometimes hold the focus better. I generally find myself landing around 1.2x the normal speed, but everyone is different, and it does depend on the narrator's style.

If you find yourself getting distracted or tired when listening while sitting or lying still, connect with Bluetooth headphones and go wandering. This can also work well for phone conversations. Whether it's pottering around your home doing low-intensity, menial tasks (tidying up, dusting/cleaning, folding clothes, ironing, laying the table, cooking, drying up, putting clothes away, and so on) or going for a nice long walk, it generally helps to move. Not only do you achieve more with your time, but the 'dual stimulation' can enhance the listening 'staying power' for many.

If you prefer to sit still while listening, try doodling/drawing or making notes to stay connected. Some find it easier to read along with the narrator, either from a hard copy or on-screen.

When it comes to work- or study-related reading, it can help to actively interact with the material as you are reading it. (See the guidance below on actively engaging with texts.)

PILLAR 4

Active reading
- Before you embark on any detailed or technical reading (on-screen or printed), get into the habit of first briefly scanning through the document before you properly immerse yourself. Read the introduction, the main headings (together with the first line or two under each heading) and any end-of-section summaries. This will provide an overview and a bit of a framework to prepare for your more detailed read.

- With your first proper read-through you can highlight, underline, circle or star key facts and important points. For some, it can help to make brief notes in the margins or using the comments function electronically. Whether it's distilling the key message of the paragraph or capturing some of your reflections as you read, this is generally time well spent. (Note: If you are working with a book and you are uncomfortable writing in it, which I understand, consider photocopying or printing off the relevant pages to allow direct annotation or highlighting.)
- When you come to the end of your 'first read' of the material, it can help to briefly glance back over the marked-up areas and any side notes to reinforce the key messages.

Probably the biggest problem people complain of when it comes to reading is the struggle to commit and get started – procrastination rearing its ugly head, yet again. There are a few strategies to counter this mental block. To start with, try laying out the reading material, opened at the relevant page. If this alone doesn't motivate you, try committing to 10 minutes, essentially giving yourself a 'get out of jail' card if it doesn't work out. Once you get rolling, there's a good chance that you will want to continue, but, if not, as soon as the 10 minutes is up, you can terminate the session without even a whisper of guilt. After all, that was the deal.

Managing post

Post management can be a real problem for adults with ADHD. The strategies I have found most useful include sticking a 'No Junk Mail' sign on your front door, close to the letterbox. It can also help to strategically position a recycling box, and a letter opener, somewhere near the front door. Limit unnecessary advertising by always opting out when purchasing goods – always read the small print carefully as companies can be sneaky! When unwanted post does slip through the net, take a moment to unsubscribe. This will involve noting the unsubscribe email address which will be printed somewhere on the letter. To reduce post more generally, where possible, request e-invoicing and set up direct debits.

Hiding among the junk mail that gets through, there will be a few important items that require an action or response. Unopened letters can present a huge source of anxiety for many adults with ADHD. This usually reflects an overestimation of the time commitment that will be involved in dealing with it or concern related to its contents. *Am I in trouble? Is it a threat or a fine? Or a bill? Have I lost my job? Is it something else to add to the list?* The simple solution is always to just OPEN IT! Try to avoid encouraging even the earliest formations of a 'post mountain' which, left unchecked, can become highly invasive. Commit to opening and sorting through the post as soon as possible after it arrives using the tips below.

PILLAR 4

Post management
- Commit 10 minutes.
- First, discard (recycle) all the junk flyers and brochures – a quick win! Avoid the 'I may need this one day' trap.
- Open all letters and deposit all envelopes and paper waste directly into the recycling box – quick win number two!
- Separate the remaining items into two piles:
  1. A 'to-file pile', which can be added to a 'to-file tray' or (ideally) immediately filed away in your paper filing cabinet. Note: Only important reference information that doesn't require an action is eligible for filing.
  2. A pile for items that will require an action.

> • As soon as you have finished opening and organising, immediately transfer the documents from these two piles to their respective next abode, then, without delay, add all new tasks to your dump-all task list and file the associated papers in a plastic sleeve in your to-do file.

Dealing with emails and texts

Keeping up with emails, and the actions that emerge from them, is a significant challenge for so many with ADHD. I would strongly recommend implementing some sort of system, rather than just rolling with it, as some do.

Some people find it useful to have different email addresses for different functions, to be able to separate things off, for example, work, social and project emails. Personally, I think having more than two emails gets confusing, so I would limit it and, at most, have a separate one for work and personal. Decide whether to merge emails or keep them separate.

It's also worth working out whether you are someone who is going to delete and file emails or retain them (read and unread) in your inbox and rely on the email's search function to find things, as required. This latter approach, which I use, may well save you lots of time. In general, the search function works well if using an email linked to a search engine, such as Gmail. If you do decide to file your emails, I encourage no more than a handful of tabs. The other thing I like about Gmail is that it arranges all incoming emails into categories: Promotions, Social and Primary. There is also an automatic prompt function that reminds you to respond to recently received emails that appear to require a response.

Schedule in a daily email review (starting from where the last review ended) for a set time of 10 minutes. If you are just starting out and this feels a bit much, begin by doing a review every other day, or even weekly. Respond there and then to any very straight-forward matters, as long as they require no more than a one-line response. Avoid getting sidetracked and lost in the detail.

Using the star or flag system, mark emails that have an associated action or that require a response. This is a convenient way of separating emails that have an action associated or that contain important reference information you will need to access later. Some find the 'mark as unread' function helpful – if selected, the email reverts to looking as though it has not yet been opened and is therefore less likely to be missed. And if you don't already, I suggest you make optimal use of the subject bar and develop an intuitive labelling approach that will save time when searching for emails.

Add all tasks (or the email itself, a function available on Gmail) to your dump-all task list during or after the review.

Some emails will inevitably slip through the net, however good your system is. If you are fortunate, someone will follow up. An important rule: *never ignore a chase!* On receipt, stop whatever you are doing and address the issue without delay.

Screen use

Excessive screen use is so often a sticky issue for adults with ADHD. The internet is like a dopamine playground: the ability to get immediate answers to questions that spontaneously pop into your mind; the lure of content cleverly tailored to your specific interests; the irresistible opportunity to escape from your other responsibilities. It's all just a bit too much for a disinhibited mind that instinctively seeks out reward and novelty. Screen-based 'traps', include:

- online (video) surfing
- social media (X, Facebook, TikTok and so on)
- news or sports feeds
- checking emails, texts or WhatsApp messages

PILLAR 4

Access to non-stop news feeds and ever-updating social media drives a pathological degree of checking, and then rechecking minutes later, just to see what's new. But this constant 'noise' is absorbing your time, narrowing your focus, draining your energy, creating stress and fostering an unhealthy and addictive relationship with your tech.

With so much of your time spent staring and swiping, you reduce your engagement in other more nourishing and health-promoting activities, such as being out in nature, moving your body, connecting with others and being 'present'. You can understand why it is vital to impose limits and boundaries (see box below).

Managing your screen time

- Schedule time in your diary dedicated to screen use. Stick to it militantly until the habit is rooted in.
- Actively banish screen time as your 'go-to', default time-filler. Every time you feel that void, often an almost imperceptible and mildly uncomfortable sense of emptiness, STOP. Impose a delay before reaching for your phone.
- In these moments, be curious and try to work out what exactly you are feeling. *Am I worried . . . or bored?* What happens if you just sit it out? Does the discomfort pass or does it build? Are you able to resist the urge and try something different?
- Go outside for a walk and some fresh air. Look around you and fully immerse yourself in the awe-inspiring beauty of nature. Breathe slowly and deeply and really try to be in the present moment.
- If you notice you've unwittingly strayed on to a screen mid-task – an 'escape behaviour' – intervene, earlier rather than later. Perhaps say out loud to yourself, 'I'm

---

procrastinating!' Then ask yourself, 'What was I intending to do right now?', referring to your diary, if necessary.

- Be bold. Experiment with using the flight mode function for extended periods. If you are feeling really brave, maybe even turn off your phone or decide not to take it out with you. Remind yourself that generations before you survived, in fact positively thrived, without a single smartphone in sight. You will be just fine and the world will keep turning. Most things can wait and, if they can't, it will probably still be okay. Enjoy the freedom it brings.

- As you enter a car, get into the habit of either switching off your phone or, if absolutely necessary, using 'car-safe' mode. Practise being mindful and enjoy the drive. Avoid putting yourself and others at an unnecessary risk – it's really not worth it.

PILLAR 4

Money management

Most adults with ADHD struggle to regulate their spending and manage their finances. How many times have you fallen into the trap of the impulse buy? The dopamine-fuelling pastime of shopping disproportionately traps people with ADHD. This is because the ADHD brain's reward centre is understimulated. It is a brain that is perpetually craving a feeding of some form and responds more excitedly when it happens.

To make things more difficult, in addition to the reward-focused 'hyperdrive', the brain's braking system is also not functioning optimally in ADHD. A regulatory problem involving the frontal part of the brain impacts its ability to inhibit or control impulse and to delay gratification. This depletes one's capacity to pull back and say 'No, thank you'. Other factors at play that negatively impact money management in ADHD include difficulties with organisation, prioritisation and sticking to a budget.

As well as overspending and impulse buying, there are a number of other common finance traps that frustrate, and occasionally floor, those with ADHD:

- **The 'Love a deal . . . it's a steal' trap:** the lure of offers that are just 'too good to miss'.
- **The 'Oh no . . . not again!' overdraft trap:** not keeping track of income and expenditure (unintentionally or out of avoidant fear) means that you may unwittingly drift into penalty-riddled overdraft territory.
- **The 'cash no-flow' trap:** whether with your business or in your home life, if you misjudge the fine balance between spending and saving you may find yourself 'in a pickle', with insufficient funds to stay afloat.
- **The 'fail to pay off' credit trap:** failing to clear your credit card balance and other bills is another common generator of infuriating fines.
- **The 'no grow scenario' trap:** being too 'in the moment' negatively impacts financial planning for the future, with little consideration of saving.

The approach to managing money is a broad topic. In the tips below, I have attempted to distil my recommendations to guide and protect you from financial harm. Like all my suggestions, I invite you to pick and choose the ideas that you haven't yet thought of, and which resonate as relevant and potentially helpful.

Five tips for (not) purchasing

1. Be extremely vigilant to the magnetic lure of an offer or a deal, however enticing it may seem. Remember, you are more vulnerable than others in this area. As a rule, if it wasn't on your list, move away from the area! And if you want to reduce the chances of an impulsive purchase, avoid handling items – the more you touch something, the more likely you are to end up buying it.

2. At the point of purchase, pause and ask yourself, 'Do I really need this item?' and 'Is now the right time to buy it?' Weigh up your current financial health and come to an informed decision rather than diving in impulsively and mindlessly. If data is your thing, you can easily keep track of your spending with money-management apps. Where possible, and especially when it comes to big purchases, try to impose a delay. Sleep on it. Take a photo of the item and, during a simmering down (akin to a cooling off) period, ask a partner, family member or friend what they think. You can always order it online at a later date.

3. Every time you buy something new, see if there is an equivalent that you no longer need or use, that you can lose. For example, throw out an old pair of shoes when you buy a new one. Designate a 'charity shop box' where you can collect items that you are ready to part with, and episodically offload it to your favourite local charity shop.

4. If you fall in love with something that you really can't justify buying for yourself, think about whether it could be a suitable gift idea for an upcoming birthday – either for someone else you care about or as a possible gift to you from others (assuming they ask). While you ponder, add it to your 'gift list', kept with your other reference lists (see page 144). You can always link the purchase to the completion of a task or project as a form of reward, if you think this approach will help motivate you to either complete the task or delay the purchase.

5. If you prefer online shopping, consider signing up to a site that allows you to save items you are especially interested in to a 'watch list', such as www.lovesales.com. You will then be alerted if, and when, the item goes down in price.

Four tips for banking

1. Meet with your bank manager. Explain that you have ADHD and struggle with organisation and money management. Ask them what help and safeguards could be put in place to

PILLAR 4

protect you. Try to establish a simple system for your banking needs, automating wherever you can.

2. Download your bank's app onto your phone and computer. At the very least, make sure you learn how to check your balance, pay bills and transfer money between accounts seamlessly, at the touch of a few buttons.

3. Get into the habit of checking your bank balance about twice a week (scheduled, with notifications, if that helps) as this should protect you from getting overdrawn. The easier it is to do this the better, and money-management apps can really streamline things.

4. Do an informal audit of your income and expenditure every now and again. It can be helpful to plug some figures into a basic spreadsheet. But if the idea of using Excel sends shivers down your spine, you can approach this caveman-style, typed into a simple Word document or even written on a napkin. It may be worth scheduling in a brief review on a rolling basis, say every three months. Becoming more aware of how your money moves allows you to identify patterns, pre-empt problems and make informed spending decisions. See below for some guidance on carrying out a self-audit.

The rough-and-ready finance self-audit
Pull out some paper, open a Word document or create a new spreadsheet.

1. First, work out and document your monthly *income* (after tax i.e., 'net income').

2. Then, tally up and breakdown all your monthly *expenditure*, dividing it into fixed expenses (rent/mortgage payments, water, gas, electricity, mobile phone bill, internet, TV, council tax, fixed travel, ISA contribution) and variable expenses (home food, eating out food, entertainment, additional travel, and so on).

3. The difference between these two figures is the extra cash (or residual funds) you have available each month to play with (that is to spend, invest or save).

Once you have been auditing things for a little while, you will be in a much stronger position to do some budgeting. Of your monthly expenditure, aim for about 50 per cent to be allocated to fixed expenses, 30 per cent to your variable expenses and reserve the remaining 20 per cent as savings. Savings can serve as a buffer to be able to clear unexpected debts.

I know there's a lot to take in in this chapter, and although you may aim high, we all know that life doesn't always play ball. One of the most important lessons to take from this book is the importance of self-compassion in everything you do. This pillar is no exception. It is important to be realistic – you may not always be fully on top of everything, but the hope is that, using these tips and strategies, you will be for more of the time. Remember, the key is small incremental changes, underpinned by an enduring self-compassionate and growth-oriented mindset. Just do your best and expect to mess up now and again. Your trajectory is the main thing.

In the next pillar, we will do a deep dive into nutrition and movement, and how important they are in the self-management of ADHD.

PILLAR 5

NOURISH AND MOVE YOUR BODY

As we explored in Part 1, the characteristic dysregulation in ADHD has a significant impact on the workings of the physical body, and the effects are cumulative. For this reason, adults with ADHD, more than most, need to actively prioritise the care and mainten-ance of their bodies and do their very best to minimise the damage.

In this pillar, we'll look at how you can nourish and strengthen your body by managing with care what you put into it and how you move.

NUTRITION AND ADULT ADHD

When writing this section, I collaborated closely with my col-league, Ingrid Kitzing, MA (Hons), Dip NT, mBant, CNHC registered, who is a respected and experienced nutritional practitioner.

There is excitement building around the theme of nutrition in adult ADHD, with increasing interest in the role of gut health, and much discussion and debate about dietary interventions that may prove helpful in ADHD. There needs to be a lot more study in this area, but what I have come to appreciate is that there are a handful of simple, basic nutritional truths, well-supported by the science and applicable to most, that can really help provide a solid nutritional grounding for adults with ADHD who, for a variety of reasons, tend to struggle in this area which is fundamentally important for brain health.

Let's explore some of the reasons for this struggle. It is important to say that, in some individuals, the medication prescribed for their ADHD can negatively impact their appetite. In most cases, however, once optimised, the treatment results in more regulated eating, and generally seems to improve the nutritional landscape. Additionally, some studies have indicated that some of the medications may themselves contribute to nutritional deficiencies.

When tired, hungry or experiencing a blood sugar dip (due to nutritionally depleted or missed meals) or when feeling low in mood, those with ADHD are more likely to slip into the pattern of self-medicating with food. Most tend to reach for high-sugar foods and quick-release carbohydrates which will provide a rapid fix, but lead to a later crash.

What is also evident is that the dysregulation inherent to ADHD predisposes you to disordered eating in a variety of guises, such as overeating, bingeing, erratic eating and missed meals. It is well-established that those with ADHD have much higher rates of obesity and binge eating disorder.

A central issue is that those with ADHD find it really hard to evaluate when they are full and when to stop eating – the signal just doesn't come through in the same way. One of the downstream effects of disordered eating is the alteration of the individual's weight 'set point', which can result in difficult-to-control weight gain.

What to do about this common problem? Well, with Ingrid's skilled oversight, I have pulled together the most relevant general truths around how to maintain a healthy, balanced diet, woven together with what we currently know about ADHD and nutrition, in order to provide you with the most practical and targeted advice possible.

PILLAR 5

There are a few specific foods and supplements that may add additional value when thinking about mental health, and ADHD in particular. I will share some of my insights in this regard too, but I caveat it with the fact that the approach you take is going to depend on individual factors. If you are serious about addressing this area properly, you may want to get some professional nutritional guidance before delving too deep.

It goes without saying, but if there is any complexity whatsoever in your situation, or any medical issues in the mix, we strongly encourage you to seek specialist advice.

I want to be clear from the outset that neither Ingrid nor I support or promote any named diets, except in a few very specific situations, usually where there is a diagnosed medical issue. Our experience tells us that radical weight loss diets simply don't work, and that they miss the point, often causing more harm than good. I am also wary of any overly restrictive interventions in ADHD, as I know they probably won't be sustained. We are both mindful that excluding important foods or food groups from the diet, unless supervised, can result in deficiencies.

What I do fully subscribe to is a diverse, balanced, unprocessed, colourful, vegetable-rich diet, embedded in a stable and consistent eating routine, with protected mealtimes that encourage mindful and undistracted eating. In terms of optimising physical and mental health, there is probably most evidence to support a **'Mediterranean-style diet'** – one that includes plenty of unprocessed, fibre-rich plant foods (fresh vegetables, fruits, nuts, seeds and legumes); moderate amounts of fish, white meat, dairy and eggs; generous amounts of extra-virgin olive oil; and only occasional red meat. Your financial situation may impose some limitations, but, as far as possible, this is something worth striving for, based on the evidence. Eating this way improves the nutrient concentration of your diet, while also helping to balance blood sugar. It also avoids many of the unhealthy foods, artificial sweeteners and food additives commonplace in the modern western diet.

I fervently believe that the food we eat should be delicious, enticing and plentiful . . . as well as healthy. As far as I am concerned, this is one of the most important bits of advice I can give you when it comes to promoting optimal health through diet, and especially relevant to adults with ADHD, given the relative intolerance of being unduly restricted and ravenous pleasure centres that refuse to stand down.

Build a nutrient-dense and plant-diverse diet

The take-home message here is that **diversity is key**. Those who eat more than 30 different types of plant-based foods a week have been shown to have a more diverse gut microbiome, with a wealth of associated health benefits, including enhanced mental well-being. Fruit is nutrient-dense and a good source of antioxidants and fibre, but you mustn't overdo it. To protect against excessive blood sugar dysregulation, it is sensible to prioritise lower glycaemic-index fruits (fruits that result in less rapid sugar spikes) such as apples, apricots, berries, cherries, kiwis and pomegranate seeds.

When to consider organic

The Dirty Dozen (and Clean Fifteen) are published annually on the Environmental Working Group website (see Resources, page 289). This list helps to prioritise the most important fruit and vegetables to buy organic, if this is an option. I do recognise the cost will be prohibitive for many and that, more generally, eating healthily on a low income can be a real challenge.

In general, the non-organic plant-based produce to avoid includes strawberries and leafy greens. Foods that generally don't need to be organic include avocados, sweetcorn and pineapple.

The more vibrant the colours of fruit and vegetables, the better. Studies indicate that blue-/purple-coloured foods are particularly helpful for brain health and mood. The colour is the result of the phytochemicals they contain, which have been shown to have a wide range of health benefits, both physical and mental. An important group of these chemicals is the polyphenols (which include the flavonoids), which are powerful antioxidants, molecules that are protective and will undoubtedly enhance the overall health profile of those with ADHD. Even switching between orange and purple carrots, and white and red onions diversifies your phytochemical intake.

Brassica vegetables, which include broccoli, Brussels sprouts, cabbage (of all varieties), cauliflower, kale, pak choi, rocket and watercress, are particularly important, with demonstrated antidepressant effects.

When it comes to protein, quality is important. Whether it is animal- or plant-based, try to include some with every meal, for reasons I will explain below. Animal proteins (fish and meat) are easier to digest and absorb, whereas plant proteins (such as beans and pulses) are particularly good sources of gut-friendly fibre. Meals that combine both plant and animal protein can work really well. For example, red lentils in a beef Bolognese add both fibre and plant protein. Eggs are an inexpensive and excellent protein source, and one of the best sources of choline (which is a key part of an important brain chemical, acetylcholine – see box below). Eat the whole egg, not just the white, as the yolk contains most of the choline and other nutrients.

Choline

Choline is an important nutrient for brain health. It is a building block of acetylcholine, an important neurotransmitter (chemical messenger) used by the calming and balancing, parasympathetic arm of the autonomic nervous system. Low levels of choline have been associated with anxiety and, as discussed, anxiety is a hallmark but underappreciated feature of ADHD.

As well as being present in eggs (with two eggs providing just over half the recommended daily intake (RDI) of choline), it is also present in high levels in organ meats (especially liver and kidney), fish (including salmon and cod), meats (beef, chicken and turkey), brassica vegetables, soya beans and shiitake mushrooms.

Organic meat has been shown to have an antidepressant effect, which may help reduce the mood-related disturbance so common in ADHD. If cost is an issue, liver (chicken or lamb) is inexpensive and quick to cook. Lamb liver is one of the best dietary sources of vitamin B12 and should be eaten regularly. Red meat is a great source of iron, but (according to the NHS in England) you should limit your intake to no more than 490g of red and processed meat a week, due to the higher risk of colon cancer above that amount. That translates to the equivalent of two meaty decks of cards, two, maximum three, times a week.

Omega-3 fatty acids (EPA, DHA and ALA), which can only be obtained from the diet, are essential for brain function. A subset of those with ADHD have low baseline levels, and supplementation has been shown to have a benefit on ADHD symptoms. Oily fish (salmon, anchovies, mackerel, trout, herring and sardines) are the best sources of EPA and DHA. It is sensible to avoid tuna (including tinned tuna) due to high concentrations of toxic heavy metals. Other tinned fish, such as sardines, salmon and mackerel, are good alternatives. Kippers (or herrings), which come filleted in most supermarkets, are quick and easy to cook, and make a low-cost omega-3-rich breakfast. Walnuts together with seeds (including chia, flaxseed and hemp) are great sources of ALA.

PILLAR 5

However, plant sources of ALA are a much less efficient way of getting your required omega-3 than fish. Those who don't eat fish are therefore likely to need to supplement with omega-3. Either way, nuts and seeds have many other health benefits and should therefore be consumed regularly. Other seafood, including oysters, crab and lobster are some of the best sources of dietary zinc, and low zinc blood levels have been linked to depressive and ADHD symptoms.

I encourage plenty of herbs and spices in the diet. They have a long and colourful history of culinary use due to their impressive benefits to human health, primarily due to their antioxidant richness which confer loads of brain benefits. Those that have a particularly high antioxidant content include cinnamon, chilli peppers, cloves, coriander, curry leaves, fenugreek, garlic, ginger, marjoram, oregano, rosemary, sage and turmeric, but don't limit it to these. Go crazy and, in true ADHD style, use more than you think you need (within reason)!

Finally, I would like to draw particular attention to fermented foods. Among others they include kefir, kimchi, kombucha, sauerkraut, miso and 'live' yoghurt. They provide an impressive range of health benefits and are often responsible for giving food a depth and complexity of flavour. Early data suggests they are also great for gut health, mood and anxiety. It is likely that, in time, we will learn that optimising the microbial balance in the gut directly improves ADHD symptoms. One caveat: individuals who have histamine intolerance or issues with mast cell activation (see page 202) may not tolerate fermented foods, as, despite being great for gut bacterial health, they are also exceptionally high in histamine.

Steer clear of ultra-processed foods (UPFs)
A recent UK government 'National Food Strategy for England' report estimates that 54.3 per cent of UK

household food purchases are ultra-processed. They include many pre-packaged meals, some breads, biscuits, cakes and breakfast cereals. UPF consumption, according to a 2022 meta-analysis study, is associated with a wide range of adverse health outcomes, including negative effects on mental health, presumably including ADHD.

They are not only deficient in nutrients, but also very often laden with chemicals such as colourings, artificial sweeteners, emulsifiers and preservatives. Get used to reading ingredient labels and, if the ingredients aren't ones that you recognise, or numbering more than a handful of items, it is probably best to steer clear.

Processed meats

Here, what I am talking about is bacon, sausages, ham and other cured deli meats, hot dogs and tinned meat. Processed meats are not good for you, despite the fact that they can taste great (apart from the tinned meat which I just can't get my head round). Remember, eating too much red and processed meat increases your risk of bowel cancer and the NHS recommends an upper limit of 70g a day (or 490g per week).

PILLAR 5

Optimise blood sugar control

Our bodies function optimally when we have good blood sugar control. This means limiting the fluctuations of sugar levels to a relatively narrow range, and avoiding large spikes and sudden and deep dips. Regulation of all forms is a real challenge in ADHD, for all the reasons we have discussed, and blood sugar control is no exception. The spikes and dips that occur initiate a toxic inflammatory cascade that increases the likelihood of many chronic illnesses.

Optimal blood sugar regulation results in more constant energy levels throughout the day, which translates into better physical and mental performance. Poor blood sugar control can drive food cravings and deplete energy levels, and it has been associated with a range of mental illnesses, including depression. While other factors such as sleep and stress obviously have an impact, diet is the major contributor to blood sugar problems.

To support good blood sugar control, every meal should include a portion of good-quality **protein** (plant or animal). Protein recommendations vary, but the current international recommended dietary allowance (RDA) equates to roughly 25–30g of protein at each meal for healthy adults (that is the equivalent to approximately 2–3 medium eggs). Protein gives you a greater sense of fullness than carbohydrates or fat, and it is broken down more gradually by the body, releasing its energy in a slower, more sustained way.

Healthy fats are an important part of a balanced diet, and they also support optimal blood sugar regulation. They include nuts, seeds, olives, extra-virgin olive oil, organic dairy (if tolerated), avocado and omega-3-rich oily fish (see page 163). You can drizzle antioxidant-rich extra-virgin olive oil on food and it will help reduce the blood sugar impact.

Fibre is not only vital for our gut microbiome, but also important for reducing blood sugar responses to food. It is estimated that our hunter-gatherer ancestors ate 100–150g fibre daily. The NHS in the UK recommends 30g daily, but few of us achieve this. Fibre slows down the rate at which sugar is absorbed and helps us to feel full for longer. Dietary fibre comes largely from wholegrains, vegetables and fruit. In general, it is preferable to try to eat wholegrains rather than refined grains – that means brown rather than white rice – and to aim for half your plate to be vegetables. Ground flaxseed is an excellent source of fibre (aim for 1–2 tablespoons daily) with benefits to health including improved blood sugar control.

Blood sugar-friendly snacks

Try to choose blood sugar-friendly snacks such as a handful of raw unsalted nuts (walnuts, hazelnuts, Brazil nuts, cashews, pecans, pistachios), an apple, hard-boiled eggs, dark chocolate (>85 per cent), protein-rich yoghurt with seeds, nuts and berries or extra-virgin olive oil hummus with raw vegetables.

Consider time-restricted eating

Time-restricted eating (which is also known as intermittent fasting) seems to be all the rage, with a growing body of research from short-term studies supporting its health benefits, though recently published longer-term studies have raised some concerns. That said, limiting your food intake to a 12-hour window, which most would consider a sensible cut-off point based on the latest findings, allows your system the space to be able to divert energy from the work of digestion to other gastrointestinal housekeeping tasks, which include important detoxification processes. The approach also helps limit unhealthy, late-night snacking. If you are going to try it out, you need to select a 12-hour eating window that works with your life, and it is okay to vary it – for example, eating between 7am and 7pm mid-week, and between 10am and 10pm at weekends – or you may prefer to maintain consistency across the week.

PILLAR 5

Protect mealtimes

Eating on the go, a hallmark feature of ADHD, not only hinders digestive functions, but research suggests that you are likely to eat more. It is so important to give yourself adequate time to enjoy your food, in a low-stress state. Give the food its deserved respect: sit down for meals, take your time and eat mindfully, noticing and appreciating the various sensations involved in both eating and drinking. To optimise the digestive process, try to get into the habit of chewing each mouthful (up to 20 chews) until it is a thick, liquid consistency. This improves the signalling around satiety, which is the awareness of fullness.

Try meal planning

A characteristic feature of ADHD is being very 'in the moment' and struggling to plan ahead. Few people, especially those with ADHD, will have the time, motivation and organisational prowess to cook every meal from scratch, especially if using fresh ingredients. Even if it feels like a foreign idea to you, experiment with meal planning for a few weeks. Get a folder (for recipes, written, printed or photocopied) and a white or blackboard (for daily menus, which can run on a weekly or fortnightly cycle). Having a routine should allow you to calculate more accurately what you need to buy in your weekly shop, and result in less waste. Meal planning clearly needs a little burst of upfront planning, but the benefits may last for years, and revolutionise your relationship with food. Finally, I suggest you always work from a list when you go food shopping and try to avoid going when you are really hungry as your choices are likely to be less healthy and more impulse-driven!

Prepping ahead

Batch cooking at the weekend can be very helpful, and fun, but you will need a freezer (and some Tupperware) to make it work well. Those with ADHD tend to work best in bursts, so when you have managed to get yourself in the cooking zone, it is worth maxing it out. Baking sourdough bread (using a live 'starter'), making a big, nutritious salad that you can use as the basis for an easy lunch throughout the week, and pickling or fermenting all manner of things, are other great weekend culinary quests that will boost health and reduce cost.

If you have a freezer, as well as freezing cooked food, have a variety of frozen vegetables and berries on hand, as well as a selection of healthy soups (bought or homemade) for a quick, last-minute nutritious meal. Remember, frozen food really retains its nutrition.

Food boxes – a helping hand

If this is feasible for you, you might like to consider getting a fruit and/or vegetable box (ideally organic, if this is an option) delivered weekly, which can supplement and nutritionally supercharge your supermarket shop.

For those who really struggle with food preparation, and who may be getting progressively more nutritionally depleted by endless fast-food surrenders, or those who despise peeling away rotting, slimy, decomposing, unused food from the back of the fridge, there is hope! There is now a selection of recipe box companies that will deliver the exact ingredients you need to cook a meal from scratch, at a cost that compares favourably to a takeaway.

PILLAR 5

Maintain sufficient hydration

The human brain is comprised of approximately 75 per cent water, and it is reliant on it for most biological functions. Dehydration negatively impacts cognitive performance and mood, sometimes dramatically, making any pre-existing cognitive vulnerabilities worse. Whenever you are not feeling quite right or your brain feels foggier than usual, hydration is one of the first things that should cross your mind.

The NHS recommends drinking about six to eight cups or glasses of fluid, ideally water, over the course of the day, but, in my opinion, you should aim for the upper end of that range. Filling up two to three bottles in the morning with (preferably) filtered water and carrying one with you whenever you leave the house can really help promote good hydration. It is better to use a glass bottle with a protective outer rubber sleeve, or a stainless steel one. Aim, at a minimum, to finish the three bottles by bedtime, and if you need to top one up for the night, that is a bonus!

Having a mug of herbal tea regularly on the go is a great way of boosting your fluid intake, with many additional nutritional benefits. My personal favourites are nettle and lemon verbena during the day and chamomile at night. Lavender and chamomile tea have been used for millennia for their calming effects, and a 2022 study showed that they also helped alleviate anxiety and depressive symptoms.

Coffee and caffeine in ADHD

Regular (good-quality and mould-free) coffee consumption is linked to many positive health benefits, likely due to its high phytochemical and antioxidant content. How people with ADHD use coffee, and cope with the caffeine it contains, varies greatly. Some rely heavily on a strong caffeine stimulant hit to get going in the morning, perhaps before their medication kicks into action. For others, it provides a welcome boost to energy and focus during the sleepy afternoon hours.

With many of my patients, however, a cup of coffee immediately makes them feel drowsy and ready for a nap, probably in part explained by the fact that they were already tired but just hadn't realised until the stimulant, through its brain regulatory effects, dampened the noise. In most, a high caffeine consumption negatively impacts sleep and increases anxiety, especially if there is already a stimulant, in the form of medication, in the mix.

Caffeine is known to be quite a 'dirty' stimulant, due to the side effects it can cause. Studies suggest that, for most people, up to three to four cups a day is beneficial to health. Many, including myself, will not tolerate anywhere near this amount, especially if also taking stimulant medication. Personally, I find one cup in the morning and, very occasionally, a second small one in the afternoon is more than enough. It is important to listen to your body and adjust your intake accordingly.

And don't forget that there is also caffeine in tea, energy drinks and chocolate. It is worth noting that studies tell us that drinking tea (especially black tea) with a meal has the effect of reducing iron absorption (by up to 80 per cent). This effect is shared with coffee, but to a lesser degree. For this reason, it is better to separate these hot drinks from meals.

Food intolerance

In terms of food intolerance, there is lots of conflicting data as to whether certain allergic (and non-allergic, but still inflammatory) responses to foods may exacerbate or even cause ADHD symptoms. It follows that restricting exposure to known triggering agents may have an effect of modifying symptoms, but the jury is out on the question of whether (restriction and) elimination diets may be useful in ADHD. The answer is probably yes, but only in those with established food intolerances, and when guided by a professional. Like other insults to the system, food intolerances (or allergies) can act as drivers of chronic inflammation, which, by virtue of its system-wide reach, will itself generate and aggravate mental health symptoms.

There are higher rates of food intolerance in ADHD. Common culprits include gluten (think BROW: barley, rye, oats and wheat), dairy (especially milk), eggs, nuts, fish, corn and soya. Increasing numbers of people across the board are presenting with features of histamine intolerance, a finding that needs to be looked at properly.

PILLAR 5

Avoid excess sugar (especially refined sugar)

There are endless debates about the impact of sugar on ADHD. The available evidence, however, suggests that sugar doesn't worsen ADHD symptoms directly. In fact, there is some evidence that a little sugar may actually improve executive function, in the short-term at least.

However, sugar is not very good for you for so many other reasons – including negatively impacting gut health, which will indirectly impact brain health – so it is best heavily restricted. It lacks any nutritional value and also severely impacts blood sugar regulation for obvious reasons. The NHS advises that adults should have no more than 30g (7 teaspoons) of added or refined sugar daily, which should be seen as an absolute maximum. It is easy to overlook the presence of sugar so be sure to read food labels carefully (particularly on breakfast cereals). Fizzy drinks are some of the worst offenders, with a single can of some colas containing 35g of sugar! Ouch.

The impact of the natural sugar that is found in fruit is very different as it comes woven together with fibre. And, separate from the sugar issue, fruit confers a whole host of other benefits. Be careful with dried fruit and fruit juice which are both pretty heavy on the sugar side and are probably best consumed in moderation.

Artificial sweeteners and food additives

The true impact of artificial sweeteners is gradually unfolding, but based on what we already know, they are clearly not great news. They have been linked to behavioural and cognitive problems, as well as increased cardiovascular disease risk. If I do have the occasional sugary fizzy drink, it will always be the original rather than the diet form.

There is also a lot of noise about the potential impact of artificial food additives, and what effect removing them from the diet has in those with ADHD. There is in fact evidence showing that certain food dyes negatively impact behaviour in some children with ADHD, and that their exclusion from the diet may reduce ADHD symptom severity. The reason for this, however, is less clear and likely to be down to several factors.

Be wary of 'low-/ no-sugar' and 'low- fat' options

Low-fat foods are very often high in sugar or salt, a commercial strategy to increase their appeal. Low- or no-sugar foods are generally packed with nasty sweeteners. The advice is to always read the label. Food manufacturers, with a few exceptions, are not always looking out for your best interests.

Optimise gut health

Poor gut health (which typically includes gut bacterial imbalance or 'dysbiosis', and intestinal hyperpermeability or 'leaky gut') is an important area of research that is really gaining momentum. These areas clearly need further investigation; however, early signals look very interesting indeed.

Studies seem to be pointing to the fact that the gut microbiome (or, more accurately microbiota, which is the correct term for the bacterial population) has relevance to the ADHD story. Our understanding is still in its relative infancy, but I envisage, in time, there being a range of evidence-based treatments for ADHD targeted at optimising gut health, using modified diets and supplementation, including pre- and probiotics.

This is a complicated area, a detailed appraisal of which is beyond the scope of this book. It is important that you understand one key premise: the bacterial balance of the gut is important and it appears to have particular relevance for mental health, so it's worth considering both probiotics and prebiotics.

PILLAR 5

Probiotic foods and supplements

There are many probiotic foods, that is, foods that contain lots of healthy bacteria, for example fermented foods (see page 164). At present, we are not entirely sure which species of bacteria are the most beneficial, and their effects may not be the same for every person. What we do know is that a diverse gut environment is important, and that probiotic foods – which typically contain a whole host of different species – are thought to help with this diversity.

There is still a lot to learn about probiotic supplementation. There are many known potentially beneficial strains of bacteria, with different combinations brought together at different concentrations and in a wide range of formulations. As well as being uncertain about which strains are best for us to consume, studies also indicate that quality varies widely. For this reason, we encourage a 'food-first' approach and, if a supplement is wanted, a multi-strain preparation from a respected brand is probably your best bet, unless you are being guided by a nutritional expert. Saying that, there is some interesting evidence suggesting that giving a particular strain of bacteria – *Lactobacillus rhamnosus* – in the first six months of life may reduce the risk of ADHD and autism down the line, but this stand-alone finding clearly needs to be replicated.

Prebiotic foods and supplements

Prebiotics, which are essentially dietary fibre, serve as the feed for the bacteria. The 2023 'Gut Feelings' trial found that the group assigned to a high-prebiotic diet fared best in terms of their mood. (Somewhat surprisingly, the probiotic groups did not appear to see any benefits.) There are a range of prebiotic supplement products available, but there has been recent research interest in partially hydrolysed guar gum (PHGG), which seems to get good bacterial-boosting results. It comes in a powder form that can be dissolved in hot drinks and doesn't negatively impact the flavour.

Consider supplementation

There's evidence to show that those with ADHD have higher rates of nutritional deficiencies (including fatty acids, magnesium, zinc and iron), some limited evidence supporting the effectiveness of individual nutrient replacement and a bit more evidence for broad-spectrum (or 'blanket') replacement using multivitamin and mineral preparations, based on studies conducted in New Zealand.

Multivitamins

A good-quality multivitamin and mineral (containing decent amounts of B vitamins) is a great way of mopping up unknown deficiencies, and an insurance policy against developing them down the line. It uses a scattergun approach (as opposed to targeted supplementation), and this is thought to be the most effective in ADHD, based on the available evidence. Ideally try to find a multivitamin in capsule form, as the quality of tablets is lower due to the additional ingredients added to bulk out the tablet. When taking a multivitamin, it is important to be cautious with additional supplementation which may already be covered. In certain cases, such as with magnesium and vitamin C, it is fine to boost the levels in the multivitamin with additional doses, but don't overdo it.

B vitamins

In terms of the B vitamins, vitamin B12 deficiency has been associated with a higher risk of depression, a known comorbidity of ADHD. The best sources of B12 are from animals (including meat, seafood, dairy products and eggs), but as more and more people exclude these from their diets, B12 deficiency is becoming increasingly common, so supplementation may be necessary. Vitamin B6 is also important for the absorption of magnesium, which is commonly deficient in ADHD.

Vitamin D

Vitamin D is essential for so many areas of health. Testing is important to help guide an appropriate dose of a vitamin D3 supplement, which can be especially important during the darker winter months. Relatively inexpensive at-home finger-prick tests are available, though it is better to be guided by a professional, and some hard data. Be sure to do a follow-up test to see how things have changed following a period of supplementation.

Omega-3 fatty acid

There is lots of evidence that supplementation with omega-3 fatty acid helps a subset of those with ADHD, possibly only those with a pre-existing fatty acid deficiency. Studies have shown a definite, but low to moderate beneficial effect. Taking omega-3 supplements may also reduce side effects, and possibly dose requirements, when used alongside prescribed ADHD medications. It is particularly important to supplement if there is an established fatty acid deficiency (you can test omega-3 levels) or if you don't eat much oily fish. Again, it is important to use a good-quality product that has been tested for purity, and you should aim for an EPA dose of around 1,000mg a day (and a slightly lower level of DHA).

Magnesium

Magnesium is an essential mineral for humans and particularly important for mental health, especially ADHD. As well as supporting neurotransmitter production, magnesium plays an important role in enzyme systems (that drive cellular processes) and energy production. I now recommend it for all my patients. Dietary magnesium intake is often inadequate due to reduced concentrations in processed foods, and levels are further depleted by alcohol and caffeine. Evolving research also suggests that chronic, modern-life stress and certain medications, possibly including stimulants, can lead to magnesium loss or deficiency. Poor sleep, anxiety and constipation are clues to magnesium deficiency.

While increasing dietary sources of magnesium (green leafy vegetables such as spinach, dark chocolate, almonds, cashews, black beans, pumpkin seeds, chia seeds and brown rice) should be the first step, supplementation is, in my view, sensible, especially given the fact that studies have found that children with ADHD are very often deficient. The (relatively small) studies that have been done in ADHD, again primarily conducted in children, suggest that magnesium supplementation may reduce some ADHD symptoms (especially hyperactivity), and that it has a calming effect on anxiety and irritability. Magnesium may also help reduce stimulant-related side effects and support sleep. It is important to be aware that vitamin B6, also available in supplement form, helps the cells to utilise the magnesium. If you are not taking a vitamin B complex, I would recommend adding some B6 – the adult dose is usually 50mg daily.

There are lots of forms of magnesium, including magnesium glycinate, citrate, taurate, L-threonate or gluconate. It is apparently better to avoid magnesium oxide (due to poor absorption and higher rates of gastrointestinal upset), but the other preparations are meant to be well tolerated, although loose stools are a possible side effect. The adult magnesium dose is usually 200mg twice a day, but preparations may vary. Epsom salt baths are thought to boost magnesium levels through skin absorption, but the evidence for this is limited.

Zinc

Zinc is important in the production of proteins, which includes enzymes. Like magnesium, zinc is also necessary for the formation of neurotransmitters, including dopamine, noradrenaline, serotonin and melatonin, and it has a nourishing effect on a key memory centre of the brain called the hippocampus. Low zinc levels have been linked with depressive and ADHD symptoms, and some (small) studies have suggested that supplemental zinc can help. In one study (in children), the lower the zinc levels, the less effective the prescribed stimulant medication was. In another, zinc added to a stimulant resulted in a greater improvement in ADHD symptoms (in children, as evaluated by their parents). The

'Zinc Taste Test' is a useful non-invasive way of checking your zinc status (see Resources, page 289).

If you are going to supplement, zinc picolinate is meant to be the best absorbed and it is probably the most researched. The usual adult dose is 30mg twice a day, taken with food. It is important to be aware that, as zinc levels go up, the levels of copper, another 'trace mineral', go down, and vice versa. So high baseline levels of copper, which can be a problem for both brain and body (among other things it blocks the production of serotonin), will almost always mean low levels of zinc. Due to its copper-lowering effect (copper deficiency is also not good for you), it is not advisable to stay on high doses of zinc for long periods of time.

Polyphenol extracts

There are a variety of flavanol-rich polyphenol supplements available, some single extract and others in combination. They may include extracts of green tea, pine bark, blueberry and grape, among others. There is some evidence that they can positively impact brain function, including in ADHD. The best studied of these types of supplements in (children with) ADHD is called Pycnogenol. Additionally, the polyphenol curcumin, the active substance in turmeric, which comes in supplement form, seems to have anti-inflammatory and antioxidant effects, and results in small to moderate improvements in the symptoms of depression, and moderate to large improvement in pain levels.

Neurotransmitter-boosting supplements

In ADHD there are lower levels of certain neurotransmitters, including dopamine, serotonin and GABA. Dopamine is an excitatory neurotransmitter and the other two are inhibitory and therefore more calming. In fact, ADHD medications work by boosting levels of dopamine. There are less dramatic ways of boosting neurotransmitter synthesis and that is by supplementing with what are called neurotransmitter precursors, essentially the building blocks of these important brain messengers. But evidence is mixed as to whether this actually translates to increased neurotransmitter release and a stronger signal, and very limited evidence that this makes a difference in ADHD. Low levels of these precursors were found in a study in children with ADHD (who had 60 per cent less tyrosine and 44 per cent less tryptophan, compared with non-ADHD children).

A 2015 systematic review of 15 studies looked at supplementation with the amino acid tyrosine (mostly using a 'loading' dose) and found benefits on working memory and information processing. To boost dopamine synthesis you can try tyrosine but it is unclear if this will impact symptoms. (As a slight aside, L-theanine, another amino acid which is found in tea leaves – green tea has particularly high levels – may also have benefits in anxiety. It is recommended to take 200–400mg/day during stressful periods, but more studies are needed to guide its more routine use.)

Vitamin D is actually a precursor of serotonin, so this is another good reason to optimise levels. The B-vitamins, especially B6 and folate (B9), are also involved in neurotransmitter formation, together with magnesium and zinc, as discussed. In fact, vitamin B6 (also called pyridoxine) is a precursor of dopamine, and in a study in adults with ADHD using a vitamin B6-based drug, there were significant improvements in sustained and selective attention. Folate is also a precursor of dopamine, and some with ADHD have a genetic mutation lowering its levels. The herb *Rhodiola rosea*, which comes in supplement form, also boosts dopamine transmission, and it has been shown in small studies to have some benefits in anxiety.

A small study in children with ADHD found over 25 per cent lower levels of the inhibitory neurotransmitter GABA and, in another study, the low GABA levels correlated with increased impulsivity. When it comes to GABA, you don't need to take a precursor, you can just take the GABA itself. However, there is a bit of controversy surrounding GABA as, taken in supplement form,

PILLAR 5

it is said not to be able to cross the blood–brain barrier, yet many who take it clearly feel its benefits and report that it has a calming effect and can promote good sleep. The dose is usually 100–200mg, taken in the evening. You never know, it may even reduce your blood pressure – a dose of 80mg did just that in one study.

The key message I want to leave you with from this section on supplements is *not* that these 'nutraceuticals', as they are known, are a cure-all for ADHD, and that you should immediately flush your ADHD medication down the toilet and go celebrating. I do, however, want to highlight some of these lesser-known findings, admittedly early-stage data and mainly from small studies in children, but findings that may nevertheless be of potential interest if you are an adult with ADHD.

In summary, I don't think we can draw many firm conclusions on the supplement landscape with regards to adults with ADHD just yet. There are many more questions than there are answers presently, but there do seem to be a few interesting signals that are deserving of more study. I think that as long as you can accept these uncertainties (and you can afford it), a cautious set of trials might not be a bad idea. For everyone with ADHD, I would recommend some supplements, like a good multivitamin and mineral, magnesium and omega-3. Other things you may need to research in more detail, and then pick and choose according to what you are looking for.

Unless you are working with a professional who is guiding you otherwise, my advice is to only introduce one new supplement at a time, and really give it the time it needs to show an effect, possibly up to two or three months in some cases. The body can take time to adjust and adapt when you make changes to its biochemistry. When trialling supplements, it is good to train and hone your sense of 'interoception' in parallel: to listen carefully to your body, to what it needs and also whether or not it likes what you are putting into it.

That's all from the nutrition side for the moment (but I encourage you to watch this space!). I will switch tack slightly now and move the focus to the important role of movement in the self-management of ADHD.

EXERCISE AS A NATURAL TREATMENT FOR ADHD

It is a well-known fact that exercise is good for our physical health, but there is also good evidence that, through its brain-boosting action, exercise supports our mental well-being too, and ADHD is certainly no exception. The available studies in ADHD (again, mainly conducted in children) show potential benefits of both stand-alone exercise sessions, and possibly also longer-term interventions (though the data is more limited here). Unfortunately, there are still few studies to draw from in adults.

Most of the studies demonstrated the benefit of a single aerobic exercise session (of moderate intensity) on ADHD symptoms and measures of executive function. Aerobic exercise is the type that raises the heart and breathing rate and brings you out in a sweat. Exercise increases blood flow to the brain and triggers the release of brain chemicals that elevate the mood and improve focus in a natural but potent way.

Further larger, well-designed randomised controlled trials are needed to answer important questions about the real-life benefits of using exercise as either an add-on or possibly as a stand-alone treatment intervention for adult ADHD. I would say that early indications are encouraging, partly extrapolating from non-ADHD studies which look more broadly at the effect of exercise on the health of the brain and body.

As exercise has similar effects on the brain to the medications used in ADHD, including its dopamine-boosting effects, it follows that doing it on a regular basis may well reduce medication dose requirements, or possibly even negate the need for medications

PILLAR 5

altogether in some, but presently there isn't the science to demonstrate that.

How much exercise is enough?

The recommendation from the NHS is to get 150 minutes (two and a half hours) of moderate-intensity activity weekly, spread evenly over 4 to 5 days of the week. So, for example, that would be 5 sessions of 30 minutes (or 4 sessions of about 40 minutes, which feels slightly more manageable). There is also a recommendation (within this quota) to do at least 2 sessions of strengthening activities a week that work all the major muscle groups.

However, the main problem for those with ADHD is the 'getting started' bit and then the 'sticking with it' bit. There are the challenges of procrastination, motivation and activation. Many recognise its value, but struggle to get going, and then, once they eventually do, to maintain consistency in practice over time.

I appreciate that the NHS guidance may sound daunting and feel unrealistic, but my advice is that something is better than nothing, and that is perfectly fine to be creative and slightly stretch the definition of exercise. Quick wins include taking the stairs instead of the lift (even if you need to walk 20 floors), getting off the bus a couple of stops early and walking the rest of the way, and always walking up a moving escalator. Together with all the running up and down stairs frantically searching for lost items, this will all count towards your daily 30 minutes.

Tips for exercising with ADHD
- Warm up properly and always stretch after vigorous exercise (see page 184 for more on stretching).
- Start low and go slow, especially if you are just getting going (or if you are hypermobile). Diving in headfirst may result in injury.

- Do not exercise just before bed or straight after food. Exercising in the morning, as we discussed in Pillar 2, is a great way to start the day and will boost your dopamine levels and sharpen the mind.
- Use creative strategies to counter ADHD-related procrastination and help maintain exercise routines:
  - Choose a form of exercise you really enjoy as you are more likely to stick with it.
  - Make it a routine – set days and set times, diarised and stuck to religiously.
  - When you are feeling unmotivated or lethargic, just do a few minutes of stretching and see how you feel afterwards.
  - If you like the idea of exercising with others, consider competitive team sports or group exercise classes.
  - Try something physical like boxing training, where you can have variable levels of contact.
  - Consider investing in some sessions with a personal trainer to establish a good routine, if this is an option financially. Having accountability like this can be a game-changer.
  - Set yourself some form of personal target (keep it realistic) or consider taking on a specific challenge, for example, a 10k race, a 20k trek or even a gentle cycle around your town.
  - Remember, exercising is much easier once you commit. Just do it!
- Short-burst, high-intensity exercise and strength training are considered particularly health-promoting; better still if done outdoors. A recent study showed clear improvements in mental health, specifically when exercising outside (possibly linked to fresh air and sunlight exposure).

PILLAR 5

> - Where possible, aim to integrate the exercise into your existing schedule, for example, cycling to and from work or college. Many with ADHD hate the idea of wasting time, and this optimises your use of it. Check with your workplace or place of study if they have shower facilities and whether they offer a 'cycle to work' scheme (which provides financial support on bike purchase).

Stretching

What many people do not appreciate is how much benefit can be gained by spending fewer than five minutes simply stretching the muscles of the body, and I find that this is a quick win in ADHD. Stretching relieves muscle tension and causes the release of chemicals that make you feel good. Try to develop, and follow, a set approach or sequence when stretching, and do it calmly and mindfully, engaging the breath.

If you are not confident in your approach, get someone who knows what they are doing to guide you through an optimal sequence (working systematically through each major muscle group) and to ensure you are doing it correctly and safely. There are also loads of great free videos online that you can follow.

Yoga (and related approaches)

Yoga is a great way to keep fit and teach yourself how to relax properly, both important goals for those with adult ADHD. It employs specific postures to stretch and strengthen the body, while using meditation practice and breathing techniques to calm and balance the mind, by stabilising the ANS (autonomic nervous system).

There are many different types of yoga, some more relaxing and meditative, and others more active and intense. Popular ones include Hatha, Ashtanga and Bikram. Kundalini yoga is growing in popularity, but take it gently as it can have quite potent emotional effects.

A few studies have looked at the effects of yoga in ADHD patients, but, as far as I'm aware, all have been in children. The results were mixed, with some demonstrating an improvement in attention and other ADHD symptoms.

I have no doubt that you already appreciate the far-reaching effects of movement and exercise on mental well-being, but, in case you haven't caught on, why not put it to the test? Make a decision to get fit and commit to a period of regular exercise, starting low and going slow and using whatever guidance I have shared that feels helpful.

In the next pillar, we'll look at toxicity, its links with ADHD and what you can do about it in your quest to live well with adult ADHD.

PILLAR 6

REDUCE YOUR TOXIC LOAD

Our modern environment is brimming with toxicity, from the air we breathe (indoor and outdoor pollution differ), the water we drink (and cook with) and the soil we grow our crops in (and graze our animals on), to the 'food' we consume and the chemicals and products our skin is exposed to. New illnesses have emerged with a delayed but predictable association with the Industrial Revolution, and it is thought that our immune and detoxification systems have simply not had enough time to catch up, from an evolutionary perspective.

'How is this relevant to ADHD?' I hear you ask. Well, together with injury, infection, illness and stress, toxicity is a potent driver of inflammation and, when the inflammation becomes chronic, it really messes with brain function. There is an increasing body of evidence linking neurodevelopmental conditions like autism and ADHD with various markers and mediators of inflammation. It is thought that the more inflammation, the more damage is done to the blood–brain barrier (which is meant to protect the brain), allowing more toxicity and harmful immune cells to enter the brain, which can spiral the situation.

Furthermore, there are established associations between ADHD and various forms of chemical toxicity. Lead, phthalates and bisphenol A (BPA) are moderately to highly associated with ADHD, and there is early and more limited evidence suggesting an association with polycyclic aromatic hydrocarbons (PAHs), flame retardants, mercury and pesticides. I suspect this is only the tip of the iceberg, and the more we look, the more we will find.

In this pillar, I will give an overview of the common sources of toxicity we encounter in everyday life, explore links with ADHD and guide you on how to reduce your exposure through simple and practical lifestyle adaptations. I debated whether to include this pillar in the book as I know some people have strong views about these things. My intention is certainly not to rub people up the wrong way or to scaremonger. However, given the established associations with toxicity and high numbers with heightened sensitivity among those with ADHD, in addition to the elevated rates of allergy, intolerance and autoimmunity, I feel it is important to share some of these learnings with you and provide some practical guidance on what you may do about it. Keep in mind that this is a relatively new area of study, with lots of conflicting findings and agendas. We don't know all the answers, but until we do, I think it makes sense to be aware of what we do know and to remain slightly vigilant.

THE IMPACT OF TOXINS ON OUR HEALTH

Environmental toxins gain entry to the body through the lungs and the gut (inhaled or ingested), or through the skin, which is more permeable than you might think. Impaired gut barrier function (known as intestinal hyperpermeability or 'leaky gut') is an important compounder of the issue, as is a leaky blood–brain barrier. Toxins that don't normally gain entry to the bloodstream and brain respectively pass through compromised barriers and cause problems. Once in, they are recognised as foreign by the host, which will trigger an immune response which, over time, can become excessive, or otherwise dysregulated, in some.

PILLAR 6

Exposed to an excessive toxic load, the nerve cells cease to function and signal normally, and cross-talk or connectivity is affected, resulting in a poorly organised and synchronised brain. Excessive glutamate, an excitatory and toxic brain chemical, is released in larger amounts and the brain becomes overstimulated and hypersensitive. The system shifts into a state of threat and hypervigilance, and is far more easily triggered into fight-or-flight or anxiety responses. In addition to their impact on the nervous and immune system, toxins can impact reproductive and hormonal systems, and there are also established links with cancer.

We are all unique in terms of our genetics, and it is this which determines how effectively we are able to clear the toxins out of our system. Various pathways for detoxification exist (mainly in the liver), which are controlled by a number of different enzymes (proteins that drive biological reactions). It is our genes that determine the effectiveness of these enzymes and, broadly speaking, they will dictate if you are a rapid or a poor metaboliser of a toxin. Poor metabolisers are more likely to get a build-up of toxicity, and more inflammation.

Importantly, toxins not only drive inflammatory processes, but they also push important nutrients out of the body. So, when addressing toxicity, as well as avoiding and in some cases removing the toxins, we also need to identify and replace the depleted nutrients.

The reality is that we can't fully eliminate toxicity from our lives, but I think it makes sense to be aware of the issues and take some steps to mitigate and reduce exposure. We don't yet have all the answers and there remain lots of divided opinions in this area, but, from my reading, there are enough clues to suggest that we could have a problem. We might like to do something about it before too much damage is done at both an individual and a societal level.

15 toxicity sources

1. **Industrial waste:** pollution from industry impacts our air and water supply, and can find its way into our food.

2. **Biocides:** toxic chemicals that affect nervous, immune, reproductive and hormonal systems include *fertilisers, pesticides, insecticides* (including pet flea drops and collars, and nit preparations), *fungicides* and *herbicides* or weedkillers (including agricultural crop spraying and spraying of green public areas by local councils).

3. **Exhaust fumes:** shown to be associated with 'toxicant-induced loss of tolerance' (TILT), which is also known as multiple chemical sensitivity (MCS).

4. **Personal care products:** includes nail varnish, some perfumes and deodorants, some types of sun protection and other body and hair products.

5. **Cleaning products:** including bleach, stain removers, air fresheners, some floor and surface cleaners, and some laundry powders and conditioners. There is a particular concern regarding aerosol use.

6. **Food-related:**
   - **Non-organic meat, vegetable and dairy produce** has a higher risk of containing pesticides, antibiotics, hormones and other growth promoters.
   - **Fish**, especially large fish such as tuna, may contain higher levels of heavy metals and other toxins.
   - **Sugar**, in addition to rotting the teeth and disrupting the microbiome, causes obesity, diabetes and related disorders, and depletes stores of minerals and vitamins.
   - **Artificial additives,** flavourings, colourings/dyes, emulsifiers, preservatives, sweeteners and substances added to food to increase its addictive potential, for example, monosodium glutamate (MSG).

PILLAR 6

- **Trans-fats and hydrogenated fats.**
- Other specific food-related issues that are loosely linked to toxicity, such as **gluten intolerance**, **lactose/dairy intolerance**, **histamine intolerance and mast cell activation disease** (see page 202).

7. **Food coverings and kitchen storage:** includes kitchen foil, cling film, plastic bags and other plastic containers, many of which can leach toxic chemicals into the food they contain.

8. **Cookware:** especially some non-stick and aluminium products.

9. **Drink-related:**
    - **Tap water:** may contain chlorine +/- fluoride as well as a range of other toxic substances.
    - **Plastic bottled drinks:** there are issues with plasticisers leaching into the drink, which is worse with direct sunlight exposure to the plastic, for example, when magnified through car windscreens.
    - **Metallic bottled drinks:** more oxidisation and leaching of metals into the liquid occurs if the drink is sugary, or acidic.
    - **Processed and sugar-heavy drinks:** as above.
    - **Alcoholic drinks:** as well as being addictive and dehydrating, alcohol breaks down to toxic intermediary products (such as acetaldehyde) and is high in histamine.

10. **Indoor toxicity:**
    - **Air fresheners**, and other **household and personal care products:** see above.
    - **Furniture and furnishings:** for example, fire retardants in curtains, sofas, mattresses and carpets; insecticides and other chemicals in carpets; stain

guard in cars, on sofas and other furnishings; house dust mites in bed sheets and pillows.

- Chemicals from **building and decorating materials and products:** especially certain high volatile organic compounds (VOC) in adhesives, fillers, paints and varnishes.

11. **Toxicity from mould and mycotoxins:**
    - Mould toxicity is an under-recognised and potentially serious issue that can cause chronic illness affecting multiple systems. It can lead to respiratory symptoms (such as asthma flares), musculoskeletal problems (such as joint pain and tendon inflammation) and a range of neuropsychiatric issues (for example, fatigue, 'ice-pick' pain and other sensory issues, anxiety, brain fog and irritability).
    - Mould is more common in damper climates and older homes, and mould-related toxicity symptoms are usually worst in September/October.
    - Mould growth is promoted by water leaks and water ingress, inherently damp environments (especially kitchens and bathrooms that don't have windows or extractor fans), rooms without adequate airflow and access to fresh air, air-conditioning units that are not serviced and carefully cleaned (at least annually) and even bedding that is not allowed to air properly (following night-time sweating). House dust mites feed off moulds and can cause a double-hit effect in sensitive individuals.
    - Independent from the mould itself, there are the toxic chemicals (mycotoxins) that the mould releases, which have particularly powerful negative effects on the immune system.

PILLAR 6

12. **Electromagnetic radiation (EMR) from electromagnetic fields (EMFs):**

- EMR is omitted from mobile phones, cordless phones, mobile phone masts (especially 5G), Wi-Fi routers, smart technology of all forms, microwaves and other electrical sources. This is considered 'physical' rather than 'chemical' toxicity.

- This remains a highly controversial area, but there is specific concern regarding the possible health impacts of 5G, the carrying of mobile phones too close to the body and the resting of laptops on laps for long periods, as well as heavy exposure at vulnerable periods during the life cycle, for example, in childhood, adolescence and pregnancy.

13. **The heavy metals:**

- The heavy metals include mercury, lead, cadmium, nickel and aluminium.

- As well as causing an inflammatory response, they also act to displace and deplete nutrients, for example, nickel depletes zinc, mercury depletes selenium, and so on.

  - **Mercury** is found in dental fillings and old thermometers, and it can result in neuropsychiatric symptoms (especially if fillings are removed unsafely).

  - **Lead** is used in industry (especially coal-burning) and found in old pipework and old paints. It can cause gastrointestinal and neuropsychiatric symptoms.

  - **Nickel** is present in stainless steel cookware, jewellery, coins, batteries, tobacco smoke and exhaust fumes. It can cause immune and hormonal dysfunction and cancers. Nickel toxicity is suggested by zinc deficiency, as well as nickel sensitivity.

- **Aluminium** is commonly present in cookware, 'tin foil', drink cans and deodorants. It can cause neuropsychiatric issues and has been linked to breast cancer.

14. **The halogens/halides:**
   - The halogens include fluorine, chlorine, bromine and iodine. They can react with other substances and convert to fluoride, chloride, bromide and iodide respectively (which are known as the halides).
   - Toxic forms, which in excess can cause various health problems including cancers, reproductive and cognitive issues, include:
      - **Chlorine**: found in tap water, cleaning products, swimming pools and PVC plastic.
      - **Bromine/bromide**: found in certain medications (including inhalers), agricultural chemicals, insecticides, dyes and fire retardants.
      - **Fluoride**: found in toothpastes, mouthwashes and tap water in certain regions of the country, for example, North-East England, West Midlands and the Republic of Ireland (among other places). The low concentration in toothpaste is argued not to be toxic, but this remains controversial in some camps.

15. **Drugs:** including prescribed, over-the-counter and illicit drugs.

I understand that the above list might seem excessive, but the aim here is really not to scare you unduly or to set unrealistic expectations. It's just to increase your awareness and to encourage you to make a few healthy changes to the way that you lead your life, and hopefully, in the process, optimise the function of your brain. This is where my ten tips to tackle toxicity come in.

TIPS TO REDUCE EXPOSURE

1. Foster a committed approach

Educate yourself properly about toxicity and take it seriously. Avoid the trap of turning a blind eye or believing 'it must be okay as everyone is doing it'. I encourage you to make a few changes to your life and, where possible, support your loved ones to do the same. The transition to a less toxic life will likely involve two phases:

1. **The clean-up phase:** the aim here is to, as far as possible and reasonable, rid your home (and possibly workplace) of some of the bigger culprits – see below for detail.
2. **The maintenance phase:** this involves incrementally and gradually adjusting and adapting your lifestyle, making better decisions (especially when replacing big items such as a mattress), so, over time, you have less and less exposure.

2. Optimise your nutrition and gut health

Vitamins and minerals work to keep toxins out of the body, and they also help detoxify the liver. As we explored in Pillar 5, where possible, they should come through the diet, but sometimes, especially when addressing a deficiency, replacement in supplement form is required (see page 175). It is also important that you work to optimise your gut flora, or microbiota (see page 173).

3. Consider getting tested for toxins

This is for those of you who are struggling with unexplained physical health issues, and where you suspect it may be linked to an exposure of some form. You will need an experienced practitioner, such as a functional medicine specialist, to interpret the results and guide management if evidence of toxicity is found. Testing could include a urine test looking for toxic metabolites, a blood test for heavy metals and another that looks at the detoxification pathways (see Resources, page 290, for details on how to access these tests).

4. Try daily juicing

Juicing is a great way of supporting detoxification and, due to the high concentration of vitamins and minerals compared with eating fruit and vegetables, boosting nutrition more broadly. Ideally, you should only juice vegetables. However, adding in a small amount of fruit (especially in the early stages) may help improve tolerability. Just as heavy metals deplete nutrients, elevating levels of nutrients through juicing can help cleanse the body of metals. For example, increasing zinc can help reduce nickel and cadmium levels.

Where possible, and in an ideal world, produce used for juicing should be organic as this reduces its exposure to environmental toxins like pesticides and fertilisers. This is more important for certain fruits and vegetables (see page 161). Ideal vegetables to juice include kale, baby spinach, watercress, parsley, lettuce leaves, celery and cucumber. In general, the darker green the leaves and the more colourful the other vegetables, the better. Carrots and beetroot add sweetness so use them sparingly.

If you need to add a bit of fruit for taste, try green apples, frozen berries and lemon juice. Nutritious and tasty add-ins include ginger (peeled if blending), seeds (including sunflower, pumpkin and chia seeds, whole or crushed into powder form) and various other nutrient-rich powders, for example, spirulina, chlorella, hemp seed and cacao.

There are a range of different types of juicers and blenders available:

- **High-speed blenders:** retain all the contents of the vegetable/fruit and make a thick smoothie-like drink, rather than a thin juice. The high fibre content is not tolerated by some.
- **Masticating juicers:** these extract the juice by pressing and 'chewing' the vegetables, retaining a higher proportion of the

nutritional content. Mastication is particularly good for leafy and fibrous vegetables such as celery, broccoli and parsley, but will work for most things.

- **Centrifugal juicers:** best to use with fruit and chunky vegetables, but can be quite expensive and bulky for home use.
- **Citrus juicers:** limited to oranges, lemons and limes.

5. Consider detoxing through sweating and soaking

Sweating

There is mounting evidence that deliberate heat exposure has many health benefits and one of these is detoxification through sweating. There is most evidence for sauna use, but exercising while wearing multiple layers of clothing (and then removing and washing them after) is likely to have similar benefits to sauna use, but it needs to be done safely. Sweating is really very good for us, so the idea of supressing it with antiperspirants is counterintuitive. Try natural aluminium-free salt deodorants instead, which still allow you to sweat but without smelling.

If you are lucky enough to have access to a sauna (perhaps at your local gym), this is a highly effective way of ridding the body of toxins, especially fat-soluble toxins (due to the layer of subcutaneous fat that lies under the skin). Ten to fifteen minutes of sauna use three times a week has demonstrated benefits. When using a sauna, it is important to wipe away the sweat from the body regularly (and then wash the used flannels/towels properly). As well as detoxification, the benefits of sauna use include boosting growth hormone and the neurotransmitters dopamine and noradrenaline, as well as an impressive reduction in cardiovascular mortality. Infrared saunas have attracted a lot of interest over recent years, and evidence supporting their use is mounting (see Resources on page 290).

It is important to use heat safely and build up tolerance gradually. It is also essential to replace the water and minerals that are lost in the sweat by drinking water (possibly with a tiny pinch of salt added if the blood pressure allows) before, during and after the heat exposure.

Soaking

Epsom salt bathing is a practice that has stood the test of time. The salts (magnesium sulphate) can be added to your bath on a regular basis (a few times a week) for a period of time (weeks to months). You should add half a cupful initially and then build up to about two to three cups. Take it slowly to avoid oxalate crystals forming in the bladder.

The soak results in the absorption of magnesium sulphate through the skin. Magnesium has many important functions, such as softening muscles, promoting relaxation and sleep, pushing heavy metals from the body and supporting essential processes including blood sugar control. As discussed in Pillar 5, it is commonly deficient in individuals with ADHD, and its replacement has been demonstrated in some studies to improve the symptoms of ADHD. The sulphate part is also helpful as it supports liver detoxification.

6. Try targeted (and safe) supplementation

We discussed supplements that may be helpful for ADHD more generally in Pillar 5. Here, we are specifically considering supplements that may support detoxification. They include:

- **Vitamin C:**
  - An excellent supplement for detoxification, and for supporting immune function more generally, due to its potent antibacterial and antiviral effects. It also benefits microbiome health and protects against heavy metals.
  - You may use reasonably high doses of vitamin C (for short stints), so it is probably worth buying it in powder form. Total daily doses can range, but aim for 1–2g a day, building up your dose gradually to avoid diarrhoea. It's not necessary to remain on these higher doses long term. As vitamin C is

water soluble it doesn't hang around long in the system, so you ideally need to dose yourself regularly, for example, twice or three times a day. Ascorbate is better tolerated than ascorbic acid.

– Increase your dose at times of increased exposure to microbes, such as when travelling abroad or when other members of the family have infections.

- **Zinc:** like vitamin C, zinc also protects against heavy metals.
- **Magnesium:** see benefits listed on page 196.
- **B vitamins:** various forms of B vitamin are helpful for detoxification so it is probably worth taking a vitamin B compound preparation. B vitamins have an important role in supporting the methylation detoxification pathway (a liver-based biochemical process where a 'methyl' group is added to a toxin to allow it to be excreted from the body).
- **Prebiotics and probiotics:** these promote a healthy microbiome, which supports the gut's barrier function, and keeps toxins out (see pages 173–4).
- Other detoxification supplements include **L-glutamine** (which can help protect against a 'leaky gut'), **milk thistle** (liver detoxification support), phosphatidylcholine (PC), **iodine/iodide**, **calcium** and **methionine**. When using these and various other supplements that bind and remove toxins, I would recommend specialist guidance.

7. Drink plenty of clean water

The NHS in the UK advises that you drink enough water that your 'pee is a clear pale-yellow colour' and recommends about six to eight glasses a day. I would suggest you aim for around 2 litres of water a day, obviously depending on what you are doing, but avoid drinking too much water as this can be harmful. A good fluid status will help dilute and flush toxins from the body.

Ideally invest in some sort of water filter, if you can, and use filtered water to cook with, as well as for drinking. Use a glass water flask to store water, to which you can add a stick of charcoal for added purification if you want to really go to town! In your home, try as far as possible to have all old lead (water) pipes removed and replaced with safer, non-toxic options. Always run the tap for five to ten seconds before filling your glass or jug to flush out the water that has been sitting in the pipes.

8. Limit your EMR exposure

This whole area has come under fierce debate, with some (usually those who have heightened sensitivity to their environment) describing characteristic symptoms when exposed to high electromagnetic radiation levels and who cite various (albeit small) studies that suggest negative health impacts, and others (often linked to industry) arguing that there is no good evidence of a problem. While the jury is out regarding this type of exposure, it feels pragmatic to impose some limits. Probably the best bit of advice is to dispose of your cordless phone if you have one (and ideally your microwave oven as well, but that's more controversial) as they are considered particularly problematic, as they emit relatively high levels of EMR. Switch off your Wi-Fi router when it is not needed (especially at night) and, where possible, use hard (ethernet) cables when using the internet. I would probably also keep your laptop off your lap as much as possible (especially if you are pregnant).

Regarding smartphones, whenever feasible, I would keep them at a reasonable distance (ideally not in your pocket or in direct contact with your body) and in 'flight mode'. Some recommend switching off the 5G function on your phone in the settings, arguing that 4G is much safer. I don't know where I stand on all this, but I have only ever used 4G and my phone has always worked without an issue. I would use the speakerphone for calls where possible, and apparently wired headphones are better for you than Bluetooth ones, but that is a difficult story to follow, and you will have to make your own decision on this one. I would try not to overload yourself with too much smart technology, especially during sleep. And, if you are light-sensitive, avoid excessive exposure to bright white LEDs and fluorescent lighting.

9. Keep your indoor air clean and dry

Try to spend less time indoors and more outdoors in the fresh air. To reduce the potential for mould growth in your home, keep the windows open and air flowing (even when the heating is on), especially in rooms where steam is produced. Install extractor fans in all bathrooms and toilets, and above cookers. I would opt for low-toxicity cleaning products, and possibly even try homemade ones, such as vinegar, lemon or bicarbonate of soda-based (there is lots of guidance on this online). Avoid aerosol sprays altogether as they are not good news.

When renovating, try to use lower VOC paints, varnishes and glues (and air rooms properly after decoration). Again, where possible, and as far as the budget allows, use natural materials (that don't 'off-gas') in the home, for example, wood, stones or tiles, and cotton. Many believe chipboard and MDF to be toxic due to the formaldehyde-based resin used in their processing. If present, have asbestos safely removed from your home, and deal with any water-related damage, water ingress or suspected mould growth properly (and early), using specialist contractors.

I have been really impressed by the benefits of using air purifiers (with HEPA filters) for bedrooms and workspaces. Some vacuum cleaners also come with these filters built in, but they are quite pricey. If you have air-conditioning or filtration units, ensure they are serviced regularly and properly.

Ask questions about the chemicals used when buying mattresses, sofas and bedding, and go for more natural options where you can when replacing, without getting militant about it. If you are sensitive to house dust mites, or find that you are stuffy and congested a lot of the time, try replacing your pillows more regularly. Fold open your bedsheets in the mornings for an hour or so (to allow the overnight body sweat to dissipate from the material), then cover for the rest of the day to limit house dust mite exposure to the sheets beneath.

If you are sensitive, try to avoid doing too much dry cleaning as it uses quite a lot of toxic chemicals. If you need to dry clean, air the clothes outside for a few hours afterwards. I would also banish any form of air freshener, whereas the vaporisation of essential oils in water is usually well tolerated. Try to use self-care products that are natural and made with essential oils.

10. Travel smart

If you tend to pick up infections quite easily, I would take extra immune-supporting supplements (see page 196) before and during travel. Ensure you get a good night's sleep before travelling, and that you remain well hydrated during the journey. Carry antibacterial gel and use it where appropriate but not excessively (and wash your hands properly when you get the chance). Avoid touching handles/buttons where possible and make an effort not to touch your mouth or nose during travel. You might like to bring along healthier alternatives to airline food, and an additional supply of nutritious snack options for your trip.

If you are staying in a hotel or apartment and using the air-conditioning in the bedroom, ideally also keep windows open to ensure a flow of fresh air. Always shower after swimming in a chlorinated pool, so the chlorine doesn't remain on your skin and get absorbed unnecessarily. If you are a natural water swimmer, there are apps that tell you the current level of toxicity in the stretch of water that you are about to swim in. If you are out in the sun, allow a little (up to about 20 minutes) direct skin exposure to the sun before applying protection to increase immune-boosting vitamin D levels. If your skin is sensitive, try to find sunscreens that are made with natural ingredients (often termed 'mineral' creams). Finally, if you happen to be staying in the vicinity of crop fields that are being sprayed with chemicals (pesticides/fertilisers, and so on), close the windows and doors of your property.

You may be feeling a little overwhelmed by these tips and questioning whether it all sounds a bit over the top. The reality is that intrusions from our environment are likely to be having a negative impact on our physical bodies, particularly in at-risk groups. What still needs to be properly established is whether ADHD is one of those groups, but it is a subject I feel we all need to engage with, without being too radical about it. The advice above is an accumulation of what I have learned on my journey over many years, which I'll go into in a little more detail below. My personal experience has provided a rare and unexpected insight into the colossal impact that environmental toxicity has on the mind–body system, especially of sensitive individuals, like those with ADHD.

MAST CELL ACTIVATION DISEASE

My interest in the body, and its relationship to ADHD, has been massively sparked over the last 10–15 years, both through the fascinating patterns of physical (somatic) health problems I began to notice in my ADHD patients, but also subsequently through my own personal health struggles which caught me off guard about 5 years ago.

After randomly getting shingles, then Lyme disease from a tick bite on a lecture tour in the Middle East, and then a few years later developing severe mould toxicity, I started showing signs of an excessive and inappropriate immune response. In time, I worked out that I was presenting with mast cell activation syndrome (or 'disease', which some argue is a more appropriate term).

Mast cells, a form of white blood cell, are a critically important part of the immune system. They are thought of as the first line of defence or the 'first responders' against external threats or attacks.

For this reason, they are particularly concentrated in bodily tissues that have direct contact with the outside world – the skin, and the mucous membranes of the eyes, ears, nose, mouth and throat, respiratory, gastrointestinal and genitourinary systems (essentially all body surfaces, inside and out). Within these barrier tissues, there is important cross-talk between mast cells and the nervous and cardiovascular systems, with mast cells clustering around nerve fibres and blood vessels.

When the mast cells register a threat, through the numerous receptors on their surface, they 'activate'. This results in what is termed 'degranulation', the release of chemical 'mediators' (usually inflammatory in nature), many of which are stored in tiny granules within the body of the cell.

The best known of these inflammatory mediators is histamine, but there are many more including cytokines. The mediators either exert their effects locally in the specific tissue or system-wide through the bloodstream. The mast cells respond by either promoting inflammation for the purpose of repair or limiting inflammation to prevent further damage.

In MCAD, the mast cells are either defective and release mediators in excess because of abnormal internal signalling, or there is some form of chronic trigger (often hidden), such as an allergy, or some form of toxic exposure, that is driving the mast cells.

It may be that genetic vulnerability, combined with increasing environmental toxicity and immune system challenge, underlies a suspected rise in problems that are thought to be underpinned or associated with mast cell activation. Could it be that ADHD, or an ADHD-like syndrome, is one of these problems?

This is a relatively new and still somewhat controversial area (which is not unusual when new presentations or understandings emerge). This controversy is fuelled by some camps believing that MCAD, in its various guises, may currently be present in up to 17 per cent of the general population, presenting in the form of allergic (including airborne and food allergies) and atopic conditions (for example, asthma and eczema), and chronic illnesses of an inflammatory nature (for example, irritable bowel syndrome (IBS), CFS/ME, fibromyalgia syndrome, migraine, and a range of autoimmune illnesses), all of which are on the rise. It is highly likely that

PILLAR 6

mental health and neurodevelopmental presentations are part of this emergent syndrome cluster, as mast cell dysfunction has an established and strong neuropsychiatric signature.

Features of MCAD

Some of the more common features include:

- Fatigue (often extreme).
- Various skin issues (especially flushing, rashes and itchiness).
- Gastrointestinal (GI), genitourinary (GU) and respiratory dysfunction (resulting from swelling of the linings of the intestines, bladder and lungs, with restricted flow).
- Neuropsychiatric dysfunction and mental health disturbance, especially headaches, anxiety (often marked, and experienced as a 'symptom' rather than an emotion), restlessness, irritability, mood changes and cognitive deficits including inattention and memory difficulties (often referred to as 'brain fog'). (Note: These features, which may mimic or aggravate the symptoms of ADHD, are likely to be driven by brain inflammation and impaired brain perfusion, which is reduced blood supply to the brain.)
- Heightened environmental sensitivity, with excessive reactions to insect bites, chemicals and medications.
- Sleep issues and disorders.
- Eye, ear, nose and throat problems, including swallowing difficulties (due to local tissue swelling).
- Palpitations and other symptoms experienced on standing (referred to as 'orthostatic' issues).
- Pain and joint issues.

In some cases, commonly in response to certain infections or toxic exposures, the mast cells can ramp up and then remain on permanent high alert causing chronic symptoms.

When the mast cells go haywire, their host often becomes extra-sensitive to their surroundings and the chemical and other toxicity within it. This is exactly what happened to me – as a result of the infections and exposures, I became highly sensitised to my environment and, over a matter of a few years, my heightened sensitivity made me a portable radar for all things toxic. So many things that I hadn't appreciated were health-depleting now showed their true colours.

For the first time in my life, I felt compelled to respect and really care for my body properly. I slowly and steadily started to integrate the recommendations outlined earlier to reduce my toxic load and inflammatory status, and create an environment conducive to repair. Can you relate to any of the descriptions above? Have you noticed other physical symptoms flaring up in line with your mental health issues? Do you happen to have hypermobility, dysautonomia or any form of autoimmunity, all of which commonly travel together with MCAD?

Whether or not you fit this picture, which is only slowly coming into focus, to really optimise brain health, I would recommend that your medium- to long-term goal be to reduce your level of toxic exposure by making small incremental tweaks and ever better decisions as to how you lead your life, and what you bring into it. I advise you to listen to your body – it will often tell you what it does or doesn't need. If you are interested in delving into toxicity and immune dysfunction further, I have included some references on page 300 and other sensible and informative resources to explore on page 290.

In the next and final pillar, I will move the focus from the body to the mind (or, more specifically, the emotional material that is emitted from it), though, as you will come to see, the line that differentiates these two entities may not be a clear-cut as we like to believe.

PILLAR 7

REGULATE YOUR EMOTIONS

Training as a doctor provided me with a unique and privileged opportunity to develop a deeper understanding of how the body functions, at both a macro and micro level. And when I started training to be a psychiatrist, I was looking at the same system, but now through the lens of our emotions, beliefs, drives and defences – transitioning from the physical to the mental, and only much later realising that they were actually one and the same.

As we saw in Part 1, emotional dysregulation is inherent to ADHD and should undoubtedly be considered a core feature of the disorder. This pillar therefore starts with an overview of the particular lie of the land in ADHD when it comes to emotions, though the majority of it will be focused on helping you to find practical, effective ways to manage and regulate emotional distress.

EMOTIONS AND EMOTIONAL DYSREGULATION IN ADHD

In adult ADHD, emotions tend to be 'hot'. Although not generally listed as a symptom, anxiety in all its manifestations is really common in ADHD, and often highly impairing. The mood characteristically shifts around, more frequently than usual, in a slightly chaotic and dysregulated manner: quick to anger, easily frustrated, excitable, low, changeable and a little unstable.

The actual emotions themselves are no different, but the intensity at which they are felt is heightened – the highs are a bit higher, and the lows a bit lower – and the fluctuations increased, but all taking place within what is considered a 'normal' range. Although there are more frequent shifts between different emotional states, with multiple changes during a single day, the mood instability, or 'mood lability' as it is sometimes called, doesn't reach the threshold of mania (or hypomania) as experienced in bipolar disorder (or 'manic depression'), unless of course bipolar is also in the mix, which it may well be.

Those with ADHD often feel restless inside, leaving them 'on edge' and unable to settle and relax. Words commonly used to describe adults with ADHD are often laden with emotional intensity too: passionate; overexcited; short-fused; bouncy; wired; intense; full-on. If an individual with ADHD perceives even subtle rejection or negativity from others, they may have a disproportionate emotional response, something that is referred to as Rejection Sensitive Dysphoria (RSD) – we'll cover this in more detail on page 209.

So, with emotional over-reactivity and mood instability, often overlaying a background state of heightened arousal; the emotional volume turned up, paired with an inability to easily shutdown and switch off; and an endlessly active mind that struggles to feel at peace, to quieten and to fall asleep, you can see how easy it could be to become overwhelmed – an experience I'm sure many of you are very familiar with.

Developing a heightened awareness of your mind–body system and being able to recognise early indicators of emotional dysregulation is key, as it allows you to put in place effective strategies to avert or manage distress. As well as learning how to better regulate emotions, it is also important to consider their meaning; to listen to what they may be trying to communicate to you.

When turmoil becomes mental illness

It can sometimes be challenging to differentiate between the normal stresses and strains of modern living (with ADHD) and an independent, co-occuring mental disorder. Normally, however, you will know if something is not right and, in these cases, you need to take some form of action, as emotional regulation work is unlikely to shift it alone. Having recurrent and inadequately treated mental illness episodes appears to have a 'kindling' effect, worsening the prognosis over the long term.

If you suspect you may be suffering from some form of mental illness, please seek professional support, initially through your GP. I know it can feel scary, but try not to ignore the presence of possible illness. Most mental disorders are now treatable, so there will likely be interventions that can significantly improve your quality of life.

Share your concerns with your doctor without feeling any shame whatsoever. You can also talk to a friend or family member (or a mental health helpline) if you need some initial support or guidance on how to proceed. There's a little more understanding around mental health than there was a few years ago; however, your experience will very much depend on how psychologically minded and understanding your GP is, what services are available locally and waiting times.

I advise my patients to ask at their GP reception which of the doctors working in the surgery are most interested and experienced in mental health, and then request to be seen by them specifically. If the dynamic is right, it is good to establish a rapport and nurture the relationship. I recognise that this may not be straightforward in the current health climate, but it's certainly worth a go.

Depending on the nature and severity of the issue, your GP may signpost or refer you for psychotherapy, initiate a medication trial or refer you to a psychiatrist. GPs are usually confident and experienced enough to prescribe some short-term sleep medication (if that is what is needed) or potentially start an anti-anxiety or antidepressant drug.

With the support of your the professionals involved in your care, approach the combined treatment of the ADHD and whatever else is going on in a structured and stepwise manner, thinking about how the treatment of each could impact the other. If you are taking or about to start taking ADHD medication, there will need to be some thought about the impact it may be having on the other condition, and potential medication interactions, as not all medications are compatible. The goal is to find an optimal balance that addresses both conditions adequately.

REJECTION SENSITIVE DYSPHORIA

'For your entire life have you always been much more sensitive than other people you know to rejection, teasing, criticism or your own perception that you have failed or fallen short?'

The question above is a brief screen for RSD, a term coined by US-based psychiatrist and ADHD specialist, Dr William Dodson, who, over recent years, has been promoting RSD as a central feature of ADHD.

Although I personally think he may be on to something important here, there have not yet been the required studies to look at this properly, so unfortunately we are unable to draw any firm conclusions as to whether or not this is 'a thing'. From a purely anecdotal perspective, and despite my initial scepticism, RSD does indeed seem to be relatively specific to ADHD, as Dr Dodson argues. I think, however, it also occurs in ASD, and that this may be even be an important driver in those with ADHD who often have a few ASD traits if not the full diagnosis. My patients resonate very strongly with the description of RSD, often feeding back that it closely captures their inner experience.

Few of us like being criticised or rejected, but, for adults with ADHD, it is often registered as an unbearable, shame-ridden and highly unpleasant experience. So much so that I think many organise their entire existence, and style of engagement with the world and others, around actively reducing the chances of it happening. That gives you a flavour of the intensity of the experience.

An 'attack' of RSD (I use the word purposefully as most describe it in those or similar terms) is usually triggered by a rejection of some form or a concern that someone might imminently withdraw their love, respect or approval in some way. It may also be activated when the individual themselves concludes that they have not met their own, often excessively high, standards of social behaviour.

RSD seems to come as a 'bolt out of the blue', and it can effectively floor an individual for hours, sometimes even days, until the episode has 'run its course.' I have heard it described as an 'emotional seizure'. It is much more than day-to-day ADHD emotional reactivity.

Ten features that characterise RSD

1. RSD usually starts in early childhood ('They're so sensitive!' others may say), but it may not properly take root until the adolescent years.
2. There is always a trigger and it is happening in real time, importantly distinguished from a fear of being rejected in the future, which has a very different character (the latter is usually a result of past abandonment or some form of early attachment disturbance).
3. Triggers include being or feeling rejected, criticised or teased, or an inner sense of having 'messed up' or 'failed' at something important.
4. The shift in state is immediate, and distress level marked (with both emotional and physical manifestations).

5. The response can either be internalised, which may appear to the outside world as low mood and restless anxiety, or externalised, quite often with impulsive anger or even rage directed towards the individual or situation that caused it.

6. It is characterised, at its core, by overwhelming feelings of intense, catastrophic shame.

7. It can sometimes present with features of dissociation (feeling detached or 'cut-off').

8. Once in full motion, it can be difficult to stem the distress, and it often needs to work its way through.

9. It seems to be a big contributor to the low self-esteem and low self-efficacy associated with adult ADHD, as episodes themselves can leave a traumatic imprint.

10. RSD appears to respond to ADHD medication, sometimes surprisingly well, and the non-stimulant medication, Intuniv (extended-release guanfacine), appears to work best in this regard, but again it hasn't been studied so we don't know for sure.

RSD can shape personality

To avoid the unbearable discomfort of RSD, individuals who have experienced it often set up their life to avoid triggering, and interact with others cautiously. This background anxiety and vigilance subtly influences decisions and choices along the way. Many carve out the avenue of least resistance, one that ruffles as few feathers as possible, to avoid waking the monster. My impression is that, over time, RSD contributes to the shaping of personality, and results in some characteristic personality styles, including:

- **People-pleasing:** many with features suggestive of RSD slip into people-pleasing mode. Huge energy is expended anticipating what others will think and how they might react, and then adapting to keep the peace. One's own needs and wishes are typically sidelined in order to please the group and maintain a sense of internal safety.

- **Perfectionistic/overachieving:** the aim here is to generate respect and, through the veil of glory, become beyond reproach by others. The individual may think, *If I really excel at . . ., then they may not notice that I am* . . . But this exhausting style of existence has no end date. The perfectionism needs to be maintained indefinitely, as 'you are only as good as your last achievement', so 'there must be no let-up'. The guard must not come down and a facade needs to be maintained at all costs.

- **Avoidance:** people with features of RSD tend to be more risk-averse, and typically avoid engaging with new challenges (and people) unless there is a high chance of success and a low chance of being shown up or exposed. It's the 'I'll take a rain check on this one' for fear of being humiliated. After all, you can't be judged if you don't get involved in the first place! Life becomes narrowed, and a hot spring of low-level paranoia often bubbles beneath the surface.

- **A conflicted sense of self:** an uncomfortable division may form between the person one presents to the outside world and the other hidden, inner, shamed version of oneself. It can all feel like an act, which can be very confusing.

Exercise: RSD and me

Do you relate to the above descriptions of RSD? Can you think of a couple of examples where you suspect that RSD was at play? Think of a recent episode, and perhaps one from your childhood or adolescent years. An awareness of the connection seems to have a protective effect and typically reduces the blame you load onto yourself, which can be a 'shame-changer'.

You can do this reflective exercise in your Thrive Journal, if you like – just find the next clean page, title it 'RSD and me', and write a paragraph or two about the experiences.

THE PHYSIOLOGY OF EMOTIONS

I think it is important and helpful to understand how and why emotions become dysregulated, and to get to grips with the basic physiology underpinning them.

At a simple level, emotions exist to communicate information and to restore balance, or 'homeostasis'. They manifest as a characteristic cluster of inner experiences, physiological changes and behaviours that are triggered by something that is important to us. They often provide the impetus to take action: to move towards or away from something. Importantly, they also serve as a form of communication with others, indicating our needs, desires, likes and dislikes. There appear to be six core emotions which exist across cultures: anger, disgust, fear, happiness, sadness and surprise, with each having a range of related emotions.

Emotions are, in part, created by different patterns of activity in the autonomic nervous system (ANS), a system of two opposing parts: the sympathetic nervous system (SNS) and the parasympathetic nervous system (PNS).

It is important to remember that emotional dysregulation can manifest both as heightened arousal (stress, anxiety, anger, rage) and in the opposite direction, with shutdown and dissociation. Let's build from the outside in and consider first the mechanisms and processes by which our remarkable system deals with external stressors or threats.

The threat-response systems

Faced with an actual or even a perceived threat, the SNS activates with the aim of kicking the body into action and preparing it to efficiently utilise metabolic reserves. Sympathetic activation primes us for *fight* (to engage and defend ourselves, with physical force if necessary) or *flight* (basically to get out of there).

Conversely, boosting parasympathetic 'tone' promotes repair, regeneration and the building up of metabolic reserves. The PNS, which is pretty much run by the important vagus nerve (which I will introduce in a bit), only really comes online when its host is in a low threat state, though it is also the PNS that is responsible for the evolutionarily more primitive *freeze* response that underpins shutdown and dissociation.

The **ANS (autonomic nervous system)** is responsible for the immediate 'stress response'. This stimulates the adrenal glands, which sit above the kidneys in the abdomen, to release adrenaline, which primes all systems (neurological, cardiovascular, musculo-skeletal and hormonal) for 'fight' or 'flight'.

Another body system, which is called the **HPA (hypothalamic-pituitary-adrenal) axis**, is the delayed threat response system. It properly comes online after the initial burst of adrenaline subsides. The output of this more protracted hormonal cascade is cortisol, also produced by the adrenal gland, which, among other functions, serves to maintain the brain on high alert. Once safety has been re-established, the cortisol levels fall, the sympathetic drive reduces and the PNS comes back to the fore to coordinate rest, repair and regeneration.

The system is evolutionarily 'designed' to deal with acute stressors; however, if the threat, or, more broadly, the state of stress (including traumatic stress), persists chronically, the SNS is continually being activated.

This persistent activation places a low-level, but continuous, strain on the cardiovascular system and increases inflammation. Chronically high cortisol levels and reduced parasympathetic

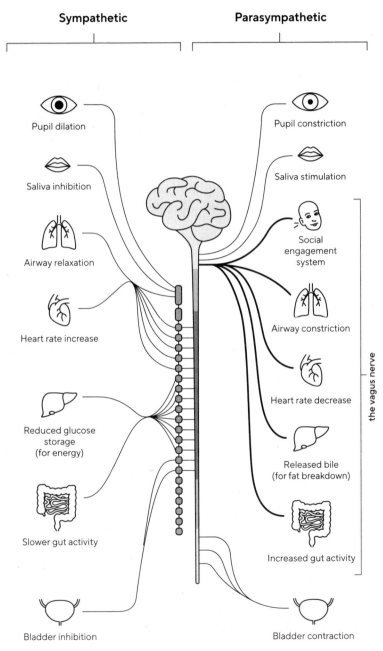

Sympathetic

Parasympathetic

Pupil dilation

Pupil constriction

Saliva inhibition

Saliva stimulation

Airway relaxation

Social engagement system

Heart rate increase

Airway constriction

Heart rate decrease

Reduced glucose storage (for energy)

Released bile (for fat breakdown)

Slower gut activity

Increased gut activity

Bladder inhibition

Bladder contraction

the vagus nerve

The autonomic nervous system (ANS)

repair will ultimately degrade health. The gut and immune system may begin to show signs of decompensation and things can spiral from there, assuming nothing changes.

Introducing the vagus nerve

The vagus nerve, often referred to as the 'wandering nerve', emerges out of the brainstem (the important interface between the brain above and the spinal cord below) and is the main parasympathetic nerve (there are in fact two of them, one on each side).

As it exits, it first shoots branches to the face and head, and then descends down the side of the neck (on both sides). It runs behind the breastbone and connects with most of the major organs of the body, throwing a net, or 'plexus', of nerve tissue around each of them. The branches of the vagus nerve that go to the head and face innervate some of the muscles of the face, the voice apparatus and quite a bit of the skin on, in and around the ears. There are also branches to the meninges, the outer layering of the brain.

Eighty per cent of the nerve fibres of the vagus are 'afferents' (think sensory) – they send information from the periphery back to the brain about the state of play out there, while 20 per cent are 'efferents', carrying data from the brain to the outside. As well as helping maintain optimal cardiovascular, gastrointestinal and re-spiratory function, particularly in the face of changing external influences, the vagus is responsible for the repair processes.

To feel safe, we require internal signals that tell us everything is in balance and no threats have been identified. Many of these safety signals come to the brain via the incoming afferent pathways of the vagus nerve. According to psychologist and neuroscientist Stephen Porges, who created 'Polyvagal Theory', when the ventral branch of the vagus nerve is activated, we are operating from the social engagement system. This system engages the use of eye contact, prosody (tone of voice), facial expression and attentive listening to essentially dampen defensive responses and avert conflict. Intonation of voice and facial expression can act as powerful magnets, pulling people into closer proximity. They help facilitate what's referred to as 'immobilisation without fear', which enables the body to feel secure enough without the need for escape (which is, of course, protective), and without becoming defensive. In the absence of this level of sophistication, we would be in a perpetual sympathetic-dominant stress state, which, as we have learned, disrupts biological processes.

Now that you understand a bit about the anatomy and physiology underpinning your emotions, let's look at some practical ways to regulate them.

HOW TO REGULATE EMOTIONS IN ADULT ADHD

People can develop both healthy and unhealthy strategies for regulating emotions. Unhealthy or 'maladaptive' strategies include:

- substance use and other addictive behaviours
- self-harm
- overworking
- risk-taking or thrill-seeking
- conflict seeking
- disordered eating
- avoidance and social withdrawal

All of the above are attempts to reduce negative emotions, through suppression, repression or escape. Although the goal is clearly to feel better, which may well be the case in the short term, these behaviours often backfire and, over time, can be a potent driver of mental and physical ill health.

There are so many healthier ways to regulate your emotions in adult ADHD. Some of these – like optimising sleep and nutrition, reducing toxicity and introducing more order, structure and routine into your day – have been covered in previous pillars, and others will be introduced here for the first time.

I have decided to focus on five specific approaches that I feel are critical to emotional regulation. They may not all be right for you, but they certainly deserve a look. I can honestly say that each of the approaches I will introduce, without exception, has changed my life for the better, enhancing my capacity to self-regulate and tolerate. And that's not to mention the hundreds of my patients who have benefitted from using them too.

1. Vagus nerve activation (or stimulation)

The vagus nerve has become an important target for a range of cutting-edge emotional regulation approaches. Vagus nerve-directed exercises have emerged as effective 'bio-hacks' which work quickly to alter your state of arousal.

Unlike some areas we stray into when considering emotional regulation, vagus nerve activation/stimulation does actually have a relatively solid evidence base, due to the ever-increasing number of studies, conducted across multiple disciplines, that monitor the impact of an intervention on something called heart rate variability (HRV). HRV is essentially a measure of autonomic function, or 'vagal tone'.

Although it's likely that the story is more subtle, stimulating the accessible areas of the body that are innervated by the vagus nerve and simply slowing the breath powerfully calms a dysregulated ANS, which is good news for those of us with adult ADHD.

Slow, deep, diaphragmatic breathing

Find a quiet and calm space. First connect with your regular breath and then, when grounded, take a few slow, deep inhalations in through your nose (as your abdomen expands) and out through your mouth (as your abdomen contracts). You ideally want to be breathing at your individual 'resonant frequency', which is usually about six breaths a minute (i.e., each full inhalation and exhalation lasting about ten seconds). Without establishing your resonant frequency using HRV monitoring software (which is readily available), you won't know for sure. You can do this breathing exercise for anything between one and ten minutes. Approaches like yoga and meditation, which work with and train the breath, can be useful practices to adopt to bring in regular breathwork. There are a range of other breathing techniques that you can try, with lots of guidance online.

As an aside, mouth taping (during sleep), which is thought to be safe, promotes nasal breathing, and has been shown to increase vagal tone and HRV. There may be other benefits including to immune and neurological function. It could be worth a try, but make sure you get tape that won't irritate your lips.

Humming or chanting

The vibrational stimulation of the laryngeal and pharyngeal branches of the vagus nerve relay messages of safety to the brain. Sounds that result in an optimal vibration of these structures include 'Ahh', 'Oooh' and 'Mmm'. Practise humming and chanting on a regular basis, possibly guided by an online video. Humming is also an effective way of circulating air through your sinuses.

Valsalva manoeuvre

The Valsalva manoeuvre involves exhaling (reasonably) forcefully against a closed airway. It is used in medicine to distinguish between various forms of cardiovascular dysfunction and as a treatment for certain types of heart rhythm disturbance. This is because increasing vagal tone slows the conduction of the heart's electrical impulse, in turn slowing its rate.

To do it you need to keep your mouth closed, pinch your nose and then gently try to exhale, which increases pressure in the inner ears, sinus cavities, chest and abdominal cavities. You may find yourself straining slightly, as if you were trying to pass a motion.

To achieve an increase in vagal tone (through the raised pressure on the vagus in the chest region), the hold should be maintained for 10–15 seconds. I advise, however, that you take it very gently to start with, and you don't do it if you have uncontrolled high blood pressure, a history of any form of stroke or any heart-related issues, or other health issues (especially eye or ear problems, due to the increased pressure it generates). Be sensible and consult with your doctor first if you have any relevant health concerns.

Ear stimulation

You can stimulate the vagus nerve by very gently touching the skin on and around the ear. There are established areas on the ear surface – in and around the entrance to the outer ear canal and behind the ear – that are directly innervated by the auricular branches of the vagus nerve.

Extremely light touch applied to these areas can have a powerfully calming effect. You know you are on the right track if, while very gently stimulating the areas, your mouth starts to moisten and you experience a pleasant fluttery sensation in your tummy. Experiment a bit and see what feels good.

Acupoint tapping on the head, face and chest

It is likely that part of the benefit experienced from acupoint tapping (on the face and trunk) is the direct result of its effects on areas innervated by the vagus nerve, although this has not yet been formally studied. See pages 230–9 for more on acupoint tapping.

Sleeping on your right side

There is some intriguing evidence that sleeping on your right side has a positive effect on HRV. Good-quality sleep has also been associated with increased HRV, and studies have also demonstrated how sleep deprivation and reduced sleep quality reduce it. Take a look back at Pillar 2 for some tips on optimising your sleep.

Electrical stimulation of the vagus nerve

There are a variety of approaches that utilise the healing potential of an electrical current. One popular device that I have quite a lot of experience with, and which I think is effective, is **Alpha-Stim**. I want to be clear from the start that it has not yet been studied in ADHD (I hope it will be soon), but anecdotally it appears very helpful indeed for emotional dysregulation and anxiety. Independently, there seems to be a growing interest in 'neuromodulatory' approaches not dissimilar to this in ADHD, as I will explain in Part 3.

Alpha-Stim's standard (AID) model uses 'cranial electrotherapy stimulation' (CES), applied via conducting ear clips. It has a solid and growing evidence base for the treatment of anxiety, and early encouraging findings in depression. It has been around for over 30 years (used in a number of different countries) and it has been studied extensively, including in the NHS.

A microcurrent of electricity (that is too mild to cause any harm or distress) is transmitted via the earlobes to the surface of the head. The electrical stimulation happens to be centred on regions of vagus nerve innervation and will undoubtedly have the effect of boosting vagal tone, but this is yet to be demonstrated.

The device is used for at least 20 minutes, most days a week, for at least a 4–6-week stint. In most people, even a single use induces a pleasant, relaxed feeling of well-being; however, when used daily for a period of a few weeks it can result in a sustained improvement in anxiety and, in my experience, far better emotional regulation. The RRP in the UK

---

is £600 (including VAT) at the time of writing, which will be out of reach for many, though some services offer a short-term rental option. See Resources, page 289 for more information.

Cold water exposure (the mammalian diving reflex)

Cold water exposure increases vagal tone. Some people favour cold water swimming or ice baths (Wim Hof style), but most just use the shower, which I suspect still confers similar benefits.

I would recommend that, halfway through your shower, you turn the water from hot to cold in three incremental steps, and then leave it on the cold setting for a further minute. The approach is thought to be more effective if you remain calm and regulated (even if inside you feel like screaming).

Cold water exposure has been demonstrated to boost immune function and reduce winter colds and flu. Studies suggest that nine minutes of cold water exposure a week is what you need to make a real difference.

Toothbrushing-linked practices

Gargling on a regular basis (which can be done either before or after brushing) will stimulate the pharyngeal muscles and, in turn, the vagus nerve that innervates them.

The gag reflex has its sensory innervation via another nerve, but the gagging action itself partially involves the pharyngeal branch of the vagus nerve. By gently stroking the brush side of your tooth-brush over your soft palate (on both sides) you will stimulate the reflex, serving as powerful training for the vagus.

Boosting levels of acetylcholine

Acetylcholine is the (anti-inflammatory) neurotransmitter used by the vagus nerve to communicate throughout the PNS network.

Foods rich in choline, a precursor of acetylcholine, include egg yolks and liver (from beef, chicken and turkey) – see page 162.

Vibrational stimulation of the vagus nerve

It is possible to activate the vagus nerve through vibration, accessing it where it passes close to bone. The **Sensate 2** device, which looks remarkably like a black pebble, is positioned over the sternum (breastbone) for a period and does just that, sending vibrations through the bone and stimulating the vagus nerve which passes beneath.

The device emits infrasonic vibrations (sound waves of a frequency too low for human hearing) which spread throughout the body and have a noticeable calming effect. At the same time, the smartphone app plays soothing sounds via headphones, synchronised with the vibrations. You can also watch an expanding and contracting image to coordinate your breathing, maintaining an optimal rate. The device costs about £200 at the time of writing (see Resources, page 290 for more information).

That brings us to the end of the vagus nerve section. The final thing I want to say is that data is power. If you have the means, consider measuring and monitoring your HRV. Over time, you will be able to work out exactly what improves it and what decreases it, mapping out trends and patterns. (See Resources, page 289, for devices that monitor HRV, as well as software that links to your computer or smartphone.) There is some evidence that simply the act of monitoring the HRV alone may improve performance and well-being!

2. Sensory modification

'Sensory processing' is one of the 'Ten Domains of Dysregulation' in ADHD that we explored in Part 1, with many (but not all) experiencing differences in the way that sensory information coming in from the outside is registered and processed. There is commonly sensory over-responsiveness (heightened sensitivity). If the issue is one of under-stimulation, individuals often seek out intense sensation as a form of compensation.

Our sensory system serves to connect us with the world, but also to protect us from it. If an individual is too sensitive, mechanisms will kick in to detach them from the noisy and oppressive outside world. This may be through behavioural adaptations such as isolation and withdrawal (sometimes into an imaginary internal world) or through addictive patterns and drug and alcohol use (often aimed at numbing the senses).

Can you relate to the experience of having been overwhelmed by incoming sensory information? Have there been times when you felt so oppressed and overloaded that you needed to 'shut off' in some way? See the box below for clues as to whether you might have sensory processing issues.

Clues to the presence of a sensory processing issue

- sensitivity to sounds or easily distracted by sounds (auditory)
- sensitivity to light (vestibular)
- sensitivity to busy environments (auditory/vestibular)
- sensitivity to clothing textures (tactile)
- sensitivity to movement (vestibular)
- sensitivity to touch from others (tactile)
- a picky eater (gustatory/tactile/olfactory)
- clumsiness, balance issues or bumping into things (proprioceptive/visual/vestibular)
- need for pressure (tactile/proprioceptive)
- need for movement (vestibular)
- need for oral input (tactile/gustatory/olfactory)

It is important to work out which stimuli dysregulate and cause you distress, and which you find calming and pleasurable, and that help regulate you. Once you understand your sensory needs, it can serve as a guide as to how you might adapt your environment and routines, so they are more aligned to these needs. So many of my patients over the years have described (typically) heightened sensitivity to their environment, yet many of them haven't appreciated its significance or considered it as a potential target for intervention.

Luckily, there is a lot that you can do to improve the quality of your life if you struggle with sensory processing issues.

Modifying your sensory inputs

We have a degree of control over what our senses are exposed to. Modifying the sensory inputs can serve as an effective form of self-soothing. How you organise your physical environment (both at home and at work) and the stimuli that you expose yourself to, influences your emotional state, how safe you feel and how much energy you expend.

I encourage you to make use of this understanding and test out some simple modifications that may help promote feelings of safety and help you better regulate your emotional world.

Where to start?

Taking time to map out your profile and identify specific triggers and sensitivities is an important first step. Then it is about creating a bespoke 'sensory diet' (or 'sensory prescription') for yourself that should ideally integrate a broad range of interventions and adjustments (see pages 226–231). It can include a variety of different strategies tailored to you and your specific needs and may also engage the use of external aids and devices. Those with more complex issues may decide to work with a sensory integration therapist.

Strategies to consider for your 'sensory diet'

Key: A= auditory (hearing), Vi= visual, O= olfactory (smell), T= tactile (touch), G= gustatory (taste), P= proprioceptive (the awareness of the body position in space), Ve= vestibular (involved in movement and balance).

- **Play calming music more often (A):** find music that relaxes you. Everyone's taste is different, but keep in mind that calming music activates the balancing PNS, whereas fast and loud music, such as dance and rock, increases the sympathetic drive. That is not to say there is not a role for music with a beat, which in some can create a light trance-like state which may aid focus. But be cautious that this is not at the expense of your stress system.
- **Expose yourself to natural beauty (Vi, A, O, T):** nature has a powerful and nourishing effect on our emotions. Open green spaces seem to be particularly important. Simply going for a walk in the park or caring for a few indoor plants can make a difference.
- **Burn or vaporise essential oils (O):** you can buy aromatherapy oil burners or vaporisers into which you put some water and a few drops of essential oil. Research online about the numerous health benefits of essential oils. There are many different oils available; some are relaxing (such as lavender) and others more stimulating (such as rosemary). You can naturally influence your emotional state and cognitive function based on the oils you decide to use.
- **Take a relaxing bath (T, O):** a hot bath with a few (ideally unscented, natural) candles is a powerful and rapid way to relax and unwind. Adding some essential oils (that are suitable for skin contact) or Epsom salts can aid relaxation, but both need to be dosed properly, so do your research.

- **Change into comfortable clothes (T, P):** a great way to 'strip' away the stresses and strains of the day (assuming you're having a quiet evening in) is to change out of your work clothes into some soft and comfortable loungewear. It will mark the transition into 'you time', which, together with the tactile sensory benefits, should help shift you into a more relaxed mood.
- **Wear tighter fitting clothing (P):** tight-fitting garments, such as compression socks, boost sensory (proprioceptive) inputs and can feel very 'containing', in my experience markedly reducing anxiety and promoting regulation. They also function to squeeze blood up the body, improving the perfusion of the brain. Body Braid, a Canadian-designed posture support brace that I love, also boosts proprioceptive feedback with powerful calming effects (see page 289).
- **Get the ambient temperature just right (T):** get to grips with your heating system and try to optimise the temperature in your home and workplace. It shouldn't be too hot or too cold as extremes of temperature promote stress in the system as your body has to compensate.
- **Limit static noise and counter external noise pollution (A):** if they are not in use, turn off your electrical items (TVs, radios, computers, mobile phones, and so on), especially those that emit a low-grade buzz, which is often only perceivable as the device is turned off. We quickly acclimatise to background sounds from the outside world – cars, trains, planes, drilling – but these intrusions act as stressors for those who are more sensitive. They impact our ability to think and, left unchecked, can affect our energy levels and mood. Consider fitting double-glazing, sound insulation or thick curtains and try noise-cancelling headphones.
- **Increase activities in natural light (Vi, Ve):** natural light elevates the mood and helps maintain the body's internal clock. Keep curtains and blinds open as much as possible during the day, work near a window and cut back overgrown garden bushes that block your light. If sensitive, try to avoid prolonged

exposure to artificial lighting, especially fluorescent tubes and bright white or blue LED lighting. Consider buying natural light or extra-warm white bulbs.

- **Avoid clutter and bring more order to your space (Vi):** look back at Pillar 4 for ways to rid yourself of the clutter around you. Making your physical environment more pleasing to the eye helps regulate the system.

- **Choose your colours carefully (Vi):** colours affect our mood and energy levels. Natural colours (blues and greens) generally make us feel more relaxed, but everyone is different so experiment and go with what works best for you.

Sensory aids

Sensory aids and devices are tools that engage the senses, support positive emotions and have a protective, calming or stimulatory effect. They can also sometimes be used to promote brain activity and develop new skills.

They come in a variety of forms and need to be tailored to the individual's unique needs. Different things suit different people, and what you try should be dictated by what you think you will find effective or enjoyable.

One of the areas with special relevance to ADHD is aids that support what I call 'dual stimulation'. Individuals with ADHD often report that they can only settle, fall asleep, concentrate or allow their creative juices to flow if they are exposed to another active stimulus at the same time – this may be the background hustle and bustle of a café (something I find helpful, but others can't tolerate), the white noise of a fan, a piece of Blu-tack to fiddle with or having the TV or radio on in the background.

Below is a **menu of sensory aids** for you to consider:

Vision
- dawn simulators and natural or colour lighting
- light boxes (can have mood-boosting effects, but can be too stimulating for some)
- blue (and red) light glasses (for protecting your sleep-wake rhythm)
- sensory lighting products, for example, colour wall washes, lava lamps
- calming colours painted on walls

Hearing
- noise reduction headphones
- sensory (concert) ear plugs
- white noise/natural sounds machine (or fan)
- padded tablecloths and sink mats to dampen noisy crockery
- rugs and insulation to limit noise in the home

Taste
- glass water bottles (with fresh herbs infusing the water)

Smell
- essential oils, and oil burners or electric vaporisers

Touch
- soft and silky bedding or nightwear (sheets, duvet covers, pillowcases, pyjamas, eye masks, and so on)
- acupuncture rings (often effective for concentrating on reading, listening or studying)
- self-massage and reflexology devices (electric and non-electric)

- fidget items, including worry beads and stress balls
- Blu-tack, clay or other squidgy materials to fiddle with
- large, comfortable pillows and beanbags
- grounding mats (for under the feet and on desk surface)
- grassy and sandy areas (for walking barefoot)
- heating or cooling pads
- reflexology insoles or socks
- sauna (including infra-red – see page 290)

Vestibular
- swings, hanging seats and hammocks
- trampolines and rebounders
- vibrating plates (for example, Power Plate – see page 289)
- balance devices, seat pads and balls
- standing desks

Proprioception
- Body Braid (posture support brace – see page 289)
- tight-fitted clothing (leggings, tops, socks)
- weighted clothing and blankets
- body brushes (also called tactile or sensory brushes)
- balls (for bouncing, throwing and catching)

Interoception
- mindfulness audio guides/Solo-Soma video (see page 289)
- Alpha-Stim AID and Sensate 2 (see pages 289–90)

3. Acupoint tapping

We touched on acupoint tapping in Pillar 1. As well as using it with great success personally, over the years I have used the main tapping approach, Emotional Freedom Techniques (EFT), with hundreds of patients, often with impressive results. Its effects are far more rapid, in my experience, than can be achieved through talking alone. You can observe emotional shifts taking place in front of your very eyes. Despite its effectiveness, though, tapping is not a cure-all. Complex problems require a skilled approach, and healing often requires time and patience.

I prefer EFT to similar trauma processing approaches such as Eye Movement Desensitisation and Reprocessing (or EMDR), which I have also trained in, because, in addition to being used as a form of one-to-one therapy, EFT can be self-applied for quick and effective stress reduction and emotional regulation. In my experience, this subtle difference empowers individuals to take back the control in managing their own emotional worlds. Knowing you can quickly reduce distress often results in a marked reduction in the anticipatory anxiety (the 'fear of the fear'), something that commonly persists even after the core problem (phobia or trauma) has been cleared from the system.

When it comes to using EFT in ADHD, there are a multitude of possible applications. It can literally be used on any form of emotional or physical distress, and, amazingly, it works (most of the time)! In Pillar 1, we explored how tapping, in a simplified form, and paired together with affirmations, can be used to address the limiting beliefs and psychological blocks that commonly arise early on in one's ADHD journey. EFT can also be used to manage and regulate emotions in the 'here and now' (see page 289 for acupoint tapping-related resources).

In my own life, there are many occasions when its timely use has successfully averted some form of emotional spiralling, or quickly recovered many a situation that felt like it was heading south. Over the years, I have regularly used it for anxiety of various flavours (there is a lot of free-floating anxiety in ADHD), but also for pain, fatigue, boredom and so much more. I will always tap before interviews and lectures, and when I need to focus my mind on an important piece of work, but find myself procrastinating and unable to settle. EFT generally never lets me down, and it has taught me a great deal about the workings of the mind.

How it works

Exactly how acupoint tapping works depends upon who you ask! A detailed analysis is beyond the remit of this book, but I will provide a brief overview. The pioneers of these approaches (Roger Callahan and Gary Craig in the US, and Phil Mollon in the UK) hypothesise that negative emotions reflect a disruption in the body's 'energy', or informational system. In the same way that acupuncture is thought to free up the flow of energy, it is argued that tapping has a similarly rebalancing and flow-enhancing effect. This explanation remains controversial and is certainly not accepted by all.

The repetitive, rhythmical stimulation does seem to be an important factor. All mammals instinctively and naturally engage this inherently calming technique. Alternately stimulating both sides of the body ('bilateral stimulation'), an approach employed by EMDR, may also play a role.

There will indeed also be 'non-specific' factors at play. The placebo effect exerts an influence in every treatment intervention and suggestibility will no doubt also influence things, but again, this doesn't mean that it fully explains the effects. It is very likely that repetitive tapping induces a light trance state, which will heighten suggestibility. Distraction, an explanation landed on by many, is in my view a gross over-simplification.

In my opinion, the calming effect on an individual's emotional state after tapping on the face and body is likely to be mediated by the ANS, with the tapping directly stimulating the vagus nerve, as discussed earlier (see page 215). A reduction in cortisol levels and an increase in dopamine levels have been demonstrated following tapping.

A certain degree of open-mindedness and patience is required to allow oneself proper exposure to these methods, and to be able to make an informed judgement of their worth. Importantly, tapping still works in those who are sceptical. I hope you experience the benefits that I and so many of my patients have.

The acupoints that are tapped

The points that are tapped on are well-established acupuncture points. The few studies that have been conducted on point location suggest that these points may have unique properties relative to surrounding skin, namely an increased density of mechano-receptors (a form of receptor that registers external stimuli) and reduced electrical resistance (i.e., increased conductivity). Studies have also demonstrated that stimulation of acupuncture points sends electrochemical impulses to the region of the brain that governs fear – the limbic area.

The most commonly used acupoints are:

1. Top of the head: on the crown of the head, a little above the hairline.
2. Eyebrow: at the beginning of either eyebrow, just above the nose.
3. Side of eye: on the bone bordering the outside corner of either eye.
4. Under the eye: on the cheekbone directly under either eye.
5. Under the nose: between the bottom of the nose and the upper lip.
6. Above the chin: under the lower lip in the indent of the chin.
7. Under the arm: under either arm, about 10cm down from the armpit.
8. Collarbone: just below the junction of the breastbone and either/both collarbones.

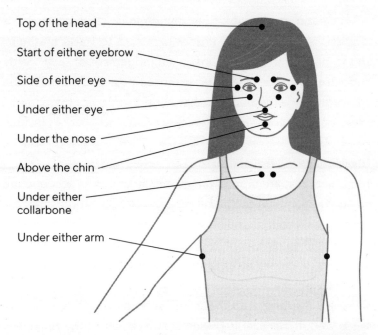

Top of the head

Start of either eyebrow

Side of either eye

Under either eye

Under the nose

Above the chin

Under either collarbone

Under either arm

Face and chest acupoints

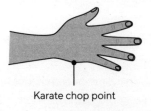

Karate chop point

Hand acupoints

There is an important point on the outer aspect of the hand (known colloquially as the 'karate chop' point – see page 76), and additional points that are sometimes used on the sides of the thumb, forefinger, middle and little fingers (see above).

The EFT procedure

Phase 1: Set-up

Identify the problem to be worked on and then focus your mind on it. Approach the problem in its entirety if it is straight-forward. If more complex and multifaceted, target a particular aspect of it:

- an emotion
- a belief
- a memory
- a physical symptom

Dealing with the 'aspects' of a problem

Most problems are made up of a variety of aspects. If we take a typical ADHD example such as a looming deadline, the aspects may include:

- The fear of falling behind and getting overwhelmed.
- The worry about how your loved ones will react if you mess up.
- The (social) anxiety of being shamed in front of others.
- The chest tightness you experience when you think about it.
- The procrastination preventing you from getting down to work.
- The words of your tutor, who told you to 'pull up your socks, or you won't progress'.
- A memory of when you failed to meet a deadline previously and had to face the consequences.

When using EFT, you need to systematically address each main aspect in turn. Often, when a critical threshold of aspects have been dealt with, the problem seems to collapse in its entirety, a phenomenon referred to as the 'generalisation effect'.

Rate the intensity of the problem on a scale of 1 to 10 (where 1 = no problem whatsoever, and 10 = the worst intensity imaginable).

Repeat the 'set-up' statement below three times while continuously tapping on the 'karate chop' point:

'Even though I have this [describe the problem in detail, for example, 'this fluttery anxiety in my chest about the deadline'], I completely accept myself/I am okay' [or a similar positive affirmation].

Phase 2: Acupoint tapping

Tap through the acupoints in a set sequence.
Ensure relatively firm contact, but not enough to hurt or bruise. Tap about eight to ten times on each: *top of head, inner eyebrow, side of eye, under the eye, under the nose, under the lip, under the arm and below the collarbone.*
Each time you move on to the next point, repeat a brief 'reminder phrase' (for example, 'this anxiety about the deadline').

Repeat the sequence two to three times.

Pause and reflect.
Take a couple of deep breaths and then reassess the intensity of the target problem, rating it again if you find this useful.

Decide on next steps.

- **If the distress is still present but less intense**, repeat the above process, but this time refer to it as 'This *remaining . . .*' (for example, 'This remaining anxiety about the deadline') in both the set-up statement and the reminder phrase.

- **If the distress associated with that aspect has been cleared** (for example, it is down to 1/10), then turn your focus to a different aspect of the problem and start the process from the beginning. Feel your way through and trust your intuition.

- **If progress is slow or definite shifts are not experienced:**
  - Consider widening the search for 'aspects'.
  - If relevant, try working on any underlying resistance to change using EFT. Common themes include:
    - a fear of change
    - a fear of it not working, leaving you without options
    - feeling unsafe using EFT
    - a fear that your problem is too big to be cleared
    - a worry that the approach looks silly
  - You can adapt the set-up statement to something like, '*Even though I'm scared to address this issue and it doesn't feel safe . . .*'

Targeting problems using EFT

When using EFT, you can focus it on:

- **Negative emotions**, such as fear, sadness, shame, anger:
  - as a stand-alone emotion
  - as a memory-linked emotion (traumatic) or situation-linked emotion (phobic).
- **Physical symptoms** for example, headache, fatigue, dizziness.
- **Charged or traumatic memories.**

> - **Dysfunctional or limiting beliefs** (usually linked to memories) **or psychological blocks.**
> - **Unwanted behaviours.**

Once you have mastered the basic approach and have become more familiar with, and sensitive to, the technique, having used it on more simple and stand-alone problems, you can try using it on slightly more multifaceted issues.

It is important to be mindful that there could be a lot going on 'under' the presenting (or most prominent) symptom. Once you process and clear the charge from whatever is at the forefront, something else (again, typically an emotion, physical symptom or memory) will often surface and take its place, as if waiting in a queue.

You need to work through the layers and be persistent. Newly emerging features or thoughts, however unrelated they may seem, are often part of the network and will require attention.

Identifying emotional shifts

There are various bodily responses and subjective experiences that are recognised in the EFT (and associated) literature as commonly being indicators of emotional processing (or 'shifts'), including:

- sighs, yawns or burps
- a feeling of fatigue or intense tiredness
- a sensation of lightness, 'floatiness' or 'openness' (especially in the chest region)
- a change in your breathing rate or depth
- a subtle change in your skin tone or colour
- changes in posture, facial expression or the tone or volume of your voice

Experiencing these subtle shifts tells you that you are on the right track, but probably the biggest clue that you are making progress is if you no longer feel the distress when you think or speak about an issue, as you did previously. This represents a reduction in the associated 'charge'.

Are there any negative effects of tapping?
Some people may experience tenderness at tapping points if they tap too vigorously, but this can be managed by changing technique. You should not tap so hard that it bruises or hurts.

It is also possible that distressing memories and emotions may surface and be 're-lived' to varying degrees, which is termed an 'abreaction' when severe. It is therefore not advisable to work on highly charged material on your own, but rather with an experienced practitioner in a contained therapeutic process.

If a strong reaction does catch you off guard, the tapping alone (without any talking) can be very balancing indeed and often results in a rapid calming of the distress. At these moments, just continue tapping through the points, rather than stop due to the distress. I find that compared with other approaches that employ the technique of 'exposure', tapping is considerably gentler.

4. Mindful release of negative states

We all experience intense and difficult emotional states and feelings. They generally come and go like the clouds in the sky, in a dynamic interplay. In ADHD, the weather systems can be a bit more changeable, and we can sometimes find ourselves overwhelmed by emotion. Wouldn't it be great if, with the flick of a switch, we could simply let go of these uncomfortable emotions?

I have come to realise that this is indeed possible, using the right approach. Many, in different guises, have explored this concept of 'letting go', or what I refer to as the mindful release of negative states or beliefs. They include Hale Dwoskin in his book

The Sedona Method and David R. Hawkins in *Letting Go*. They share similar themes in terms of the ingredients they cite that are necessary to shed unwanted states. There is clear overlap with mindful practice as well as the powerful idea that you are separate from your emotions or beliefs, despite them feeling an integral part of your fabric. I have experimented with these approaches over the years and feel quite confident that, with a bit of practice, they work for most people, and again they don't require you to believe in the approach!

In a nutshell, the technique for letting go of distress involves a phase of *awareness and acceptance*, followed by a phase of *release*, with a discharging of any associated resistance. At this point, as Hawkins describes, 'the energy behind it dissipates'.

When I first read about these techniques, they sounded patronisingly simple; however, I have found them to be extremely effective and personally invaluable. Below are a few practical pointers so you can try it for yourself:

- As soon as you become aware of the presence of a negative state (thought, belief, feeling or emotion), it is important to first get below the level of thoughts and get in touch with the underlying feelings and emotions themselves. Thoughts tend to lead to more thoughts, all in an attempt to explain the presence of the feeling.
- Try not to become overly caught up with the external events that may have caused the feelings. Commonly these are latched on to by the mind and used as a vehicle to give expression to the feelings that need releasing.
- Once below the thought and connected with the feeling, accept it is there and briefly stay with it and really feel it. See if you can identify any resistance to it.
- Then set a clear intention to release it, to let it go. At that moment, allow your body to fully relax and soften, while trying to stay connected to the feeling. Notice as it quickly loses its

power and dissipates. It is virtually impossible to experience distress when your body is relaxed.

Surrendering to a feeling often means loosening your attachment to any particular outcome: it will be what it will be. In my experience, true freedom involves letting go of attachments. We might enjoy or desire something, but we shouldn't *need* it to feel okay. In my view, the goal should be to try to progressively reduce your dependence on, or attachment to, *all* things, including other people and, importantly, the views they hold.

These days, if I am triggered by something, I try to assume a more observing stance, as opposed to taking on a victim role. I find it helpful to tap into what I think of as my 'deeper wisdom' – that subconscious 'self' which, for me, has a spiritual aspect. However you think of your own true self – perhaps the spirit, soul or psyche – you may find it helpful to pay greater attention to its guidance. I encourage you to actively seek out opportunities to experiment with letting go. It may take a bit of time and practice to really see the full benefits, but, with curiosity and perseverance, it will likely foster a heightened sense of freedom and a stronger relationship with self.

5. Solo-Soma morning movement meditation

Personally, I have always struggled with meditation-based approaches that require me to sit still. 'Solo-Soma' is an active, body-focused meditation practice that I developed and refined over a number of years to address this challenge, and that was initially intended for my use only. The name is from the Latin, *solo* – alone – and *soma* – with your body. When I realised how profound its ANS-rebalancing effects were, I decided to start teaching it to others.

It has not been formally evaluated yet, but it appears to work very well. Its creation was the output of many years of intuitive self-exploration and therapeutic experimentation on my own body and mind. It is underpinned by a scientific and trauma-informed foundation, and years of experience working creatively, with a strong body (somatic) focus.

Solo-Soma is an efficient 20-minute, self-applied, sensory-based meditation. Think of it as an autonomic nervous system reboot or balancer. Personally, I usually extend it to a 30–40-minute practice, as I enjoy and benefit from it so much. It functions at multiple levels – among other things, it engages movement, touch and the breath. It is intended to be used daily as part of your morning self-care routine, to help launch the day on a positive footing.

I have noticed that many of my patients with ADHD find it particularly effective and grounding. Given that dysregulation is the central issue in ADHD, it follows that an approach which has been designed with mind–body regulation at its heart will have tangible benefits in this neurodivergent group.

The approach draws from a variety of existing healing, emotional regulation and trauma-processing methods – some very old and passed down from ancient times, such as yoga, acupressure (Tui Na) and Qigong, and others more contemporary such as vagus nerve activation, EMDR, EFT and other cutting-edge trauma-focused and energy psychology techniques. I have integrated some physiological interventions such as calf pumping, lymphatic drainage support, Valsalva (see page 219) and inversion exercises (designed to shift blood around the body and encourage optimal brain perfusion) and cognitive approaches that engage affirmation, gratitude, intention and awe.

Solo-Soma promotes calm and balance in the system, and its profound effects are likely to be underpinned by a range of mechanisms. There is a strong emphasis on activating the vagus nerve, which, as we have learned, enhances PNS functioning, with calming effects. Individual components of Solo Soma have been previously studied (by others) and have been shown to improve measures such as HRV. Touch, including self-touch, has been demonstrated to increase levels of oxytocin and endorphins.

Regular practice fosters a heightened connectedness with one's own physical body and, in turn, with others through an increasingly attuned sensory and bioenergetic system. Mindful practice, with all its demonstrated benefits, lies at its heart.

I have included six taster exercises that form part of Solo-Soma below. If you are keen to learn the whole routine properly, an instructional video is available on The Grove website (see Resources, page 288).

Please take this guidance as it has been intended: not as a proven cure for anything, but simply as an efficient way to calm and regulate the ANS, and an invitation to explore your physical body creatively, enquiringly and unashamedly . . . and hopefully, along the way, to tap into its considerable healing potential.

Practicalities

Solo-Soma is generally practised soon after waking. Most will do it wearing soft clothes and while standing (but it can be adapted for sitting or lying if necessary).

If you have long hair, you may wish to tie it back, but this is not essential. Hair clips, glasses and jewellery should ideally be removed. If you have any injuries or vulnerable body regions, or if you have issues with balance (or any other relevant medical problem), I strongly encourage you to take things cautiously and listen to your body.

If you are hypermobile (about half of those with ADHD are), be very careful not to overstretch your vulnerable joints, especially your neck. If you are prone to dizziness or light-headedness, you need to be extra vigilant, especially when doing the exercises that involve inversion. Please ensure that you have sufficient space around you, especially when doing the exercises which involve arm swinging.

It goes without saying, but if you feel unwell in any way, or it is too much for you, take a break and, if necessary, find a way to modify the routine.

Solo-Soma morning movement meditation taster

1. Shaking things up

- While standing with your legs shoulder-width apart, spend 30 seconds or so gently and continuously shaking the body, as if there was a minor earthquake rumbling inside of you.
- You can then either rock rhythmically from foot to foot while continuing to shake your whole torso, or gently bounce at your knees creating the shake from there. You could even rock forward slightly on to your toes and gently bounce at the ankle joint if this comes naturally and you are stable enough.
- At some point, you should let your shoulders also bounce freely, while gently shaking both hands at the same time, as if you were gently flicking water off them.

Shaking things up

'Shaking things up' has a powerful grounding effect, stimulates the lymphatic system and wakes up the musculoskeletal system, releasing tension.

2. Cross crawl

- Raise your arms, lift your left knee and bring your right elbow down and across to meet it. Repeat on the opposite side.
- Continue alternating for about 30 seconds, exhaling with a vigorous 'Ooh' sound with every movement (expelling air from your lungs in the process).

Anecdotally, cross-lateral activity (that is crossing the midline of the body in a co-ordinated way) is said to strengthen integration between the two hemispheres of the brain. It's meant to be good for reading, focus, co-ordination and balance. It is also a great way of getting the whole body moving and warmed up after a period of inactivity.

Cross crawl

3. Qigong arm swinging

- Raise both arms above your head. As you bend at the knees, allow your arms to fall forward and then swing them down either side, and then behind the body. (Important: Make sure to keep your neck in line with the rest of your spine at all times.)
- Then, from a squat position, immediately reverse the movement and raise both arms back up above and over your head (while breathing in deeply) creating a nice full body stretch.
- Repeat, continuing for about 30 seconds.
- As you let your arms fall, and while exhaling fully, make a releasing 'Ahhh' sound.

It is claimed that this movement increases energy, mood and mental clarity, as well as improving blood and lymphatic circulation. It also strengthens the knees, hips and shoulders.

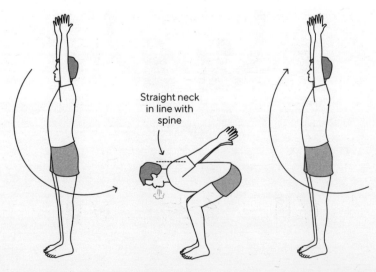

Straight neck in line with spine

Arm swinging

4. Flow exercise

· Place your hands on opposite shoulders, crossing your arms in front of your body. Gripping the opposite shoulders gently, slide both hands down the upper and then lower arms. The forearms, then palms, then fingertips meet with contact being maintained between arms/hands throughout.

· Pause, then slide your hands back up your arms in the opposite direction, without breaking contact. Repeat this up-and-down sequence about ten times.

· Start the exercise by taking a deep inhale. Then, as you slide downwards, exhale fully. As you slide back up, inhale deeply.

· As long as you are able to maintain good balance, gently bend at the knees and sink into a squat position as you exhale (and slide down the arms), then, as you inhale, reverse the movement (sliding back up the arms) and return to the upright position.

· On the last exhale, end with your hands meeting in a firm grip while maintaining a fixed squat position.

· While gripping, hold and lock the breath for about ten seconds (in what's called a Valsalva manoeuvre – see page 219), before releasing both the hands and the breath. You will probably need to take a moment to recover your strength and breath after this one.

Flow exercise

As well as the benefits associated with touch, the squatting and the Valsalva manoeuvre are thought to confer health benefits. Both are good for boosting core strength and, as we've seen, the latter supports cardiovascular health through its actions on the vagus nerve (it lowers blood pressure and heart rate and increases HRV). Do please check with your doctor whether it is safe to do the Valsalva if you have any relevant health issues (see page 219).

5. Acupoint stimulation (and horizontal eye movements)

- Bend fully at the waist and hang your arms down towards your feet. Using a pointed, tensed middle finger of each hand, pulse repeatedly and reasonably firmly on the 'Liver 3' acupressure point on each foot for about 30 seconds, with a gentle bouncing action. To locate this point, run your middle finger towards you along the space between the big and second toe. The acupoint lies in the dip just before the inverted V-shaped

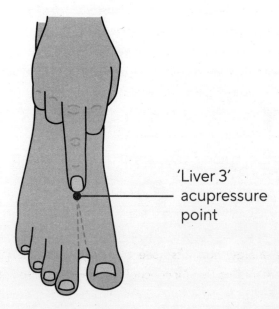

'Liver 3' acupressure point

Foot acupoint

meeting of the two (metatarsal) bones that extend to the big and second toe.

- While bent over in the inverted position, pulsing with your fingertips, do repeated alternate horizontal eye movements. Start moving your eyes left – then right – then left – then right, and so on, briefly fixing your vision on a defined point in each direction, while limiting your head movement.

Stimulating this point has a calming effect, reducing anxiety, and the eye movements are effective at processing traumatic charge.

6. Midline tapping

- Using the index and middle fingers of both hands, start tapping down from the crown of the head, in the midline, to the area directly between the eyebrows.
- Continue tapping outwards in opposite directions over both eyebrows and around both eyes, coming round to the front of the cheeks (pausing briefly on the cheekbones, directly under both eyes); then continue tapping down and around both nostrils, with your fingertips meeting in the middle (over the philtrum) below the nose; then tap around the lips, again meeting in the middle (in the crease of the chin) under the lower lip. You can imagine you are tracing the shape of a flower or even a butterfly (around the eyes, nose and mouth).
- Then, very slowly, work your way from the chin down the midline of the neck, chest and abdomen, tapping with the fingers of both hands continuously (either at the same time or alternately – try both). Continue down to the level of the bladder (just below the belly button). As you descend, focus particularly on the midline energy 'hotspots' (see overleaf) – the chakras and important midline Ren (or conception) meridian acupoints. The seven chakras include (in ascending order): root, sacral, solar plexus, heart, throat, third eye and crown.

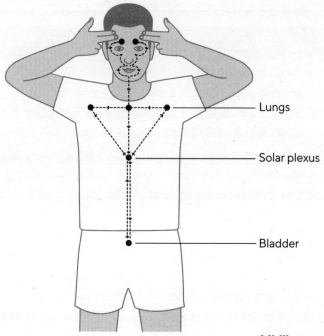

Midline tapping

- Once you have reached the level of the bladder, reverse the direction and continue tapping back up the midline of the body. When you reach the level of the breastbone (at the solar plexus), splay upwards and outwards, creating a V shape with your tapping, ending up under the outer aspect of the collarbones (an important lung acupuncture point). Then, stimulating lymphatic drainage points along the way tap horizontally and reasonably firmly across the upper chest (under the collarbones) meeting back in the midline, and closing the triangle.

Acupoint tapping is thought to have a number of benefits, including the reduction of anxiety and the processing of trauma (go back to page 230 for more on tapping). Stimulation of areas around the face, neck and upper chest may also improve lymphatic drainage.

7. 'Shield-up' (to finish)

- To end the movement meditation practice, bend at the hips again and hang down, dropping your hands down towards your feet. If you are sufficiently balanced, stable and flexible, slide both hands (palms facing up) under the soles of both feet, creating a continuous circular loop with your body. If this is not possible or you feel unstable, simply hang your arms down towards your feet, making contact if possible.
- While maintaining this inverted position, take three slow, deep breaths, feeling the wonderful stretch across your whole spine.
- Then, gently release your hands from (under) your feet and gradually, while rolling back up, vertebra by vertebra, run the fingertips of both hands up, over the tops of your feet and up the front of your legs. Allow your fingertips to come together and meet around the level of the bladder.
- Continue tracing up the midline of the front of the body, over the chest, neck and face as if doing up a zip. At the level of the crown (the highest point on the head), open and raise your arms (think flower blooming) and look up towards the sky.
- Hold this open and energising position for a few seconds, while thinking of (and possibly stating out loud) one thing, person or situation that you feel gratitude for, allowing the subject of the gratitude to emerge naturally if possible.

The action of 'zipping up' is designed to symbolise a form of protective shield and is a nice way of bringing the practice to a close. The inversion, the breathwork and the practice of gratitude that are part of the 'shield-up' phase, all have demonstrated health benefits.

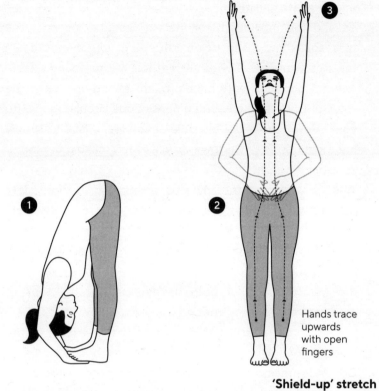

Hands trace
upwards
with open
fingers

'Shield-up' stretch

We have come to the end of our tour through some of the most effective techniques for regulating emotions, based on my experience. I hope these approaches have a positive and stabilising effect on your life and they help reduce distress levels.

This completes Part 2, and we will now transition to the third and final part of the book, that gives an overview of the more traditional treatments available for adult ADHD and also explores some of the barriers and residual difficulties you may come up against, and what you can do about them.

PART 3

MOVING FORWARD

I see ADHD less like something one 'has' (like diabetes, perhaps) and more as an integral part of you, akin to your personality, but somewhat more malleable. The reality is that, once established, ADHD will likely accompany you through the trials and tribulations that constitute the fabric of life, shaping your experience along the way.

Optimal ADHD management indisputably requires a lifelong commitment, and the ability to adapt skilfully along the way.

You've already gone some way to managing your ADHD and stabilising the ship and hopefully you have already seen a real difference in many areas. Things should be feeling a little more in control and less frantic.

As you emerge into this clearer and less oppressive landscape, it is easier to see the big picture and to evaluate your next steps.

For some of you, managing your ADHD is likely to require the use of medication, while for others, non-medication treatment options may be the route of travel. In a moment, we will be exploring the medical management of ADHD so you can evaluate which approach, if any, may be right for you.

In the final chapter, we will explore stubborn symptoms and common pitfalls that you may encounter along the way. I'll introduce some additional creative workarounds and clever 'hacks' that should help you to mop up some of those residual difficulties, edging you ever closer to that thrive zone.

I feel it's important to remind you here that, even with a committed approach, things are never going to be perfect; life with ADHD is inherently challenging and endlessly frustrating. I often tell my patients that the goal is to do your best to stay 'on track', but with the knowledge, and acceptance, that this will not always be possible.

THE MEDICAL MANAGEMENT OF ADULT ADHD

Whether to try medication for your ADHD or to stick to a more therapeutic and lifestyle-oriented approach is obviously a very personal decision. As you read through this chapter, I want to encourage you to keep an open mind and to really investigate the options properly before deciding either way.

To get a balanced perspective of the various treatment options and approaches, it is sensible to do a bit of digging and self-study. There is a fair amount of misinformation out there in relation to ADHD and its treatment, as well as a great deal of scaremongering, so you may be pleased to know that I have done most of the heavy work for you.

When it comes to what you decide, I have absolutely no agenda – my primary objective is to provide you with impartial and accurate information to support your decision-making. I will try my very best to concisely summarise what I think is important, but a lot will depend on what is available locally and, if the NHS has nothing to offer, whether or not you have the means to cover the cost of private care.

MEDICATION FOR ADULT ADHD

The National Institute for Health and Care Excellence (NICE) guidelines in the UK state quite clearly that medication is the 'first line' recommended treatment for ADHD in adults. Multiple studies have demonstrated that medication, when used responsibly, is a reasonably safe and very effective intervention. In fact, ADHD medication ranks among the most effective available in mental health, across the board.

Though there remain some important and very pertinent questions as to the longer term health impact of ADHD medication, which I briefly address later in the chapter, there is a tsunami of data demonstrating that ADHD medications are effective in the short term, and that they dramatically reduce the risk of a range of adverse outcomes.

In my professional experience, medication has driven obvious and sometimes dramatic improvements to the quality of life of scores of my patients. It has literally saved lives in some cases (not to mention the relationships, careers and reputations resurrected along the way).

I feel it is only right to briefly share my personal experience at this stage too. Following my diagnosis in my early to mid-thirties, it took me a few years and trials of a range of different stimulant and non-stimulant medications (obviously under psychiatric supervision) before I 'landed'. This experience gave me a unique insider's perspective and I have no doubt that it has made me a better prescriber.

Common misconceptions and myths relating to ADHD medications

1. ***Adults with 'so-called' ADHD are just trying to get stimulant medication to get 'high' or to give them an advantage.*** ADHD commonly co-occurs with substance use disorder and, in general, treating the former improves the latter. Most of those who take stimulants for their ADHD use them appropriately. However, given that these

medications do have abuse potential, caution is required to prevent 'diversion' for abuse or, more commonly, for cognitive enhancement.

2. ***ADHD medications have terrible side effects and they are addictive.*** In general, medications prescribed for ADHD are well tolerated, and typically only cause mild to moderate adverse effects. And, when used appropriately, ADHD medications are not addictive. In fact, quite the opposite – there is data indicating that they are actually protective against addiction.

3. ***Taking ADHD medication reduces creativity.*** This is a commonly cited concern, but, in my experience, it is not generally the case. For most, assuming that the dose has been optimised properly, medication typically facilitates the expression of the individual's creativity where it previously couldn't shine through. There are some, for example comedians and musicians, who report that they perform better when they are not medicated, but this is only a minority.

The medications prescribed for ADHD can be very effective, but they do need to be treated with respect, and only initiated by a specialist prescriber in ADHD. They must be used safely and appropriately, with the necessary monitoring. I really do not recommend trying medication given to you by a friend or family member. This unsupervised use can be risky, as you are likely to misjudge the dosing and, regardless, it usually takes weeks to find an optimal dose. Additionally, despite what you may have been told, taking a single dose of stimulant medication is not a reliable way of working out whether you have ADHD. The 'Ten Domains of Dysregulation' explored in Part 1 are a much better guide.

Start low, and go slow

A brief but important and personal aside, as I think there is a crucial learning point here: for reasons that I explained in Pillar 6 (see pages 203–4), I am very sensitive to medication. It took a little while, and a few bumps along the way, for me to realise that I only needed tiny doses of stimulant, otherwise the side effects obscured any benefits.

After many years working in this field, I can tell you that I am not alone in this regard. Many adults with ADHD are super sensitive, again for complicated and fascinating reasons. I suspect that a fair number may have been unduly scared off by inexperienced and over-zealous prescribers. In order to identify and appropriately adjust for those who are more sensitive, it is vital to 'start low, and go slow'.

Medication that is prescribed for ADHD falls into two broad categories: **stimulants** and **non-stimulants**. They are very different indeed, and there is good evidence to support the use of both types, but more and stronger evidence when it comes to stimulants.

Unless there is a good reason *not* to use them, the first-line choice has traditionally been stimulant medication (the 'extended-release' or long-duration form specifically – see opposite for detail). This is due to the weight of evidence supporting their use and the fact that multiple studies have shown them to be more effective than non-stimulants.

The stimulants include methylphenidate and dexamphetamine. The commonly used non-stimulant medications include atomoxetine, bupropion and guanfacine. (Of these, there is most evidence for atomoxetine. Guanfacine, and to a lesser extent atomoxetine, can have mildly sedative and anti-anxiety effects in some.) NICE has some useful information on medications commonly prescribed in the UK on its website, as does the website medicines.org.uk/emc (see Resources, page 288).

Be aware that medication options and dosing guidance may differ between countries.

Stimulant medications

One way these medications work is by increasing the availability of the chemicals dopamine and noradrenaline across the brain. These 'neurotransmitters' are dysregulated in ADHD. Stimulant medications work quickly, in a similar way to caffeine, and their effects wear off after a few hours. Exactly how long they remain active for, along with how much is 'loaded' upfront (relative to how much is released gradually over the subsequent hours) defines the preparation's 'release profile'. Your prescriber should recommend a preparation based on your specific needs in terms of coverage and, of course, local availability.

Due to their potential for abuse (only) if misused, all stimulants are classified as 'controlled drugs'. This means there are specific rules that govern exactly how they are prescribed and dispensed. In the UK, these rules include the requirement for the prescription to be written in a particular way, and the fact it becomes invalidated after 28 days if it hasn't been used. The duration of the prescription is limited to no more than 30 days, unless 'exceptional circumstances' are documented. Controlled medications are kept locked away by the pharmacy, and there may be a little more scrutiny by the dispensing pharmacist until they get to know you.

You can either get stimulant preparations with a short duration (called 'immediate release') or ones that have a longer duration (called 'extended or modified release').

Immediate-release (IR) preparations

These are usually taken three – occasionally four – times a day, typically in the morning, lunchtime and mid-afternoon. The effects of a single dose last between three and five hours, depending on the drug (IR dexamfetamine, e.g. *Amfexa*, lasts a bit longer than IR methlyphenidate, e.g. *Ritalin*). They are fiddlier to manage and, because of the multiple dosing points, sticking to the schedule can be a challenge for those with ADHD, and dosing timings need to be firmly anchored into your daily schedule, with visual (and, if necessary, alarm) reminders. Some, however, prefer the degree of control these preparations confer and, in the right hands, the regimen can be carefully tailored to one's requirements. IR preparations don't tend to be offered as a 'first-line' medication for ease but also safety as they can be more easily manipulated and misused. Extended-release preparations require less frequent dosing and are easier to manage.

Extended-release (ER) preparations

ER stimulants, such as lisdexamfetamine (e.g. *Elvanse Adult*) and a range of preparations of methylphenidate (e.g. *Equasym XL, Medikinet XL, Concerta XL, Delmosart XL* and so on), give between 6 and 14 hours coverage, depending on the release profile. They may provide sufficient coverage alone as a once-daily dose, taken in the morning. However, in adults, they are commonly 'topped up' with an IR, to extend the coverage by a few hours. In some, two successive doses of ER preparations (usually not the longer acting ones) are used to ensure sufficient coverage. Remember that most of these ER medications were originally designed for children, with the school day in mind. It is understandable, therefore, that the way they are used may need to be adapted for adults who will often need to focus well into the early evening hours.

If there is a poor response to the first stimulant tried, you would typically try the other one, before possibly moving to a trial of one of the non-stimulants.

The IR stimulants usually take about 20–30 minutes to start showing an effect, while the ER stimulants take a little longer – anything from 45 to 60 minutes and they take an hour or two to reach peak concentrations in the bloodstream, and then the effects are sustained for a period.

As the stimulant levels in the blood start waning, you will start to notice your underlying ADHD symptoms resurfacing. For most, this is a gradual and nonintrusive transition, but for others it feels like 'falling off a cliff edge'. Where there is a dramatic or uncomfortable 'kick back' as the effects of the medication wear off, people are said to experience 'rebound symptoms'. This can sometimes be effectively managed by adding in a small dose of IR medication to soften the gradient of the drop-off.

Everyone's metabolism, which is genetically determined, is different. It is not yet possible to accurately establish who will respond best to which medication. It is also not possible to predict dose requirements and, importantly, it is not influenced by your weight or size, as you might expect. This is another reason why it is sensible to start with a low dose and increase gradually.

Non-stimulant medications

These act more like antidepressants, working in similar but slightly different ways to the stimulants. Importantly, none of them are controlled drugs, as they cannot be abused. These medications take much longer to show their full effect (weeks to months), but, once established, they have more sustained and consistent levels in the blood than stimulants, typically providing round-the-clock coverage. Unlike the stimulants, these medications do not exert their effects over the whole brain, explaining their lack of abuse potential.

Non-stimulants are generally considered third-line, after both of the stimulants have been tried and have either been ineffective or were not tolerated (causing unacceptable side effects, like severe anxiety). There are, however, reasons why some choose them over stimulants:

- If there is a coexistent anxiety disorder (and concerns about aggravating it).
- If medication adherence is a concern (timing is less critical with non-stimulants).
- Where there are concerns about stimulant misuse or diversion, or the individual doesn't feel comfortable taking stimulants (for example, if they have struggled with street stimulant misuse in the past).
- If stable, 24-hour control of symptoms is specifically required (for example, to protect against evening substance use).

Safety of ADHD medications

As discussed, stimulants (especially IR stimulants) do have abuse potential, and with prolonged use of unnecessarily high doses, or when misused, they are likely to cause tolerance and dependence. In my experience, this is not such a common issue clinically, but, by definition, the patients I see have a clinician carefully overseeing things, which may mitigate this risk.

Taking higher than prescribed doses of stimulants, using them in an irresponsible fashion or in a way that they were not designed is clearly unwise. They may trigger other serious mental health problems including addiction and, in those with additional risk factors, could result in cardiovascular dysfunction.

When it comes to the cumulative direct health impact of ADHD medication, a 2023 study showed that long-term exposure was associated with an increased risk of cardiovascular disease, especially high blood pressure, and its bedfellow, arterial disease. It did suggest that obesity and smoking seemed to mediate the risk, which is important to know. There was no increased risk of heart rhythm problems, which was a reassuring finding.

There is no good evidence to indicate that ADHD medications permanently change the levels of brain chemicals or receptors in the brain, but there are some early and somewhat concerning findings (from a 2019 US database study) that they may be associated with an increased risk of Parkinson's disease, a finding that needs further investigation.

When weighing up whether or not to try ADHD medication, you may find yourself worrying about these possible long-term adverse effects, but it is very important that you counterbalance these (not as yet fully founded) concerns against those already very well-documented complications and negative outcomes that are associated with untreated ADHD, that we've explored throughout this book, and the considerable body of evidence that shows that medication significantly reduces these risks. Like everything in life, there is a sensitive balance to be struck.

When it comes to ADHD with moderate to severe levels of impairment, based on the available science, and if used responsibly, I believe the benefits of trying ADHD medication probably still outweigh the risks. This may of course change with further study.

Side effects of ADHD medications

Stimulant and non-stimulant medications are associated with a range of potential side effects, which are typically reported as mild and self-limiting.

Common side effects of stimulant medications include:

- a slight increase of blood pressure and pulse
- headache
- reduced appetite (possibly with associated weight loss)
- palpitations
- nausea/vomiting/stomach ache
- diarrhoea
- dry mouth
- insomnia
- irritability/mood changes

- cough/inflammation of the nose or throat
- sexual side effects (for example, erectile dysfunction, reduced libido)

Common side effects associated with atomoxetine, the most commonly used non-stimulant, include:

- nausea
- decreased appetite
- dry mouth
- headache
- insomnia
- fatigue
- erectile dysfunction
- a slight increase of blood pressure and pulse

Is medication something I should consider?

Taking medication is not for everyone, but it can be very helpful for many. For some, it can be a game-changer. I have heard it described as being like 'putting on prescription glasses for the first time'. Importantly, by trying it out you are not committing to taking it long term.

The truth of the matter is that, for many, medication can come at a slight cost. This may be in terms of the side effects it causes (see above), but also factors like stigma, cost and the potential physical health problems that *may* be associated with taking the medication long term, such as the strain stimulants may be putting on the cardiovascular system. As already stated, I am generally in favour of offering medication to patients where it feels clinically indicated. I suggest, however, that my patients do their own reading around the topic, and that they do not rush into the decision.

Some just don't seem to tolerate medication well and, despite best efforts, can't find a drug that hits that all-important 'sweet spot'; essentially, a medication that does what it is meant to do, and doesn't have troubling side effects. If you are really lucky, you may 'hit gold' on your first medication trial, with no obvious nega-tive effects or downsides, but this is not that common. If you decide to try medication, this must happen under the guidance of an ADHD specialist. You will need your blood pressure, pulse and weight checked to get a baseline (off medication), and then rechecked with every dose change and then at six-monthly inter-vals once stable. It is important to ensure that these parameters remain within the normal range. Stimulants and some non-stimulants can cause a slight increase to blood pressure and pulse, which is generally not a problem unless the readings are already high, or borderline high.

There is obviously an upfront investment of your time when trying out ADHD medication. However, once you have identified the drug and dose that suits you best, you may not need to make any further changes for years to come. In my experience, used correctly, it is uncommon for people to develop significant toler-ance to their ADHD medication, including stimulant medication, which would be indicated by increasing dose requirements over time.

I have supported quite a few ADHD patients over the years who have made the decision not to take medication for a variety of reasons, including:

- concern about side effects
- fear of 'getting addicted'
- worry about long-term negative effects
- anxiety about one's personality being altered or feeling 'controlled'

Instead, they rely on non-medication interventions – including some of those explored in the seven pillars. I have seen examples of this working reasonably well, particularly when the individual has the right mindset, is sufficiently motivated and committed to change, and they follow a structured approach.

Why non-medication interventions are important in ADHD

1. Non-medication interventions, some of which have been demonstrated to improve the quality of life of patients, should (according to the NICE guidelines) always form part of the standard 'multimodal' treatment approach in ADHD.
2. Some of those who try medication either don't respond or respond poorly.
3. Even with a decent response to medication, there are usually residual symptoms and difficulties that will need addressing.

ADHD is a strongly genetic condition that involves disordered brain physiology. Particularly for those with more severe forms of the disorder, it is sometimes not possible to override these powerful biological drives, however much positive thinking willpower and strategising you throw into the mix. If psychosocial interventions alone are going to work, I think there needs to be a well thought through and multi-faceted approach.

THERAPIES AND COACHING

Therapies and coaching for adult ADHD include the following:

- psychoeducation
- cognitive behavioural interventions
- coaching-based approaches

- group-based, dialectical behavioural therapy (DBT)
- mindfulness-based interventions

Most of these approaches share common threads, such as:

- self-care and lifestyle management
- self-development (often employing a strengths-based approach)
- emotional regulation
- problem-solving (and the application of compensatory strategies that target problem areas)
- communication skills training and other practical (executive function) skills training (such as organisational skills and time management)

Unfortunately, there is not presently a great deal of compelling data to support the apparent value of some of these approaches in reducing the symptoms of ADHD. In most of the well-conducted studies, the benefits are no real comparison to medication and, in some cases, any clear benefit is yet to be properly demonstrated.

In defence of the therapies, this is quite a tricky area to study well. Perhaps the right variable is not yet being measured or the right questions asked. Admittedly, there is a lot less data overall for these approaches, primarily because there are far fewer industry-sponsored studies. There is no getting away from the fact, however, that the available data generally indicates relatively small gains (mainly impacting quality of life), in the absence of concurrent medication.

There is probably most evidence supporting what we call 'psychoeducation' (this includes learning about the disorder, understanding how it affects the brain/mind and exploring how best to manage it), which is very much the thrust of this book.

There is some evidence supporting individual and group-based cognitive behavioural interventions (with a degree of extrapolation to coaching-based approaches, which similarly focus on executive function skills for life management). There is also some limited evidence supporting group-based therapy, DBT, and early but cautiously encouraging data in support of meditation-based interventions, such as mindfulness training.

I suspect, however, that when you take a more multidimensional approach to intervention, and combine structured, high-quality ADHD-specific psychotherapy or coaching with committed lifestyle optimisation, creative and targeted workarounds, and the right mindset, the subject of the seven pillars, the results may prove to be a little more impressive. This is in line with my observations, both in terms of my own personal journey and my patients' experiences.

If you are lucky enough to get as far as the diagnosis stage, the unfortunate reality on the ground is that you are unlikely to be offered a comprehensive menu of non-medication-based interventions. Most individuals seeking support through the NHS can expect a primary focus on prescribing, and little else. Things may be slightly better in the private sector. This reality is the main reason I decided to write this book, so try not to lose hope.

Technologies

There is unfortunately currently not enough evidence to confidently recommend the use of **neurofeedback** (a form of 'biofeedback' in which people respond to a display of their own brain waves, often in the form of a computerised game, boosting activity in certain ADHD brain regions in the process) or **brain training** (which specifically targets 'working memory' faculties and the brain's ability to inhibit or slow down). These approaches are, however, being refined and enhanced.

There is some very early but reasonably interesting data on **neuromodulation**, a group of approaches that use electrical current (and in some cases magnetism) in various applications. The 'neuromodulatory' approaches that seem to hold promise in ADHD include:

- Transcranial Magnetic Stimulation (TMS)
- Transcranial Direct Current Stimulation (tDCS)
- Transcranial Random Noise Stimulation (TRNS)

You may be relieved to learn that electroconvulsive therapy or ECT (the barbaric-looking electric shock treatment portrayed in films like *One Flew Over the Cuckoo's Nest*) is not one of them!

There is early but pretty robust data supporting the use of Alpha-Stim as a treatment for generalised anxiety (see page 220 and Resources, page 289), and the NHS is exploring its wider application beyond this indication at the time of writing. Where I have used it in my ADHD patients (as a treatment for coexistent anxiety), it has appeared to have broader-reaching regulatory effects, impacting other ADHD symptoms in a positive way. I have seen quite compelling results in the domains of emotion, activity and sleep. It clearly needs further study before it can be routinely recommended for ADHD, but it may be worth a try if you also struggle with anxiety.

As you can see, there are a range of options for treating ADHD, but, at present, medication is by far the most commonly employed one, due to the weight of evidence behind it. Optimal management is more nuanced than shifting the biology alone, though, and there is undoubtedly a role for both therapeutic interventions and lifelong self-management, underpinned by high-quality psychoeducation.

In the next and final chapter, we will think about when things don't quite go to plan, and what you can do about it.

CREATIVE WORKAROUNDS FOR STUBBORN SYMPTOMS

Taken together, the seven pillars in Part 2 provide a framework for living well with adult ADHD. Medication may have also taken you part of the journey. However, even with what might be considered an optimised treatment approach, invariably there will be some lingering symptoms and problem behaviours left in place. The good news is that, once the ground has been cleared and some of the symptoms have been modified using the approaches that have been discussed, these leftover problems can be more easily evaluated and effectively targeted with focused interventions.

Problems that prove particularly stubborn and difficult to shift may get in the way of long-term stability. It is crucial, therefore, to identify these barriers as early as possible, with a generous serving of honesty and humility. In my experience, some of the more persistent symptoms and behaviours include the following. Perhaps you can relate to some of these?

- procrastination
- time blindness
- forgetfulness
- episodic impulsive mishaps
- tendency to feel overwhelm (especially at times of stress)
- addiction-related issues
- low self-esteem/self-belief

Exercise: Identify your barriers
In your Thrive Journal, take some time now to map out your current areas of difficulty or struggle. You can then try to target them systematically with creative workarounds and compensatory strategies, which we'll look at next.

It Is vitally important to work out what went wrong and to forgive yourself when you occasionally trip up. Your challenge is to find novel and creative counterstrategies that really work for you, adapting them over time, or perhaps to simply accept that you can't win them all and get on with it.

CREATIVE WORKAROUNDS

A few years after my diagnosis, when I understood myself and my ADHD better, I made the decision to cease endlessly battling to overcome certain challenges that had plagued my life for years, and instead started trying to find workarounds. And rather than only working to change myself, I shifted the emphasis onto making the necessary adaptations to my external world, so that I no longer had to do the things I really struggled with (as much).

A creative workaround sometimes involves finding a way of not having to deal with a problem anymore, but not in a manner that will have any negative consequences.

On the next page, I introduce a handful of creative workarounds that may help with issues such as procrastination, time blindness, forgetfulness, impulsive mishaps, overwhelm and low self-esteem. Please remember this is not an exhaustive list. These are some of the main clusters of workarounds, but of course, there are scores more. On page 276, I have provided some tips on dealing with addiction-related issues, as this is such a common area of difficulty in those with adult ADHD (see page 46).

Making use of automation and notifications

It is great practice to automate as many routine tasks as possible. This can involve the use of technology, including AI, but automation may be as simple as setting a series of notifications and reminders on your phone. This is particularly useful for prescription alerts, dental appointments, car service prompts and birthday or anniversary reminders. It is a good idea to routinely request reminder texts or emails for all appointments and renewals, where this is an option. Make sure the devices you use synchronise and talk to each other, and that data can be easily shared with others where necessary.

You can minimise late-payment chases by setting up direct debits and standing orders to make it all happen automatically (automated payments), and make use of apps which alert you before you go into the red zone in your bank account. Where possible, I would recommend that you arrange for your salary to get paid directly into your account, simplifying processes and cutting out the need for you to do anything, leaving less room for error (or diversion of funds for impulsive end-of-month spending sprees). Apps that monitor and limit screen time or access to social media can be really helpful if this is an area of vulnerability for you.

AI tools like virtual assistants and ChatGPT, if used creatively, can save you lots of time. Whether it is managing schedules or organising tasks and information, there are increasingly sophisticated approaches out there that, in time, are likely to prove invaluable for those with ADHD. Try to get on board with the latest technology to give yourself an edge during this transitional period. A note of caution however: try to keep tech solutions really simple, at least when getting started.

Outsourcing (or delegating)

Where necessary, and possible, you may judge that it is preferable to employ or pay others to do jobs you really hate or particularly struggle with. This could include things like ironing, bookkeeping, gardening, home repairs or keeping you active (via a personal trainer), and so on. This clearly depends on your financial situation and is not an option for everyone. When weighing up whether to retain or outsource responsibility, it helps to determine what monetary value you assign to your time and work out what your priorities are.

In a work or educational setting, if you are fortunate enough to have resource to help minimise your impairment, bring people in who will be able to provide support in the areas that you struggle with most. Be sure to approach this outsourcing with abundant humility and without any shame whatsoever.

Skill-sharing/trading

Another creative way of outsourcing is to trade your time and expertise with friends, colleagues or family members who have different, and perhaps complementary, skills and interests. If your best friend loves numbers and spreadsheets, and you can't think of anything better than being outside in nature and getting your hands dirty, why don't you consider trading the completion of your tax return with a day's work clearing weeds in their garden? Then everyone's a winner!

Co-working, body doubling and accountability partnering

These deceptively simple and remarkably effective strategies are increasingly recognised within the adult ADHD community as a way of boosting efficiency and productivity. The shared concept is simple: the presence of another person (or people) in your immediate environment (in person or on-screen) increases your ability to focus, get tasks done and achieve goals. It can encourage a 'flow state', a term defined by psychologist Mihaly Csikszentmihalyi that describes a low-anxiety state where you feel 'in the zone'.

It is partly to do with accountability, but may also be a result of the physiological safety blanket of co-regulation – the containment and security felt when in the proximity of others. You can 'body double' with friends, family members or even complete strangers (there are apps designed for this – see Resources on page 291), but it is important to limit chit-chat during sessions.

Let it be seen (or heard) at the point of action

The problem in ADHD is usually in the execution of tasks, rather than a lack of awareness of what needs to be done. It can be helpful to place reminders and 'messages to self' at the point of action in a tangible form; something that can be seen or heard, to make you pause, reflect and, where required, redirect yourself. Those messages may be in the form of a pre-programmed notification on your phone, a Post-it note strategically located, a blob of Blue-tack stuck to your bank card (to remind you to question purchases), the jolting buzz of a timer to bring you out of hyperfocus or even a whispered code word or gesture from a loved one. The point is to make you stop and *think* (to inhibit), perhaps averting a knee-jerk response which may have damaging downstream consequences.

Exercise: Identify your hotspots

Take a moment to think about some of your 'hot-spots' – situations or activities where things have gone wrong in the past. What learnings have you extracted from these recurring mishaps? What could you have done differently? What reminders could you put in place at the point of action for next time? Try to vividly imagine the alternative scenario, engaging positive emotions like joy and relief. Remember, strong emotion often serves to supercharge motivation.

Admitting your struggle to others

When you are really overwhelmed and not sure where to turn, sometimes the best thing is to just open up and share what's going on for you with select others. Whether it is a partner, parent or family doctor, let them know that you are in need of some extra support. Asking for help is not weakness. Far from it. In my book, it is a true sign of strength and an essential ingredient when nurturing the growth-oriented mindset we discussed in Pillar 1.

Taking time out to 'reset'

When everything feels like it is getting a bit too much, another strategy is to take a break. When you are feeling uncomfortably 'full' it is often a sign that you need to take some leave from work – or do something to break the cycle, to change things up and reboot. If you are able to get away for a few days, even better. Where you can, try to leave things in your wake in a healthy state, handing projects over to others, if this is an option.

Scheduling daily or weekly check-ins

If there is someone who you want or need to stay in touch with, and you know you struggle in this area, you may want to consider scheduling a rolling, daily or weekly call (or video conference call) at a fixed time. This way it is far more likely to happen (and you don't need to think about it). This strategy can be particularly helpful in a work or academic setting, with agreed brief weekly or daily check-ins with your up-line or supervisor. You can set goals and review progress, making it much more likely that you will stay on track.

TACKLING ADDICTION

As we've discussed, addiction and addictive behaviours are such complex and multifaceted problems, with so much potential to sabotage progress in those with ADHD. I am, of course, aware that not everyone with ADHD will struggle in this area, but many do, and a surprising number do not even realise that they have an addiction issue or are too ashamed to admit it to themselves.

Adults with ADHD often migrate to substances that have a stimulant effect, like nicotine, caffeine and cocaine, in addition to those that have more of a 'depressant' or calming effect, such as cannabis. In addition to alcohol, I also see quite a lot of misuse of benzodiazepines (such as Valium and sleeping tablets).

As well as substance-related addictions, there are a broad range of behavioural or 'process' addictions, such as those outlined on page 46. The truth is that you can get addicted to just about anything! It's all about dopamine, and how quickly it spikes in the blood and, in turn, the brain. Individuals may find that using these substances or behaviours helps them to function in situations they previously struggled in, but sometimes at a significant cost.

Below are my **top tips for approaching addiction**:

1. Addiction is a self-perpetuating cycle: withdrawal drives usage, which generates withdrawal, and so on . . . At some point, this never-ending cycle will need to be interrupted and broken. It is important to recognise that **to make a change you are going to need to be proactive**. Once you are stuck in the addictive loop, nothing is going to happen without a clear-cut decision to make a change.

2. If you are struggling to decide what to do, take a few moments to **weigh up the pros and cons of your struggle** (ideally on paper, in black and white, and possibly in discussion with an understanding loved one). Be truthful about the downsides and negatives, but also about the things that benefit you and keep you going back for more. Develop a curiosity about your behaviours and drives, but ensure you keep the self-compassion rolling at all times. It is not your fault that you are

in this situation, but it is your responsibility to try to navigate out of it.

3. Prior to making the decision to abstain from something, preferably with the **support of others** (either within one-to-one therapy or a group programme), try to **acknowledge, understand and address the psychological aspects** of the addiction. Be sure to maintain that support throughout the recovery process. And remember, there are two separate stages to navigate: (i) the giving up phase, and (ii) the maintenance phase.

4. When you ultimately decide to stop doing something, you are going to need to commit to it fully. Don't waste your time and energy looking back and grieving your loss. And **do not question your decision**, as it was made with the benefit of a clear and rational perspective, over a period of time. You have already established that it is the right decision, so the job now is simple and unambiguous – to stick with it.

5. To avoid being triggered it is sensible to **keep your distance from those who are actively engaging in the behaviour you are trying to avoid**. This can be difficult if your friendships have formed around your addiction, and you may need to avoid certain people, at least for a period. The reality is that friendships often change when making such a transformative shift in the way you lead your life. If a friend doesn't accept your decision to abstain, and they actively try to entice you back in (which is often the case, and primarily linked to their fear of being left alone in the ditch), then you really need to discuss this openly with them, and, if they persist, question how much of a friend they really are.

6. Don't forget that the very essence of addiction is an inability to regulate or manage certain behaviours, with obvious overlaps with ADHD. It is important to get it very clear in your mind that, once you have decided to stop, **there is no such thing as 'just one more ...'** and no 'special occasion' that warrants you

abandoning ship! Remember, when it comes to addiction you are often either 'in' or 'out'.

7. **If you are struggling with your decision to remain abstinent:**
   - In the moment, try to breathe and stay present. Avoid making any rash decisions.
   - Call someone you can speak openly with about how you are feeling, which will impose an all-important delay.
   - Just take one day at a time . . . and keep going.
   - Try to reframe how you think about your decision. Rather than viewing it as a 'loss', spend your time emphasising the very real gains.
   - If finances are an issue, and you think it will help motivate you, calculate how much money you have saved on a weekly or monthly basis.
   - If you are a visual person, keep a calendar on the wall and tick off each day you maintain abstinence.
   - It helps to expect, but not fear, a period of mild withdrawal-linked discomfort that occurs after you give up something your system has acclimatised to – you may experience anxiety, irritability, frustration, sometimes intense but usually brief cravings, desperate loneliness, sleep disruption and even depression. It may help to redefine any discomfort you experience as your body ridding itself of nasty toxins, and remind yourself that it is short-lived.
   - Drink plenty of water, eat well and exercise daily if possible.
   - Be mindful not to replace one addiction with another, which is a common pitfall!

8. **Try not to fall into the trap of waiting for something to happen.** For this reason, it is generally not a good idea to set yourself a goal of staying abstinent for x months, as, when you meet this target, you may feel as if you have 'arrived', unwittingly giving yourself permission to 'celebrate' your achievement with the very thing you gave up.

9. **Be particularly vigilant at times of high stress, personal crisis or loss.** When you are feeling desperate or fearful, your guard will be down and you will be far more vulnerable to relapse.

10. **If you do relapse** (or lapse, the term used for a brief relapse), **try not to beat yourself up.** By its very nature, addiction is a relapsing and remitting condition, so it may well happen. If you do have a slip-up, what is important is that you learn from it and consider what you might have done differently. This will help to refine your approach and hopefully protect against it happening again.

If you are struggling with addiction of any form, there is absolutely nothing to feel shameful about, and there are plenty of organisations out there to help (see Resources, page 287).

When faced with any of these stubborn residual difficulties, especially where you believe you have exceeded your personal resources, it may be time to **ask for help**. Depending on the issue, maybe chat with your GP, arrange to see an adult ADHD coach or look for a group programme to join. It can be validating and de-stigmatising to meet others who can relate to your struggles and provide support.

CONCLUSION:
A PATH FORWARD ILLUMINATED

A wave of profound emotion hits me as I sit here, putting pen to paper for the last time, as I guide this book to its close. I imagine how you may be feeling right now. So many words to digest and ideas to grapple with. And so much to do! *Where to start?* You may be thinking. I get it!

An ancient philosophical idea I came across many years ago left a real impression on me; so much so that I wish to share it with you at this poignant moment. It relates to the manner in which change, and personal growth, often manifests. It is a story of *two lights*.

The first light is a spectacularly bright light, and it represents the output of the first phase of a process of change. Sometimes, following only a minimal input of effort, things may suddenly appear to be going to plan. For what turns out to be a brief window, the first light shines brightly and fills the space. Then, without warning, the plug is pulled, and the light brutally withdrawn. The rug has been ripped from under you.

To illustrate my point, I want you to imagine a determined toddler who, with great effort, manages to claw himself up the arm of the sofa and then stand, unaided. His father quickly takes his hand and supports him to take a few magical steps. The child's excitement is palpable, pure ecstasy in his eyes. But then, his father gently detaches and the child stumbles and tumbles to the ground, incensed. The bright light, representative of his sheer delight, has been all but extinguished.

Something important, though, has taken place. The experience represented by this extreme but short-lived illumination has given the child direction. It has highlighted the endpoint, the goal, mapping out a path that was not previously obvious. It is now that the real work begins, and this is where the second light comes into the frame.

This time the light begins as a mere, almost imperceptible glow, and only very slowly and gradually brightens. This time round it takes sustained effort, and a good deal of patience, to get anywhere near the previous level of brightness, and it is not so straightforward getting there.

The child in our story, due to his father's bittersweet intervention, has been shown what he needs to do, where he needs to go. A path has been lit, energised by that moment of elation, however brief, now etched into the conscious and subconscious pathways of his developing brain, serving as a guiding force. The child works hard but it is slow going, with frustrating setbacks. He knows where he is headed now, though. He realises that it is possible, and that if he is prepared to put in the effort, he can get there.

I encourage you to see your first read of this book as the first light – a brief illumination of the road ahead, a look at how the land lies and a menu of options open to you. Having reached this point, you should certainly feel a sense of achievement. Even if you retain only a scattering of the material I have shared, you will be in a stronger position, with a clearer idea of where you are headed (unless, that is, you have just started reading, and jumped straight to the end to see how the book finishes – funny old thing ADHD!)

As you broach these closing words, instead of thinking the job is done and preparing to move on to other endeavours, I challenge you instead to shift to phase two of this lightshow. This is where the work really begins but, hopefully, the journey feels less daunting now. There are the makings of a plan of action. It is going to take a little work and perseverance, but that's okay.

My recommendation is, that after a brief period of reflection, you turn back to Pillar 1 and initiate your second read, with the goal of reviewing, integrating and implementing. Small incremental shifts, unfolding gradually one after another. Keep writing in your Thrive Journal and making tweaks and refinements to how you manage things to work best for you. The light might seem small right now, but think where it can go – a glittering palace of possibilities and potential, drawing you in, one small step at a time.

APPENDIX:
DSM-5 CRITERIA FOR ADHD

Below, I have included the specific wording of the six *DSM-5* criteria (**Criteria A to E**) that must be met in order for a diagnosis of ADHD to be made, which we discussed in Part 1 (see pages 59–63). Some of the examples shown in brackets after each listed symptom relate to adults.

CRITERIA A

A persistent pattern of inattention and/or hyperactivity-impulsivity that interferes with functioning or development, as characterised by (1) and/or (2):

1. **Inattention:** Six (or more) of the following symptoms have persisted for at least six months to a degree that is inconsistent with developmental level and that negatively impacts directly on social and academic/occupational activities:
    [Note: The symptoms are not solely a manifestation of oppositional behaviour, defiance, hostility or failure to understand tasks or instructions. For older adolescents and adults (age 17 and older), at least five symptoms are required.]
    a. Often fails to give close attention to details or makes careless mistakes in schoolwork, at work or during other activities (e.g., overlooks or misses details, work is inaccurate).

b. Often has difficulty sustaining attention in tasks or play activities (e.g., has difficulty remaining focused during lectures, conversations or lengthy reading).

c. Often does not seem to listen when spoken to directly (e.g., mind seems elsewhere, even in the absence of any obvious distraction).

d. Often does not follow through on instructions and fails to finish schoolwork, chores or duties in the workplace (e.g., starts tasks but quickly loses focus and is easily sidetracked).

e. Often has difficulty organising tasks and activities (e.g., difficulty managing sequential tasks; difficulty keeping materials and belongings in order; messy, disorganised work; has poor time management; fails to meet deadlines).

f. Often avoids, dislikes or is reluctant to engage in tasks that require sustained mental effort (e.g., schoolwork or homework; for older adolescents and adults, preparing reports, completing forms, reviewing lengthy papers).

g. Often loses things necessary for tasks or activities (e.g., school materials, pencils, books, tools, wallets, keys, paperwork, eyeglasses, mobile phones).

h. Is often easily distracted by extraneous stimuli (for older adolescents and adults, may include unrelated thoughts).

i. Is often forgetful in daily activities (e.g., doing chores, running errands; for older adolescents and adults, returning calls, paying bills, keeping appointments).

2. **Hyperactivity and impulsivity:** Six (or more) of the following symptoms have persisted for at least six months to a degree that is inconsistent with developmental level and that negatively impacts directly on social and academic/occupational activities:

[Note: The symptoms are not solely a manifestation of oppositional behaviour, defiance, hostility or failure to understand tasks or instructions. For older adolescents and adults (age 17 and older), at least five symptoms are required.]

a. Often fidgets with or taps hands or feet or squirms in seat.

b. Often leaves seat in situations when remaining seated is expected (e.g., leaves their place in the classroom, in the office or other workplace, or in other situations that require remaining in place).

c. Often runs about or climbs in situations where it is inappropriate. (Note: In adolescents or adults, may be limited to feeling restless.)

d. Often unable to play or engage in leisure activities quietly.

e. Is often 'on the go', acting as if 'driven by a motor' (e.g., is unable to be or uncomfortable being still for an extended time, as in restaurants or meetings; may be experienced by others as being restless or difficult to keep up with).

f. Often talks excessively.

g. Often blurts out an answer before a question has been completed (e.g., completes people's sentences; cannot wait for turn in conversation).

h. Often has difficulty waiting their turn (e.g., while waiting in line).

i. Often interrupts or intrudes on others (e.g., may butt into conversations, games or activities; may start using other people's things without asking or receiving permission; for adolescents and adults, may intrude into or take over what others are doing).

CRITERIA B

Several inattentive or hyperactive-impulsive symptoms were present prior to age 12 years.

CRITERIA C

Several inattentive or hyperactive-impulsive symptoms are present in two or more settings (e.g., at home, school or work; with friends or relatives; in other activities).

CRITERIA D

There is clear evidence that the symptoms interfere with, or reduce the quality of, social, academic or occupational function.

CRITERIA E

The symptoms do not occur exclusively during the course of schizophrenia or another psychotic disorder, and are not better explained by another mental disorder (e.g., mood disorder, anxiety disorder, dissociative disorder, personality disorder, substance intoxication or withdrawal).

RESOURCES

ADDICTION SUPPORT

Alcoholics Anonymous
National: 0800 917 7650, London: 020 7407 9217
https://www.alcoholics-anonymous.org.uk/

FRANK (Drugs)
0300 123 6600
https://www.talktofrank.com/

MIND
https://www.mind.org.uk/information-support/types-of-mental-health-problems/recreational-drugs-alcohol-and-addiction

Narcotics Anonymous
0300 999 1212
https://ukna.org/

The NHS Stopping Smoking Service
0300 123 1044
https://www.nhs.uk/better-health/quit-smoking/

The Samaritans
116 123
https://www.samaritans.org/

ADHD MEDICATION INFORMATION

Electronic Medicines Compendium
https://www.medicines.org.uk/emc

National Institute for Health and Care Excellence
https://bnf.nice.org.uk/treatment-summaries/attention-deficit-hyperactivity-disorder/

HRV MONITORING

HeartMath Institute
https://www.heartmath.org/

Oura Ring
https://ouraring.com/

WHOOP wristband
https://www.whoop.com/gb/en/

NUTRITION

Environmental Working Group (for Dirty Dozen and Clean 15)
https://www.ewg.org/

Ingrid Kitzing (Functional Medicine practitioner)
https://www.ingridkitzingnutrition.co.uk/

Supplements
http://www.amritanutrition.co.uk (for 10% off, register on first visit to the website using the invite code THRIVE)

SENSORY AIDS AND EMOTIONAL REGULATION

Acupoint tapping (Emotional Freedom Techniques)
https://www.thetappingsolution.com/ (for learning basic EFT)
https://www.theenergytherapycentre.co.uk/ or https://www.thegrovepractice.com/courses (for training in EFT for ADHD)

Alpha-Stim (Cranial Electrotherapy Stimulation)
https://themicrocurrentsite.co.uk/ (15% discount code: THRIVEADHD)

Body Braid
https://bodybraid.com/ (10% discount code: THRIVEADHD)

Power Plate
https://powerplate.co.uk/

Regulate Training (advanced emotional regulation skills for professionals)
https://www.thegrovepractice.com/training/regulate

Sensate 2
(10% discount code: THRIVEADHD)
https://www.getsensate.com/THRIVEADHD (non-USA)
https://www.us.getsensate.com/THRIVEADHD (USA)

Solo-Soma (for full video download)
https://www.thegrovepractice.com/self-study-courses/

TESTING

ADHD questionnaires and screening tools
https://www.caddra.ca/etoolkit-forms/

Genova Diagnostics
https://www.gdx.net/

Lifecode G^x
https://www.lifecodegx.com/

Mosaic Diagnostics
https://mosaicdx.com/

Zinc Taste Test
https://www.lambertshealthcare.co.uk/minerals/zinc/zincatest/

TOXICITY AND ALLERGY

Allergy support (testing, purifiers and more)
https://www.allergybestbuys.co.uk/

Book: Goodman, J., *Staying Alive in Toxic Times: A seasonal guide to lifelong health* (Yellow Kite, 2021)

Dr Sarah Myhill
https://www.drmyhill.co.uk/

Infrared Sauna
https://www.sunlighten.com/ (Enter promo code THRIVEADHD on the 'Get Pricing' form to receive an additional £200 off your purchase)

USEFUL ORGANISATIONS AND CHARITIES

AADD-UK
https://aadduk.org/

ADDISS (support for parents and families affected by ADHD)
http://www.addiss.co.uk/

ADDitude Magazine
https://www.additudemag.com/

ADHD Aware (monthly online drop-in sessions)
https://adhdaware.org.uk/

ADHD Europe
https://adhdeurope.eu/

Canadian ADHD Resource Alliance (CADDRA)
https://www.caddra.ca/public-information/adults/

The Flow Club (offers remote co-working sessions)
https://www.flow.club

Relationships and ADHD (Melissa Orlov – online counselling)
https://www.adhdmarriage.com/counseling
Book: Orlov, M., *The ADHD Effect on Marriage* (Specialty Press/
A.D.D. Warehouse, 2010)

Simply Wellbeing
https://www.simplywellbeing.com/

THRIVE programme at The Grove
https://www.thegrovepractice.com/training/thrivewithadultadhd

Totally ADD
https://totallyadd.com/

UK Adult ADHD Network (UKAAN) (for professionals working
with adult ADHD
https://www.ukaan.org/

REFERENCES

KEY REFERENCES

Adamou, M. et al., 'The Adult ADHD Assessment Quality Assurance Standard (AQAS)' (2024), doi:10.31219/osf.io/dksqw

Faraone, S.V. et al., 'The World Federation of ADHD International Consensus Statement: 208 Evidence-based conclusions about the disorder'. *Neuroscience & Biobehavioral Review* 128 (2021): 789–818, doi: 10.1016/j.neubiorev.2021.01.022

Kooij, J.J.S. et al., 'European consensus statement on diagnosis and treatment of adult ADHD: The European Network Adult ADHD'. *BMC Psychiatry* 10 (67), (2010): doi.org/10.1186/1471-244X-10-67 and 'Updated European Consensus Statement on Diagnosis and Treatment of Adult ADHD'. *European Psychiatry* 56 (2019): 14–34 doi:10.1016/j. eurpsy.2018.11.001

National Institute for Health and Care Excellence, 'Attention deficit hyperactivity disorder: diagnosis and management'. *NICE* (2019), https://www.nice.org.uk/guidance/NG87

OTHER REFERENCES BY TOPIC

Prevalence of ADHD

Fayyad, J. et al., 'The descriptive epidemiology of DSM-IV Adult ADHD in the World Health Organization, World Mental Health Surveys'. *Attention Deficit Hyperactive Disorder* 9 (1), (2017): 47–65, doi: 10.1007/s12402-016-0208-3

Song, P., et. al., 'The prevalence of adult attention-deficit hyperactivity disorder. A global systematic review and meta-analysis'. *Journal of Global Health* (2021), doi:10.7189/jogh.11.04009

Willcutt, E.G., 'The prevalence of DSM-IV attention-deficit/hyperactivity disorder: a meta-analytic review'. *Neurotherapeutics* 9 (3), (2012): 490–9, doi: 10.1007/s13311-012-0135-8

ADHD in women

Dorani, F. et al., 'Prevalence of hormone-related mood disorder symptoms in women with ADHD'. *Journal of Psychiatric Research* 133 (2021): 10–15, doi:10.1016/j.jpsychires.2020.12.005

Ter Beek, L.S., Böhmer, M.N., Wittekoek, M.E. and Kooij, J.J.S., 'Lifetime ADHD symptoms highly prevalent in women with cardiovascular complaints. A cross-sectional study'. *Archives of Women's Mental Health* 26 (6), (2023): 851– 855, doi:10.1007/s00737-023-01356-7

Willcutt, E. G., 'The Prevalence of DSM-IV Attention-Deficit/ Hyperactivity Disorder: A Meta-Analytic Review'. *Neurotherapeutics* 9 (3), (2012): 490–9, doi: 10.1007/s13311-012-0135-8

Young, S. et al., 'Females with ADHD: An expert consensus statement taking a lifespan approach providing guidance for the identification and treatment of attention-deficit/ hyperactivity disorder in girls and women'. *BMC Psychiatry* 20 (1), (2020), doi: 10.1186/ s12888-020-02707-9

ADHD across the lifespan

Faraone, S.V. et al., 'The age-dependent decline of attention deficit hyperactivity disorder: a meta-analysis of follow-up studies'. *Psychological Medicine* 36 (2), (2006): 159–65, doi: 10.1017/ S003329170500471X

Franke, B. et al., 'Live fast, die young? A review on the developmental trajectories of ADHD across the lifespan'. *European Neuropsychopharmacology* 28 (10), (2018): 1059–88, doi: 10.1016/j. euroneuro.2018.08.001

Adverse outcomes of ADHD (and effect of medication)

Chang, Z. et al., 'Risks and Benefits of Attention-Deficit/Hyperactivity Disorder Medication on Behavioral and Neuropsychiatric Outcomes: A Qualitative Review of Pharmacoepidemiology Studies Using Linked Prescription Databases'. *Biological Psychiatry* 86 (5), (2019): 335–43, doi: 10.1016/j.biopsych.2019.04.009

Faraone, S.V. et al., 'The World Federation of ADHD International Consensus Statement'.

Adaptive/positive aspects of ADHD

Sedgwick, J.A., Merwood, A., Asherson, P., 'The positive aspects of attention deficit hyperactivity disorder: A qualitative investigation of successful adults with ADHD'. *ADHD Attention Deficit and Hyperactivity Disorders* 11 (3), (2019): 241–53, doi:10.1007/s12402-018-0277-6

Mental health comorbidity (including addiction)

Choi, W.S. et al., 'The prevalence of psychiatric comorbidities in adult ADHD compared with non-ADHD populations: A systematic literature review'. *PLOS ONE* 17(11), (2022), doi: 10.1371/journal.pone.0277175

Deberdt, W., Thome, J., Lebrec, J. et al., 'Prevalence of ADHD in nonpsychotic adult psychiatric care (ADPSYC): A multinational cross-sectional study in Europe'. *BMC Psychiatry* 15 (2015): 242. doi:10.1186/s12888-015-0624-5

Faraone, S.V. et al., 'The World Federation of ADHD International Consensus Statement'.

Groenman, A.P., Janssen, T.W.P. and Oosterlaan, J., 'Childhood Psychiatric Disorders as Risk Factor for Subsequent Substance Abuse: A Meta-Analysis'. *Journal of the American Academy of Child & Adolescent Psychiatry* 56 (7), (2017): 556–69, doi:10.1016/j.jaac.2017.05.004

Jacob, C.P. et al., 'Co-morbidity of adult attention-deficit/hyperactivity disorder with focus on personality traits and related disorders in a tertiary referral center'. *European Archives of Psychiatry and Clinical Neuroscience* 257 (6), (2007): 309–17, doi: 10.1007/s00406-007-0722-6

Jensen, C.M., Steinhausen, H-C., 'Comorbid mental disorders in children and adolescents with attention-deficit/hyperactivity disorder in a large nationwide study'. *ADHD Attention Deficit and Hyperactivity Disorders* 7 (1), (2015): 27–38, doi: 10.1007/s12402-014-0142-1

Marx, I. et al., 'ADHD and the Choice of Small Immediate Over Larger Delayed Rewards: A Comparative Meta-Analysis of Performance on Simple Choice-Delay and Temporal Discounting Paradigms'. *Journal of Attention Disorders* 25 (2), (2021): 171–87, doi:10.1016/j.eurpsy.2017.01.578

Rommelse, N. N. et al., 'Comorbid problems in ADHD: degree of association, shared endophenotypes, and formation of distinct subtypes. Implications for a future DSM'. *Journal of Abnormal Child Psychology* 37 (6), (2009): 793–804, doi:10.1007/s10802-009-9312-6

van Emmerik-van Oortmerssen, K. et al., 'Prevalence of attention-deficit hyperactivity disorder in substance use disorder patients: a meta-analysis and meta-regression analysis'. *Drug Alcohol Dependence* 122 (1–2), (2012): 11–19, doi:10.1016/j.drugalcdep.2011.12.007

Physical health (somatic) comorbidity

Faraone, S.V. et al., 'The World Federation of ADHD International Consensus Statement'.

Allergy, asthma, autoimmunity and ADHD

Chen, M.H. et al., 'Comorbidity of Allergic and Autoimmune Diseases Among Patients With ADHD'. *Journal of Attention Disorders* 21 (3), (2017): 219–27, doi:10.1177/1087054712474686

Cortese, S. et al., 'Association between attention deficit hyperactivity disorder and asthma: A systematic review and meta-analysis and a Swedish population-based study'. *Lancet Psychiatry* 5 (9), (2018): 717–26, doi:10.1016/S2215-0366(18)30224-4

Hegvik, T.A. et al., 'Associations between attention-deficit/hyperactivity disorder and autoimmune diseases are modified by sex: A population-based cross-sectional study'. *European & Child Adolescent Psychiatry,* 27 (5), (2018): 663–75, doi:10.1007/ s00787-017-1056-1

Schans, J.V. et al., 'Association of atopic diseases and attention-deficit/ hyperactivity disorder: A systematic review and meta analyses', *Neuroscience Biobehavioral Review* 74 (Pt A), (2017): 139–48, doi:10.1016/j.neubiorev.2017.01.011

Binge eating disorder and ADHD

Sevilla Vicente, J. et al., 'Adult ADHD diagnosis and binge eating disorder'. *European Psychiatry* 41 (S1), (2017), doi:10.1016/j. eurpsy.2017.01.578

Covid (and Long Covid) and ADHD

Merzon, E. et al., 'ADHD as a Risk Factor for Infection with Covid-19'. *Journal of Attention Disorders* 25 (13), (2021): 1783–90, doi: 10.1177/1087054720943271

Merzon, E. et al., 'Clinical and Socio-Demographic Variables Associated with the Diagnosis of Long COVID Syndrome in Youth: A Population-Based Study'. *International Journal of Environmental Research and Public Health* 19 (10), (2022), doi: 10.3390/ ijerph19105993

Wang, Q., Xu, R. and Volkow, N.D., 'Increased risk of COVID-19 infection and mortality in people with mental disorders: Analysis from electronic health records in the United States'. *World Psychiatry* 20 (1), (2021): 124–30, doi: 10.1002/wps.20806

Diabetes (type 2) and ADHD

Chen, M., Pan, T., Hsu, J., Huang, K., Su, T., Li, C. et al., 'Risk of Type 2 Diabetes in Adolescents and Young Adults with Attention-Deficit/ Hyperactivity Disorder'. *Journal of Clinical Psychiatry* 79 (2018):3, doi: 10.4088/JCP.17m11607

Dysautonomia/POTS and ADHD

Csecs, J.L.L. et al., 'Joint Hypermobility Links Neurodivergence to Dysautonomia and Pain'. *Frontiers in Psychiatry* (2022), doi:10.3389/ fpsyt.2021.786916

Raj, V. et al., 'Psychiatric profile and attention deficits in postural tachycardia syndrome'. *Journal of Neurology, Neurosurgery & Psychiatry* 80 (3), (2009): 339–44, doi:10.1136/jnnp.2008.144360

Epilepsy and ADHD

Bertelsen, E.N. et al., 'Childhood Epilepsy, Febrile Seizures, and Subsequent Risk of ADHD'. *Pediatrics* 138 (2), (2016), doi:10.1542/peds. 2015-4654

Chou, I. et al., 'Correlation between Epilepsy and Attention Deficit Hyperactivity Disorder: A Population-Based Cohort Study'. *PLOS ONE* 8 (2013): 3, doi: 10.1371/journal.pone.0057926

Fatigue and ADHD

Rogers, D.C., Dittner, A.J., Rimes, K.A. and Chalder, T., 'Fatigue in an adult attention deficit hyperactivity disorder population: A trans-diagnostic approach'. *British Journal of Clinical Psychology* 56 (1), (2017): 33–52, doi:10.1111/bjc.12119

Sáez-Francàs, N. et al., 'Attention-deficit hyperactivity disorder in chronic fatigue syndrome patients'. *Psychiatry Research* 200 (2012): 2–3, doi:10.1016/j.psychres.2012.04.041

Migraine and ADHD

Arruda, M., Arruda, R., Guidetti, V. and Bigal, M., 'ADHD Is Comorbid to Migraine in Childhood: A Population-Based Study'. *Journal of Attention Disorders* 24 (2020):7, doi:10.1177/ 1087054717710767

Neuroinflammation and mast cell activation disease +/- ADHD

Afrin, L.B. et al., 'Characterization of mast cell activation syndrome'. *American Journal of Medical Science* 353 (2017): 207–15, doi:10.1016/j. amjms.2016.12.013

Afrin, L.B. et al., 'Diagnosis of mast cell activation syndrome: A global "consensus-2"'. *Diagnosis* 8 (2), (2020): 137–52, doi: 10.1515/dx-2020-0005

Afrin, L.B., et al., 'Mast cell activation disease: An underappreciated cause of neurologic and psychiatric symptoms and diseases'. *Brain Behavior, and Immunity* 50 (2015): 314–21, doi: 10.1016/j.bbi.2015.07.002

Afrin, L.B. Butterfield, J.H., Raithel, M. and Molderings, G.J., 'Often seen, rarely recognized: Mast cell activation disease – a guide to diagnosis and therapeutic options'. *Annals of Medicine* (2016), doi:10.3109/07853890. 2016.1161231

Kölliker-Frers, R. et al., 'Neuroinflammation: An Integrating Overview of Reactive-Neuroimmune Cell Interactions in Health and Disease'. *Mediators of Inflammation* (2021), doi: 10.1155/2021/9999146

Molderings, G.J. et al., 'Familial occurrence of systemic mast cell activation disease'. *PLOS ONE* 8 (9), (2013), doi:10.1371/journal. pone.0076241

Seneviratne, S.L., Maitland, A. and Afrin, L.B., 'Mast cell disorders in Ehlers-Danlos syndrome'. *American Journal of Medical Genetics Part C Seminars in Medical Genetics* 175 (1), (2017): 226–36, doi:10.1002/ ajmg.c.31555

Song, Y. et al., 'Mast cell-mediated neuroinflammation may have a role in attention deficit hyperactivity disorder', *Experimental and Therapeutic Medicine* 20 (2), (2020): 714–26, doi: 10.3892/etm.2020.8789

Weiler, C.R. et al., 'AAAAI Mast Cell Disorders Committee Work Group Report: Mast cell activation syndrome (MCAS) diagnosis and management'. *Journal of Allergy and Clinical Immunology 144 (4)*, (2019): 883–96, doi: org/10.1016/j.jaci.2019.08.023

Obesity and ADHD

Chen, Q. et al., 'Common psychiatric and metabolic comorbidity of adult attention-deficit/hyperactivity disorder: A population-based cross-sectional study'. *PLOS ONE* 13 (2018): 9, doi:10.1371/journal.pone.0204516

Cortese, S. et al., 'Association Between ADHD and Obesity: A Systematic Review and Meta-Analysis'. *American Journal of Psychiatry* 173 (2016): 1, doi:10.1176/appi.ajp.2015.15020266

Pain/fibromyalgia and ADHD

van Rensburg, R., Meyer, H.P., Hitchcock, S.A. and Schuler, C.E., 'Screening for Adult ADHD in Patients with Fibromyalgia Syndrome'. *Pain Medicine* 19 (9), (2018): 1825–31, doi:10.1093/ pm/ pnx275

Stickley, A., Koyanagi, A., Takahashi, H. and Kamio, Y., 'ADHD symptoms and pain among adults in England'. *Psychiatry Research* 246 (2016): 326-331, doi:10.1016/j.psychres.2016.10.004

Sexually transmitted diseases and ADHD

Chen, M.H. et al., 'Sexually Transmitted Infection Among Adolescents and Young Adults With Attention-Deficit/Hyperactivity Disorder: A Nationwide Longitudinal Study'. *Journal of the American Academy of Child & Adolescent Psychiatry* 57 (1), (2018): 48–53, doi:10.1016/j.jaac.2017.09.438

Environmental toxicity +/- ADHD

Balmori, A., 'Electromagnetic pollution from phone masts. Effects on wildlife'. *Pathophysiology* 16 (2–3), (2009): 191–99, doi: 10.1016/j.pathophys.2009.01.007

Faraone, S.V. et al., 'The World Federation of ADHD International Consensus Statement'.

Lewis, A.C., Jenkins, D., Whitty, C.J.M., 'Hidden harms of indoor air pollution – five steps to expose them'. *Nature* 614 (7947), (2023): 220–23, doi: 10.1038/d41586-023-00287-8

Moore, S. et al., 'The Association between ADHD and Environmental Chemicals – A Scoping Review'. *International Journal of Environmental Research and Public Health* 19 (5), (2022), doi:10.3390/ijerph19052849

Pall, M.L., 'Microwave frequency electromagnetic fields (EMFs) produce widespread neuropsychiatric effects including depression'. *Journal of Chemical Neuroanatomy* 75 (Pt B), (2016): 43–51, doi:10.1016/j.jchemneu.2015.08.001

Zhang, J., Sumich, A., Wang, G.Y., 'Acute effects of radiofrequency electromagnetic field emitted by mobile phone on brain function'. *Bioelectromagnetics* 38 (5), (2017): 329–38, doi: 10.1002/bem.22052

Sleep +/- ADHD

Bjorvatn, B. et al., 'Adults with Attention Deficit Hyperactivity Disorder Report High Symptom Levels of Troubled Sleep, Restless Legs, and Cataplexy'. *Frontiers in Psychology* 8 (2017): 1621, doi: 10.3389/fpsyg.2017.01621

Blume, C. et al., 'Effects of calibrated blue-yellow changes in light on the human circadian clock'. *Nature Human Behaviour* 8 (3), (2024): 590–605. doi: 10.1038/s41562-023-01791-7

Cheah, K.L. et al., 'Effect of Ashwagandha (Withania somnifera) extract on sleep: A systematic review and meta-analysis', *PLOS ONE* 16 (9), (2021) doi:10.1371/journal.pone.0257843

Coogan, A.N. et al., 'Circadian rhythms and attention deficit hyperactivity disorder: The what, the when and the why'. *Progress in Neuro-psychopharmacology & Biological Psychiatry* 67 (2016): 74–81, doi:10.1016/j.pnpbp.2016.01.006

Dunster, G.P., Hua, I., Grahe, A. et al., 'Daytime light exposure is a strong predictor of seasonal variation in sleep and circadian timing of university students'. *Journal of Pineal Research* 74 (2), (2023), doi: 10.1111/jpi.12843

Faraone, S.V. et al., 'The World Federation of ADHD International Consensus Statement'.

Hesselbacher, S., Aiyer, A.A., Surani, S.R., Suleman, A.A, Varon, J., 'A Study to Assess the Relationship between Attention Deficit Hyperactivity Disorder and Obstructive Sleep Apnea in Adults'. *Cureus* 11 (10), (2019): e5979, doi: 10.7759/cureus.5979

Kim, J., Lee, G.H., Sung, S.M., Jung, D.S., Pak, K.,' Prevalence of attention deficit hyperactivity disorder symptoms in narcolepsy: A systematic review' [published correction appears in *Sleep Medicine* 107 (July 2023): 100]. *Sleep Medicine* 65 (2020): 84–8. doi:10.1016/j.sleep.2019.07.022

Lugo, J. et al., 'Sleep in adults with autism spectrum disorder and attention deficit/hyperactivity disorder: A systematic review and meta-analysis'. *European Neuropsychopharmacology* 38 (2020): 1–24, doi:10.1016/j.euroneuro.2020.07.004

Schredl, M., Bumb, J.M., Alm, B. and Sobanski, E., 'Nightmare frequency in adults with attention-deficit hyperactivity disorder'. *European Archives of Psychiatry and Clinical Neuroscience* 267 (1), (2017): 89–92, doi:10.1007/s00406-016-0686-5

Souto-Souza, D. et al., 'Is there an association between attention deficit hyperactivity disorder in children and adolescents and the occurrence of bruxism? A systematic review and meta-analysis'. *Sleep Medicine Reviews* 53 (2020), doi:10.1016/j.smrv.2020.101330.

Surman, C.B. et al., 'Association between attention-deficit/hyperactivity disorder and sleep impairment in adulthood: evidence from a large controlled study'. *Journal of Clinical Psychiatry* 70 (11), (2009): 1523–9, doi:10.4088/ JCP.08m04514

van Andel, E. et. al, 'Attention-Deficit/Hyperactivity Disorder and Delayed Sleep Phase Syndrome in Adults: A Randomized Clinical Trial on the Effects of Chronotherapy on Sleep'. *Journal of Biological Rhythms* 37 (6), (2022): 673–89, doi:10.1177/07487304221124659

Wynchank, D. et al., 'Adult Attention-Deficit/Hyperactivity Disorder (ADHD) and Insomnia: An Update of the Literature'. *Current Psychiatry Reports* 19 (12), (2017): 98, doi:10.1007/s11920-017-0860-0

Yoon, S.Y., Jain, U., Shapiro, C., 'Sleep in attention-deficit/hyperactivity disorder in children and adults: past, present, and future'. *Sleep Medicine Reviews* 16 (4), (2012): 371–88, doi: 10.1016/j.smrv.2011.07.001

Youssef, N.A., Ege, M., Angly, S.S., Strauss, J.L., Marx, C.E., 'Is obstructive sleep apnea associated with ADHD?'. *Annals of Clinical Psychiatry* 23 (3), (2011): 213–24.

Nutrition +/- ADHD

Faraone, S.V. et al., 'The World Federation of ADHD International Consensus Statement'.

Farsad-Naeimi, A. et al., 'Sugar consumption, sugar sweetened beverages and Attention Deficit Hyperactivity Disorder: A systematic review and meta-analysis'. *Complementary Therapies in Medicine* 53 (2020), doi: 10.1016/ j.ctim.2020.102512

Lange, K.W., Lange, K.M., Nakamura, Y. and Reissmann, A., 'Nutrition in the Management of ADHD: A Review of Recent Research'. *Current Nutrition Reports* 12 (3), (2023): 383–94, doi: 10.1007/s13668-023-00487-8

Pinto, S. et al., 'Eating Patterns and Dietary Interventions in ADHD: A Narrative Review'. *Nutrients* 14 (20), (2022), doi:10.3390/nu14204332

Shareghfarid, E., Sangsefidi, Z.S., Salehi-Abargouei, A., Hosseinzadeh, M., 'Empirically derived dietary patterns and food groups intake in relation with Attention Deficit/Hyperactivity Disorder (ADHD): A systematic review and meta-analysis'. *Clinical Nutrition ESPEN* 36 (2020): 28–35, doi: 10.1016/j.clnesp.2019.10.013

Food dyes and ADHD

Miller, M.D. et al., 'Potential impacts of synthetic food dyes on activity and attention in children: A review of the human and animal evidence'. *Environmental Health* 21 (45), (2022), doi: 10.1186/s12940-022-00849-9

Nigg, J.T., Lewis, K., Edinger, T. and Falk, M., 'Meta-analysis of attention-deficit/hyperactivity disorder or attention-deficit/hyperactivity disorder symptoms, restriction diet, and synthetic food color additives'. *Journal of the American Academy of Child & Adolescent Psychiatry* 51 (1), (2012): 86–97, doi: 10.1016/j.jaac.2011.10.015

Rambler, R.M. et al., 'A Review of the Association of Blue Food Coloring with Attention Deficit Hyperactivity Disorder Symptoms in Children'. *Cureus* 14 (9), (2022), doi: 10.7759/cureus.29241

Nutritional deficiencies in ADHD

Effatpanah, M. et al., 'Magnesium status and attention deficit hyperactivity disorder (ADHD): A meta-analysis'. *Psychiatry Research* 274 (2019): 228–34, doi:10.1016/j.psychres.2019.02.043

Greenblatt, J.M., Delane, D.D., 'Micronutrient Deficiencies in ADHD: A Global Research Consensus'. *Journal of Orthomolecular Medicine* 32 (6), (2017), https:// isom.ca/ article/ micronutrient-deficiencies-adhd-global-research-consensus

Kamal, M., Bener, A. and Ehlayel, M.S., 'Is high prevalence of vitamin D deficiency a correlate for attention deficit hyperactivity disorder?'. *ADHD Attention Deficit Hyperactive Disorders* 6 (2), (2014): 73–8, doi: 10.1007/s12402-014-0130-5

Landaas, E.T. et al., 'Vitamin levels in adults with ADHD', *BJPsych Open* 2 (6), (2016): 377–84, doi:org/10.1192/bjpo.bp.116.003491

Skalny, A.V. et al., 'Serum zinc, copper, zinc-to-copper ratio, and other essential elements and minerals in children with attention deficit/ hyperactivity disorder (ADHD)'. *Journal of Trace Elements in Medicine and Biology* 58 (2020), doi:10.1016/j.jtemb.2019.126445

Sucksdorff, M. et al., 'Maternal Vitamin D Levels and the Risk of Offspring Attention-Deficit/Hyperactivity Disorder'. *Journal of the American Academy of Child & Adolescent Psychiatry* 60 (1), (2021): 142–51, doi:10.1016/j.jaac.2019.11.021

Viktorinova, A. et al., 'Changed Plasma Levels of Zinc and Copper to Zinc Ratio and Their Possible Associations with Parent- and Teacher-Rated Symptoms in Children with Attention-Deficit Hyperactivity Disorder'. *Biological Trace Element Research* 169 (1), (2016): 1–7, doi:10.1007/ s12011-015-0395-3

Wang, Y., Huang, L., Zhang, L., Qu, Y. and Mu, D., 'Iron Status in Attention-Deficit/Hyperactivity Disorder: A Systematic Review and Meta-Analysis'. *PLOS ONE* 12 (1), (2017), doi: 10.1371/journal.pone.0169145

Zhou, F. et al., 'Dietary, nutrient patterns and blood essential elements in Chinese children with ADHD'. *Nutrients* 8 (6), (2016): 1–14, doi:10.3390/ nu8060352

Omega-3 supplementation in ADHD

Bloch, M.H., Qawasmi, A., 'Omega-3 fatty acid supplementation for the treatment of children with attention-deficit/hyperactivity disorder symptomatology: systematic review and meta-analysis'. *Journal of the American Academy of Child & Adolescent Psychiatry* 50 (10), (2011): 991–1000, doi: 10.1016/j.jaac.2011.06.008

Chang, J.P., Su, K.P., Mondelli, V. and Pariante, C.M., 'Omega-3 Polyunsaturated Fatty Acids in Youths with Attention Deficit Hyperactivity Disorder: A Systematic Review and Meta-Analysis of Clinical Trials and Biological Studies'. *Neuropsychopharmacology* 43 (3), (2018): 534–5, doi:10.1038/npp.2017.160

Hawkey, E., Nigg, J.T., 'Omega-3 fatty acid and ADHD: blood level analysis and meta-analytic extension of supplementation trials'. *Clinical Psychological Review* 34 (6), (2014): 496–505, doi:10.1016/ j.cpr.2014.05.005

Probiotic supplementation in ADHD

Pärtty, A. et al., 'A possible link between early probiotic intervention and the risk of neuropsychiatric disorders later in childhood: A randomized trial'. *Pediatric Research* 77 (6), (2015): 823–8, doi:10.1038/pr.2015.51

Vitamin/mineral supplementation in ADHD

Bhagavan, H.N., Coleman, M. and Coursin, D.B., 'The effect of pyridoxine hydrochloride on blood serotonin and pyridoxal phosphate contents in hyperactive children'. *Pediatrics* 55 (3), (1975): 437–41

Rucklidge, J.J., Frampton, C.M., Gorman, B. and Boggis, A., 'Vitamin-mineral treatment of attention-deficit hyperactivity disorder in adults: double-blind randomised placebo-controlled trial'. *British Journal of Psychiatry* 204 (2014): 306–15, doi:10.1192/bjp.bp.113.132126

Yorbik, O. et al., 'Potential effects of zinc on information processing in boys with attention deficit hyperactivity disorder'. *Progress in Neuro-Psychopharmacology and Biological Psychiatry* 32 (3), (2008): 662–7, doi:10.1016/j.pnpbp.2007.11.009

Polyphenol supplementation in ADHD

Weichmann, F., Rohdewald, P., 'Pycnogenol® French maritime pine bark extract in randomized, double-blind, placebo-controlled human clinical studies'. *Frontiers in Nutrition* 11 (2024), doi: 10.3389/fnut.2024.1389374

Weyns, A-S. et al., 'Clinical investigation of French maritime pine bark extract on attention-deficit hyperactivity disorder as compared to methylphenidate and placebo: Part 1: Efficacy in a randomised trial', *Journal of Functional Foods* 97 (2022), doi:10.1016/j.jff.2022.105246 and 'Part 2: Oxidative stress and immunological modulation'. *Journal of Functional Foods* 97 (2022), doi:1016/j.jff.2022.105247

Restriction and elimination diets and ADHD

Nigg, J.T. et al., 'Meta-analysis of attention-deficit/hyperactivity disorder or attention-deficit/hyperactivity disorder symptoms, restriction diet, and synthetic food color additives'. *Journal of the American Academy of Child & Adolescent Psychiatry* 51 (1), (2012): 86–97, doi: 10.1016/j.jaac.2011.10.015

Pelsser, L.M. et al., 'Effects of a restricted elimination diet on the behaviour of children with attention-deficit hyperactivity disorder (INCA study): A randomised controlled trial'. *Lancet* 377 (9764), (2011): 494–503, doi:10.1016/S0140-6736(10)62227-1

Ultra-processed foods (not specific to ADHD)

Department for Environment, Food & Rural Affairs. 'National food strategy for England' (2020), https://www.gov.uk/government/publications/national-food-strategy-for-england

Elizabeth, L. et al., 'Ultra-Processed Foods and Health Outcomes: A Narrative Review'. *Nutrients* 12 (7), (2020), doi:10.3390/nu12071955

Hecht, E.M. et al., 'Cross-sectional examination of ultra-processed food consumption and adverse mental health symptoms'. *Public Health Nutrition* 25 (11), (2022): 3225–34, doi: 10.1017/S1368980022001586

Time-restricted eating (not specific to ADHD)

Meng, C. et al., 'Association Between Time-Restricted Eating and All-Cause and Cause-Specific Mortality'. *Circulation* 149 (Suppl. 1), (2024), doi:10.1161/circ.149.suppl_1.P192

Regmi, P., Heilbronn, L.K., 'Time-Restricted Eating: Benefits, Mechanisms, and Challenges in Translation'. *iScience* 23 (6), (2020), doi: 10.1016/j.isci.2020.101161

Caffeine benefits (not specific to ADHD)

Poole, R. et al., 'Coffee consumption and health: umbrella review of meta-analyses of multiple health outcomes'. *British Medical Journal* 359 (2017), doi: 10.1136/bmj.j5024

Water intake guidance – NHS (not specific to ADHD)

National Health Service. 'Water, drinks and hydration' (2023), https://www.nhs.uk/live-well/eat-well/food-guidelines-and-food-labels/water-drinks-nutrition

Exercise (and the effect of natural environments)

Bowler, D.E., Buyung-Ali, L.,M., Knight, T.M., Pullin, A.S., 'A systematic review of evidence for the added benefits to health of exposure to natural environments'. *BMC Public Health* 10 (2010), doi: 10.1186/1471-2458-10-456

Coon, J.T. et al., 'Does participating in physical activity in outdoor natural environments have a greater effect on physical and mental wellbeing than physical activity indoors? A systematic review', *Environmental Science & Technology* 45 (5), (2011): 1761–72, doi:10.1021/es102947t

National Health Service. 'Physical activity guidelines for adults aged 19 to 64' (2024), https://www.nhs.uk/live-well/exercise/physical-activity-guidelines-for-adults-aged-19-to-64/

Shaner, A.A. et al., 'The acute hormonal response to free weight and machine weight resistance exercise'. *Journal of Strength & Conditioning Research* 28 (4), (2014): 1032–40, doi:10.1519/JSC.0000000000000317

Vysniauske, R., Verburgh, L., Oosterlaan, J. and Molendijk, M.L., 'The Effects of Physical Exercise on Functional Outcomes in the Treatment of ADHD: A Meta-Analysis'. *Journal of Attention Disorders* 24 (5), (2020): 644–54, doi: 10.1177/1087054715627489

Zang, Y., 'Impact of physical exercise on children with attention deficit hyperactivity disorders: Evidence through a meta-analysis'. *Medicine* 98 (46), (2019), doi:10.1097/MD.0000000000017980

Emotional regulation and well-being

Emotional dysregulation in ADHD

Faraone, S.V. et al., 'Practitioner Review: Emotional dysregulation in attention-deficit/hyperactivity disorder – implications for clinical recognition and intervention'. *Journal of Child Psychology and Psychiatry* 60 (2), (2019): 133–50. doi: 10.1111/jcpp.12899

Skirrow, C., Asherson, P., 'Emotional lability, comorbidity and impairment in adults with attention-deficit hyperactivity disorder'. *Journal of Affective Disorders* 147 (1–3), (2013): 80–6. doi: 10.1016/j.jad.2012.10.011

Surman, C.B. et al., 'Understanding deficient emotional self-regulation in adults with attention deficit hyperactivity disorder: A controlled study'. *ADHD Attention Deficit and Hyperactive Disorders* 5 (3), (2013): 273–81. doi: 10.1007/s12402-012-0100-8

Rejection Sensitive Dysphoria in ADHD (no available studies)

Cleveland Clinic, 'Rejection Sensitive Dysphoria (RSD)' (2022), https://my.clevelandclinic.org/health/diseases/24099-rejection-sensitive-dysphoria-rsd

Dodson, W., 'New Insight Into Rejection Sensitive Dysphoria', *ADDitude* (2024), https://www.additudemag.com/rejection-sensitive-dysphoria-adhd-emotional-dysregulation/

Sensory processing issues in ADHD

Ghanizadeh, A., 'Sensory processing problems in children with ADHD, a systematic review'. *Psychiatry Investigation* 8 (2), (2011): 89–94. doi: 10.4306/pi.2011.8.2.89

Use of the breath (not specific to ADHD)

Nestor, J., *Breath: The New Science of a Lost Art* (Riverhead Books, 2020)

Zaccaro, A. et al., 'How Breath-Control Can Change Your Life: A Systematic Review on Psycho-Physiological Correlates of Slow Breathing'. *Frontiers in Human Neuroscience* 12 (353), (2018), doi:10.3389/fnhum.2018.00353

Gratitude, awe and flow state (not specific to ADHD)

Csikszentmihalyi, M., *Flow: The Psychology of Optimal Experience* (Harper Perennial, 1991)

Komase, Y. et al., 'Effects of gratitude intervention on mental health and well-being among workers: A systematic review'. *Journal of Occupational Health* 63 (1), (2021), doi: 10.1002/1348-9585.12290

Monroy, M., Keltner, D., 'Awe as a Pathway to Mental and Physical Health', *Perspectives on Psychological Science* 18 (2), (2023): 309–20, doi:10.1177/17456916221094856

Heart Rate Variability and vagus nerve activation (not specific to ADHD)

Balzarotti, S., Biassoni, F., Colombo, B. and Ciceri, M.R., 'Cardiac vagal control as a marker of emotion regulation in healthy adults: A review'. *Biological Psychology* 130 (2017): 54–66, doi: 10.1016/j.biopsycho.2017.10.008

Bonaz, B., Bazin, T. and Pellissier, S., 'The Vagus Nerve at the Interface of the Microbiota-Gut-Brain Axis'. *Frontiers in Neuroscience* 12 (2018):49, doi:10.3389/ fnins.2018.00049

Jungmann, M., Vencatachellum, S., Van Ryckeghem, D. and Vögele, C., 'Effects of Cold Stimulation on Cardiac-Vagal Activation in Healthy Participants: Randomized Controlled Trial'. *JMIR Formative Research* 2 (2), (2018), doi: 10.2196/10257

Kim, H.G. et al., 'Stress and Heart Rate Variability: A Meta-Analysis and Review of the Literature'. *Psychiatry investigation* 15 (3), (2018): 235–45, doi:org/10.30773/pi.2017.08.17

Kok, B.E. and Fredrickson, B.L., 'Upward spirals of the heart: autonomic flexibility, as indexed by vagal tone, reciprocally and prospectively predicts positive emotions and social connectedness'. [Published correction appears in *Biological Psychology*, 117 (May 2016): 240] *Biological Psychology* 85 (3), (2010): 432–36. doi: 10.1016/j.biopsycho.2010. 09.005

Mäkinen, T.M. et al., 'Autonomic nervous function during whole-body cold exposure before and after cold acclimation'. *Aviation, Space, and Environmental Medicine* 79 (9), (2008): 875–82, doi: 10.3357/asem.2235.2008

Mercante, B., Deriu, F. and Rangon, C.M., 'Auricular Neuromodulation: The Emerging Concept beyond the Stimulation of Vagus and Trigeminal Nerves'. *Medicines* 5 (1), (2018), doi: 10.3390/medicines5010010

Porges, S.W., 'Polyvagal Theory: A Science of Safety'. *Frontiers in Integrative Neuroscience* 16 (2022), doi:10.3389/fnint.2022.871227

Ramirez-Yañez, G., 'Mouth Breathing: Understanding the Pathophysiology of an oral habit and its consequences'. *Medical Research Archives* 11 (1), (2023), doi:11. 10.18103/mra.v11i1.3478

Sandercock, G.R., Bromley, P.D., Brodie, D.A., 'Effects of exercise on heart rate variability: inferences from meta-analysis'. *Medicine & Science in Sports & Exercise* 37 (3), (2005): 433–9, doi: 10.1249/01.mss.0000155388.39002.9d

Spiegelhalder, K. et al., 'Heart rate and heart rate variability in subjectively reported insomnia', *Journal of Sleep Research* 20 (1 Pt 2), (2011): 137–45, doi: 10.1111/j.1365-2869.2010.00863.x

Yang, J.L., Chen, G.Y. and Kuo, C.D., 'Comparison of effect of 5 recumbent positions on autonomic nervous modulation in patients with coronary artery disease'. *Circulation Journal* 72 (6), (2008): 902–8, doi:10.1253/circj.72.902

Young, H.A., Benton, D., 'Heart-rate variability: a biomarker to study the influence of nutrition on physiological and psychological health?'. *Behavioural Pharmacology* 29 (2 and 3), (2018): 140–51, doi: 10.1097/ FBP.0000000000000383

Effects of heat and cold exposure (not specific to ADHD)

Esperland, D., de Weerd, L. and Mercer, J.B., 'Health effects of voluntary exposure to cold water - a continuing subject of debate'. *International Journal of Circumpolar Health* 81 (1), (2022): 2111789, doi: 10.1080/ 22423982.2022.2111789

Janssen, C.W. et al., 'Whole-body hyperthermia for the treatment of major depressive disorder: a randomized clinical trial'. *JAMA Psychiatry* 73 (8), (2016): 789–95, doi: 10.1001/jamapsychiatry.2016.1031

Jungmann, M., et. al, 'Effects of Cold Stimulation on Cardiac-Vagal Activation in Healthy Participants: Randomized Controlled Trial'

Laukkanen, T. et al., 'Sauna bathing is associated with reduced cardiovascular mortality and improves risk prediction in men and women: a prospective cohort study'. *BMC Medicine* 16 (1), (2018), doi:10.1186/s12916-018-1198-0

Mäkinen, T.M. et al., 'Autonomic nervous function during whole-body cold exposure before and after cold acclimation'.

Masuda, A. et al., 'Repeated thermal therapy diminishes appetite loss and subjective complaints in mildly depressed patients'. *Psychosomatic Medicine* 67 (4), (2005): 643–7, doi: 10.1097/01. psy.0000171812.67767.8f

Podstawski, R. et al., 'Endocrine Effects of Repeated Hot Thermal Stress and Cold Water Immersion in Young Adult Men'. *American Journal of Men's Health* 15 (2), (2021), doi: 10.1177/15579883211008339

Soejima, Y. et al., 'Effects of Waon therapy on chronic fatigue syndrome: a pilot study'. *Internal Medicine* 54 (3), (2015): 333–8, doi: 10.2169/ internalmedicine.54.3042

Šrámek, P. et al., 'Human physiological responses to immersion into water of different temperatures'. *European Journal of Applied Physiology* 81 (2000): 436–42, doi:10.1007/s004210050065

Touch and oxytocin (not specific to ADHD)

Li, Q., Zhao, W. and Kendrick, K.M., 'Affective touch in the context of development, oxytocin signaling, and autism'. *Frontiers in Psychology* 13 (2022): 967791, doi: 10.3389/ fpsyg.2022.967791

Acupoint tapping (not specific to ADHD)

Al-Hadethe, A., Hunt, N., Al-Qaysi, G. and Thomas, S., 'Randomized controlled study comparing two psychological therapies for post-traumatic stress disorder (PTSD): Emotional freedom techniques (EFT) vs. narrative exposure therapy (NET)'. *Journal of Traumatic Stress Disorders and Treatment* 4 (4), (2015): 1–12, doi:10.4172/2324-8947.1000145

Bach, D. et al., 'Clinical EFT (Emotional Freedom Techniques) Improves Multiple Physiological Markers of Health'. *Journal of Evidence-Based Integrative Medicine* (2019), doi: 10.1177/2515690X18823691

Church, D., Sparks, T. and Clond, M., 'EFT (Emotional Freedom Techniques) and resiliency in veterans at risk for PTSD: A randomized controlled trial'. *Explore: The Journal of Science and Healing* 12 (5), (2016): 355–65, doi.org/10.1016/j.explore.2016.06.012

Clond, M., 'Emotional Freedom Techniques for Anxiety: A Systematic Review With Meta-analysis'. *Journal of Nervous and Mental Disease* 204 (2016): 388–95. doi: 10.1097/ NMD.0000000000000483

Feinstein, D., 'Acupoint stimulation in treating psychological disorders: evidence of efficacy'. *Review of General Psychology* 16 (2012): 364–380, doi:10.1037/a0028602

Hui, K.K. et al., 'Acupuncture, the limbic system, and the anticorrelated networks of the brain'. *Autonomic Neuroscience* 157 (1–2), (2010): 81–90, doi:10.1016/j.autneu.2010.03.022

Karatzias, T. et al., 'A controlled comparison of the effectiveness and efficiency of two psychological therapies for post-traumatic stress disorder: Eye movement desensitization and reprocessing vs. emotional freedom techniques'. *Journal of Nervous and Mental Disease* 199 (6), (2011): 372–8, doi: 10.1097/NMD.0b013e31821cd262

Ma, S.X., 'Low Electrical Resistance Properties of Acupoints: Roles of NOergic Signaling Molecules and Neuropeptides in Skin Electrical

Conductance'. *Chinese Journal of Integrative Medicine* 27 (8), (2021): 563–9. doi: 10.1007/s11655-021-3318-5

Maharaj, M.E., 'Differential gene expression after Emotional Freedom Techniques (EFT) treatment. A novel pilot protocol for salivary mRNA assessment'. *Energy Psychology: Theory, Research, and Treatment* 8 (1), (2016): 17–32. doi: 10.9769/ EPJ.2016.8.1.MM

Nelms, J. and Castel, D., 'A systematic review and meta-analysis of randomized and non-randomized trials of emotional freedom techniques (EFT) for the treatment of depression'. *Explore: The Journal of Science and Healing* 12 (2016): 416–26, doi:10.1016/ j.explore.2016.08.001

Sebastian, B. and Nelms, J., 'The effectiveness of emotional freedom techniques in the treatment of post-traumatic stress disorder: A meta-analysis'. *Explore: The Journal of Science and Healing* 13 (2017): 16–25, doi:10.1016/j.explore.2016.10.001

Stapleton, P. et al., 'A feasibility study: Emotional freedom techniques for depression in Australian adults'. *Current Research in Psychology* 5 (1), (2014): 19–33, doi:10.3844/crpsp.2014.19.33

Stapleton, P. et al., 'An Initial Investigation of Neural Changes in Overweight Adults with Food Cravings after Emotional Freedom Techniques'. *OBM Integrative and Complementary Medicine* 4 (1), (2019), doi:10.21926/obm.icm.1901010

Stapleton, P. et al., 'Effectiveness of school-based emotional freedom techniques intervention for promoting student well-being'. *Adolescent Psychiatry* 7 (2), (2017): 112–26, doi: 10. 2174/2210676607666171101165425

Stapleton, P. et al., 'Reexamining the Effect of Emotional Freedom Techniques on Stress Biochemistry: A Randomized Controlled Trial', *Psychological Trauma: Theory, Research, Practice, and Policy* 12 (8), (2020): 869–77, doi: 10.1037/tra0000563

Mindfulness and yoga-based therapies

Chimiklis, A.L. et al., 'Yoga, Mindfulness, and Meditation Interventions for Youth with ADHD: Systematic Review and Meta-Analysis'. *Journal of Child & Family Studies* 27 (2018): 3155–68, doi:10.1007/s10826-018-1148-7

Gunaseelan, L. et al., 'Yoga for the Management of Attention-Deficit/ Hyperactivity Disorder'. *Cureus* 13 (12), (2021), doi:10.7759/cureus.20466

Zhang, J., Díaz-Román, A. and Cortese, S., 'Meditation-based therapies for attention-deficit/hyperactivity disorder in children, adolescents and adults: a systematic review and meta-analysis'. *Evidence-Based Mental Health* 21 (3), (2018): 87–94, doi: 10.1136/ebmental-2018-300015

Zhang, Z. et al., 'The Effect of Meditation-Based Mind-Body Interventions on Symptoms and Executive Function in People With ADHD: A Meta-Analysis of Randomized Controlled Trials'. *Journal of Attention Disorders* 27 (6), (2023): 583–97, doi:10.1177/10870547231154897

Xiao, Z. et al., 'The benefits of Shuai Shou Gong (SSG) [arm swinging] demonstrated in a Randomised Control Trial (RCT) study of older adults in two communities in Thailand'. *PLOS ONE* 18 (5), (2023), doi:10.1371/journal.pone.0282405

Other non-medication approaches for adult ADHD

Cortese, S. et al., 'Cognitive training for attention-deficit/hyperactivity disorder: meta-analysis of clinical and neuropsychological outcomes from randomized controlled trials'. *Journal of the American Academy of Child & Adolescent Psychiatry* 54 (3), (2015): 164–74 [published correction appears in 44(5): 433], doi: 10.1016/j.jaac.2014.12.010

Hirvikoski, T. et al., 'Psychoeducational groups for adults with ADHD and their significant others (PEGASUS): A pragmatic multicenter and randomized controlled trial'. *European Psychiatry* 44 (2017): 141–52, doi: 1 0.1016/j.eurpsy.2017.04.005

Knouse, L.E, Teller, J. and Brooks, M.A., 'Meta-analysis of cognitive-behavioral treatments for adult ADHD'. *Journal of Consulting and Clinical Psychology* 85 (7), (2017): 737–50, doi: 10.1037/ccp0000216

Lam, A.P. et al., 'Long-term Effects of Multimodal Treatment on Adult Attention-Deficit/Hyperactivity Disorder Symptoms: Follow-up Analysis of the COMPAS Trial'. *JAMA Network Open* 2 (5), (2019), doi:10.1001/jamanetworkopen.2019.4980

Pedersen, H. et al., 'Psychoeducation for adult ADHD: a scoping review about characteristics, patient involvement, and content'. *BMC Psychiatry* 24 (1), (2024): 73, doi: 10.1186/s12888-024-05530-8

Philipsen, A. et al., 'Effects of Group Psychotherapy [Dialectical Behavioural Therapy], Individual Counseling, Methylphenidate, and

Placebo in the Treatment of Adult Attention-Deficit/Hyperactivity Disorder: A Randomized Clinical Trial'. *JAMA Psychiatry* 72 (12), (2015): 1199–1210 [published correction appears in *JAMA Psychiatry* 73 (1), (2016): 90], doi: 10.1001/jamapsychiatry.2015.2146

van Doren, J. et al., 'Sustained effects of neurofeedback in ADHD: a systematic review and meta-analysis'. *European Child & Adolescent Psychiatry* 28 (3), (2019): 293–305, doi: 10.1007/s00787-018-1121-4

Young, Z., Moghaddam, N. and Tickle, A., 'The Efficacy of Cognitive Behavioral Therapy for Adults With ADHD: A Systematic Review and Meta-Analysis of Randomized Controlled Trials'. *Journal of Attention Disorders* 24 (6), (2020): 875–8, doi:10.1177/1087054716664413

Medication management of ADHD

Efficacy, tolerability and approach

Cortese, S. et al., 'Comparative efficacy and tolerability of medications for attention-deficit hyperactivity disorder in children, adolescents, and adults: a systematic review and network meta-analysis'. *Lancet Psychiatry* 5 (9), (2018): 727–38, doi: 10.1016/S2215-0366(18)30269-4

Kooij, J.J.S. et al., 'Updated European Consensus Statement on diagnosis and treatment of adult ADHD'. *European Psychiatry* 56, (2019): 14–34, doi:10.1016/j.eurpsy.2018.11.001

National Institute for Health and Care Excellence, 'Attention deficit hyperactivity disorder: diagnosis and management'.

Impact of medication on substance use

Chang, Z. et al., 'Stimulant ADHD medication and risk for substance abuse'. *Journal of Child Psychology and Psychiatry* 55 (8), (2014): 878–85, doi: 10.1111/jcpp.12164

Faraone, S.V. et al., 'The World Federation of ADHD International Consensus Statement'.

Quinn, P.D. et al., 'ADHD Medication and Substance-Related Problems'. *American Journal of Psychiatry* 174 (9), (2017): 877–85. doi: 10.1176/appi.ajp.2017.16060686

Srichawla, B.S., Telles, C.C., Schweitzer, M. and Darwish, B., 'Attention Deficit Hyperactivity Disorder and Substance Use Disorder: A Narrative Review'. *Cureus* 14 (4), (2022), doi: 10.7759/cureus.24068

Impact on cardiovascular health

Habel, L.A. et al., 'ADHD medications and risk of serious cardiovascular events in young and middle-aged adults'. *JAMA* 306 (24), (2011): 2673–83, doi: 10.1001/jama.2011.1830

Zhang, L. et al., 'Attention-Deficit/Hyperactivity Disorder Medications and Long-Term Risk of Cardiovascular Diseases'. *JAMA Psychiatry* 81 (2), (2024): 178–87, doi: 10.1001/jamapsychiatry.2023.4294

Impact on brain health

Baumeister, A.A., 'Is Attention-Deficit/Hyperactivity Disorder a Risk Syndrome for Parkinson's Disease?'. *Harvard Review of Psychiatry* 29 (2), (2021): 142–58, doi: 10.1097/ HRP.0000000000000283

Becker, S., Sharma, M.J. and Callahan, B.L., 'ADHD and Neurodegenerative Disease Risk: A Critical Examination of the Evidence', *Frontiers in Aging Neuroscience* 13 (2021), doi: 10.3389/ fnagi.2021.826213

Fan, H.C. et al., 'The Association Between Parkinson's Disease and Attention-Deficit Hyperactivity Disorder'. *Cell Transplant* 29 (2020), doi: 10.1177/0963689720947416

OTHER IMPORTANT QUESTIONS AND THEMES

Is ADHD a brain disorder?

Demontis, D. et al., 'Genome-wide analyses of ADHD identify 27 risk loci, refine the genetic architecture and implicate several cognitive domains'. *Nature Genetics* 55 (2), (2023): 198–208, doi:10.1038/ s41588-022-01285-8

Is ADHD genetic?

Faraone, S.V., Larsson, H., 'Genetics of attention deficit hyperactivity disorder'. *Molecular Psychiatry* 24 (4), (2019): 562–75, doi:10.1038/ s41380-018-0070-0

Is there such a thing as adult-onset ADHD?

Taylor, L.E., Kaplan-Kahn, E.A., Lighthall, R,A. and Antshel, K.M., 'Adult-Onset ADHD: A Critical Analysis and Alternative Explanations'. *Child Psychiatry in Human Development* 53 (4), (2022): 635–53, doi:10.1007/s10578-021-01159-w

Intelligence and ADHD

Rommelse, N., Antshel, K., Smeets, S. et al., 'High intelligence and the risk of ADHD and other psychopathology'. *British Journal of Psychiatry* 211 (6), (2017): 359–64, doi:10.1192/ bjp.bp.116.184382

Is ADHD a new disorder?

Esteller-Cucala, P. et al., 'Genomic analysis of the natural history of attention-deficit/hyperactivity disorder using Neanderthal and ancient Homo sapiens samples'. *Scientific Reports* 10 (1), (2020): 8622, doi:10.1038/s41598-020-65322-4

ADHD on a continuum

Greven, C.U. et al., 'The opposite end of the attention deficit hyperactivity disorder continuum: genetic and environmental aetiologies of extremely low ADHD traits'. *Journal of Child Psychology and Psychiatry* 57 (4), (2016): 523–31, doi:10.1111/jcpp.12475

ADHD links with adversity and trauma

Björkenstam, E., Björkenstam, C., Jablonska, B. and Kosidou, K., 'Cumulative exposure to childhood adversity, and treated attention deficit/hyperactivity disorder: a cohort study of 543 650 adolescents and young adults in Sweden'. *Psychological Medicine* 48 (3), (2017): 498–507, doi:10.1017/S0033291717001933

Ouyang, L. et al., 'Attention-deficit/hyperactivity disorder symptoms and child maltreatment: a population-based study'. *The Journal of Pediatrics* 153 (6), (2008): 851–6, doi:10.1016/j.jpeds.2008.06.002

ACKNOWLEDGEMENTS

When I was 17 and about to submit my application for medical school, one of my teachers took me aside. He expressed well-meaning concern as to whether I would meet the grades I needed and encouraged me to rethink medicine as a career, something I'd set my sights on since childhood. Thanks to a positive upbringing which had shaped a 'can-do' mindset, rather than succumb and accept defeat, I decided to assertively take a stand. I was determined to prove him wrong and, after months of raw hyperfocus and intense study, I did just that. I am truly grateful to Mr Older for unwittingly helping me to crystallise my vision, which provided a privileged gateway into the fascinating world of medicine and then explorations of the mind.

Along the way on this eventful journey, I have had the privilege of meeting and engaging with a succession of truly amazing and awe-inspiring individuals – brilliant minds and mature souls who have generously taught me and expanded my horizons in many different directions. I would like to extend a warm literary embrace to a handful of those life-guiding teachers, mentors and friends.

Firstly to my tutor, Andy Sparrow, at the University of Nottingham School of Medicine, whose educational prowess and creative approach to teaching was like nothing I'd ever experienced.

To Jeremy Pfeffer, a wonderful and experienced psychiatrist who has now sadly passed away, who, despite having a more traditional approach, helped me realise that psychiatry really was my calling, and mentored me during those formative days.

To Phil Mollon, an esteemed author, true visionary and global authority in the world of energy psychology, who generously gave of his time and wisdom to patiently introduce me to, and orientate me in, this new healing dimension. And the many others who have helped me hone and develop these sensitive and awesome skills and techniques, including Judy Byrne, Richard Morris and Ashley Meyer.

To the wonderful and skilled mind and body therapists who have supported me to effectively clear some of the emotional baggage from my own life, freeing me up to be more available, present and open. Among others, they include Jill, Julia, Ashley, Heather, Anthea, Tim, Gilian and Werner. Thank you for your care.

To Alan Hakim and Anne Maitland who have guided and mentored me in my knowledge acquisition in the important fields of hypermobility and immunology respectively, both global leaders in their fields, truly special individuals and now good friends.

To Margaret Weiss, Sandra Kooij and Iris Manor, thought leaders, clinicians, innovators and researchers in the field of adult ADHD, who believed in me and the new ideas I was bringing to the speciality in relation to the emergent pattern of somatic (physical health) links with ADHD.

To my esteemed colleagues at UKAAN and in particular to its previous president, Philip Asherson, who, more than anyone else, has got adult ADHD firmly onto the map in the UK. I thank you for your wise counsel, unparalleled experience, warm friendship and care and attention when it came to my personal journey.

And to my colleagues at The Grove, whose brilliant work in mental health education remains right at the cutting edge. Thank you for giving me the space to develop our groundbreaking 'Regulate' programme for mental health professionals, a programme that is already positively impacting the lives of many. Its content, and the research that went into building it, has heavily informed some of the content of this book.

To Akiva Tatz, who, through our regular learning sessions in past times, taught me so much about life and the bigger picture; deep and complex ideas and insights that have helped shape and mature my spiritual understanding, with various themes permeating through this book.

To the thousands of patients and clients who I have worked with over the years, who have taught me the majority of what I know and who have trusted me with their care and repair (and have tolerated me often running just a few minutes behind).

A special thanks to sleep specialist psychiatrist, Hugh Selsick, and functional medicine practitioner, Ingrid Kitzing, who I collaborated with in the writing of the sleep and nutrition pillars respectively, both bringing world-class expertise to the table.

And to Jenny Goodman and Caroline Sherlock who, in different ways and at different times, have taught me about the huge, often hidden, impact of environmental toxicity and its effect on the body and mind, and have helped on my quest to nurture more of an integrated and nutrition-focused practice.

I also want to extend a heartfelt thank you to the wonderful editors at Vermilion, Anya, Leah, Marta and especially Julia Kellaway, who have respectfully helped guide the shaping of this book. Their skill, attention to detail and professionalism have been second to none and I have learned a great deal. Thank you all, and I look forward to building on what we have produced here.

Most importantly of all, I would like to thank my amazing and supportive family. My parents, for instilling in me a solid moral compass, a love of life and a growth-oriented mindset that continues to serve me well. My wife Natalie, for loving me unconditionally, for believing in me and for tolerating my, at times, slightly different ways. We have been through some difficult experiences together over recent years, but ones that have strengthened our bond and our family. Thank you for unselfishly allowing me the space to explore my passions and develop my vocation, and the time to immerse myself in the writing of this book. I value, beyond words, the containment and support you provide me. And to my two gorgeous girls, Mia and Sophie, who bring me endless joy and, in different ways, have taught me so much. May you both emit love and joy and navigate safely through this troubled and complex world. I hope, when the time is right, you will read and integrate into your own lives some of the more general life lessons I introduce in this book, and that you both continue to flourish.

INDEX

Page numbers in **bold** refer to diagrams.

5G 192, 199